Twilight
Volume 3:
The New Centurions

Joann SFAR, Lewis TRONDHEIM, story
Art for New Centurions: KERASCOET
Art for Revolutions: OBION

NANTIER • BEALL • MINOUSTCHINE
Publishing inc.
new york

Also available in Dungeon:
Dungeon, Zenith, vols. 1, 2: $14.95 each, 3: $12.95
Dungeon Early Years, vols. 1, 2: $12.95
Dungeon, Twilight, vols. 1, $12.95, 2: $14.95
Dungeon, Parade, vols. 1, 2: $9.95 each
Dungeon, Monstres, vols. 1, 2: $12.95 each
Also by Trondheim:
Little Nothings, vols. 1, 2, 3: $14.95 each
Mr. I, $13.95
with Thierry Robin:
Li'l Santa, $14.95
Happy Halloween, Li'l Santa, $14.95

Add $4 P&H first item $1 each additional.

Write for our complete catalog
of over 200 graphic novels:
NBM
40 Exchange Pl., Suite 1308
New York, NY 10005
www.nbmpublishing.com

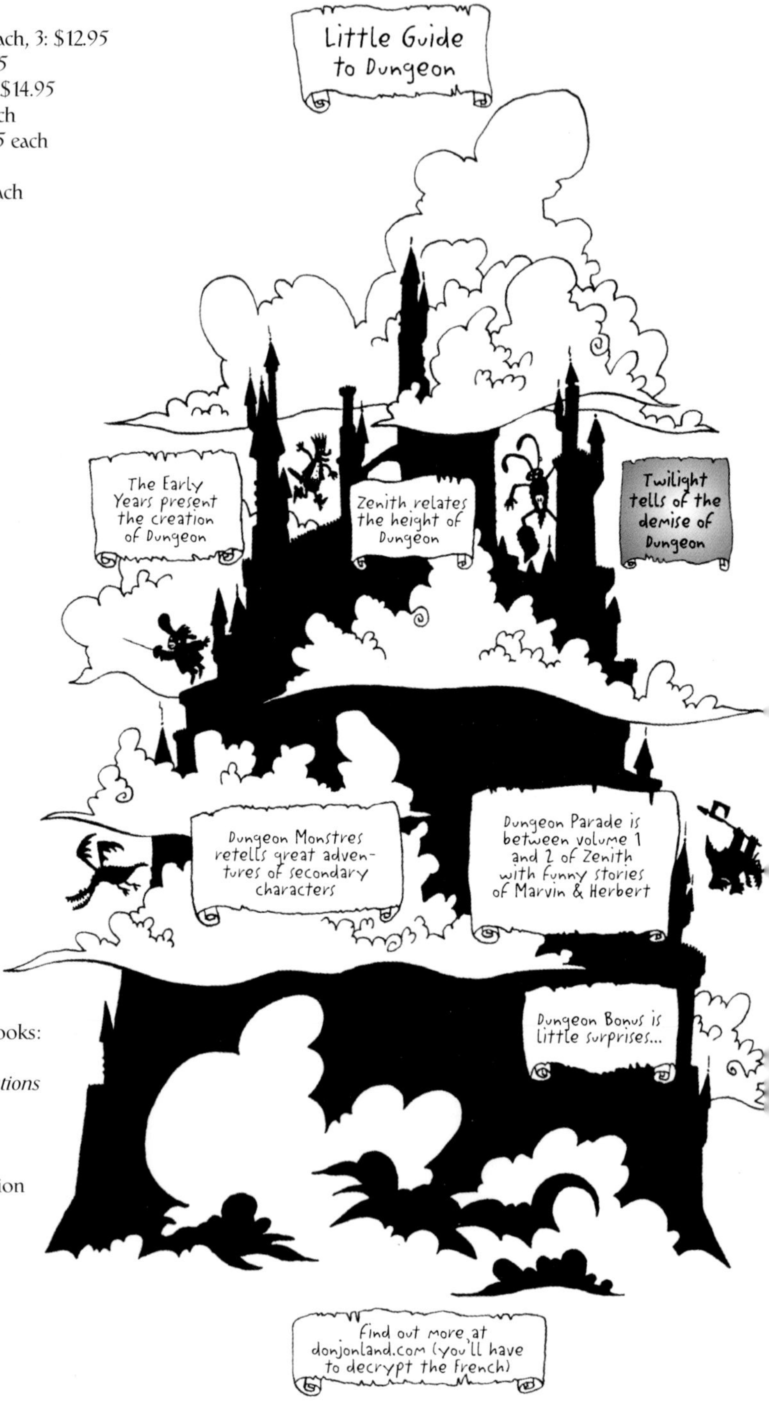
Little Guide to Dungeon
The Early Years present the creation of Dungeon
Zenith relates the height of Dungeon
Twilight tells of the demise of Dungeon
Dungeon Monstres retells great adventures of secondary characters
Dungeon Parade is between volume 1 and 2 of Zenith with funny stories of Marvin & Herbert
Dungeon Bonus is little surprises...
Find out more at donjonland.com (you'll have to decrypt the French)

Originally published in French in 2 books:
Donjon Crepuscule:
Les Nouveaux Centurions and *Revolutions*
ISBN: 978-1-56163-578-8

Translation by Joe Johnson
Lettering by Ortho
Printed in Singapore

3 2 1

Library of Congress Control Number: 2007276175

The New Centurions

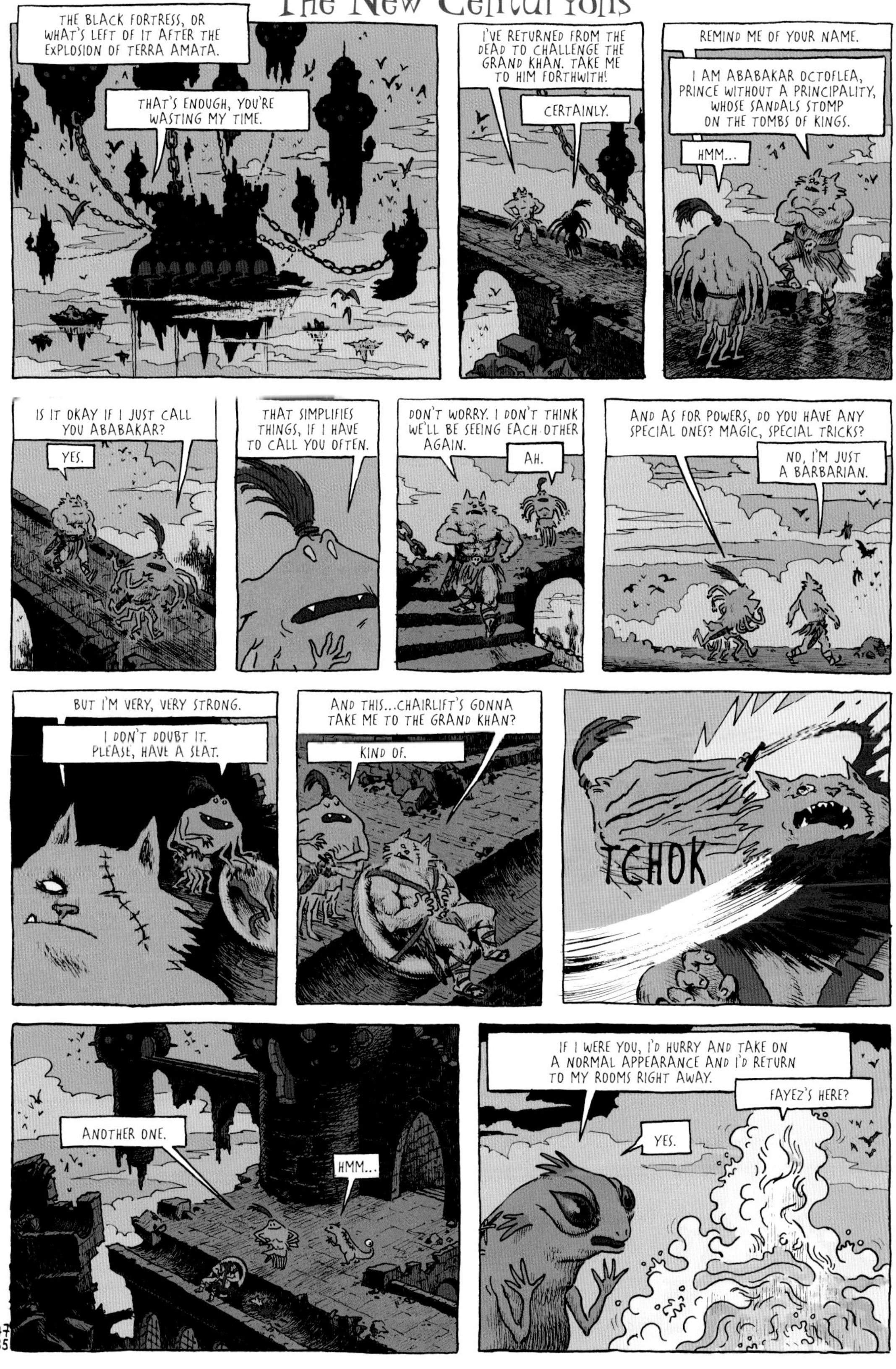

THE BLACK FORTRESS, OR WHAT'S LEFT OF IT AFTER THE EXPLOSION OF TERRA AMATA.
THAT'S ENOUGH, YOU'RE WASTING MY TIME.
I'VE RETURNED FROM THE DEAD TO CHALLENGE THE GRAND KHAN. TAKE ME TO HIM FORTHWITH!
CERTAINLY.
REMIND ME OF YOUR NAME.
I AM ABABAKAR OCTOFLEA, PRINCE WITHOUT A PRINCIPALITY, WHOSE SANDALS STOMP ON THE TOMBS OF KINGS.
HMM...
IS IT OKAY IF I JUST CALL YOU ABABAKAR?
YES.
THAT SIMPLIFIES THINGS, IF I HAVE TO CALL YOU OFTEN.
DON'T WORRY. I DON'T THINK WE'LL BE SEEING EACH OTHER AGAIN.
AH.
AND AS FOR POWERS, DO YOU HAVE ANY SPECIAL ONES? MAGIC, SPECIAL TRICKS?
NO, I'M JUST A BARBARIAN.
BUT I'M VERY, VERY STRONG.
I DON'T DOUBT IT. PLEASE, HAVE A SEAT.
AND THIS...CHAIRLIFT'S GONNA TAKE ME TO THE GRAND KHAN?
KIND OF.
TCHOK
ANOTHER ONE.
HMM...
IF I WERE YOU, I'D HURRY AND TAKE ON A NORMAL APPEARANCE AND I'D RETURN TO MY ROOMS RIGHT AWAY.
FAYEZ'S HERE?
YES.

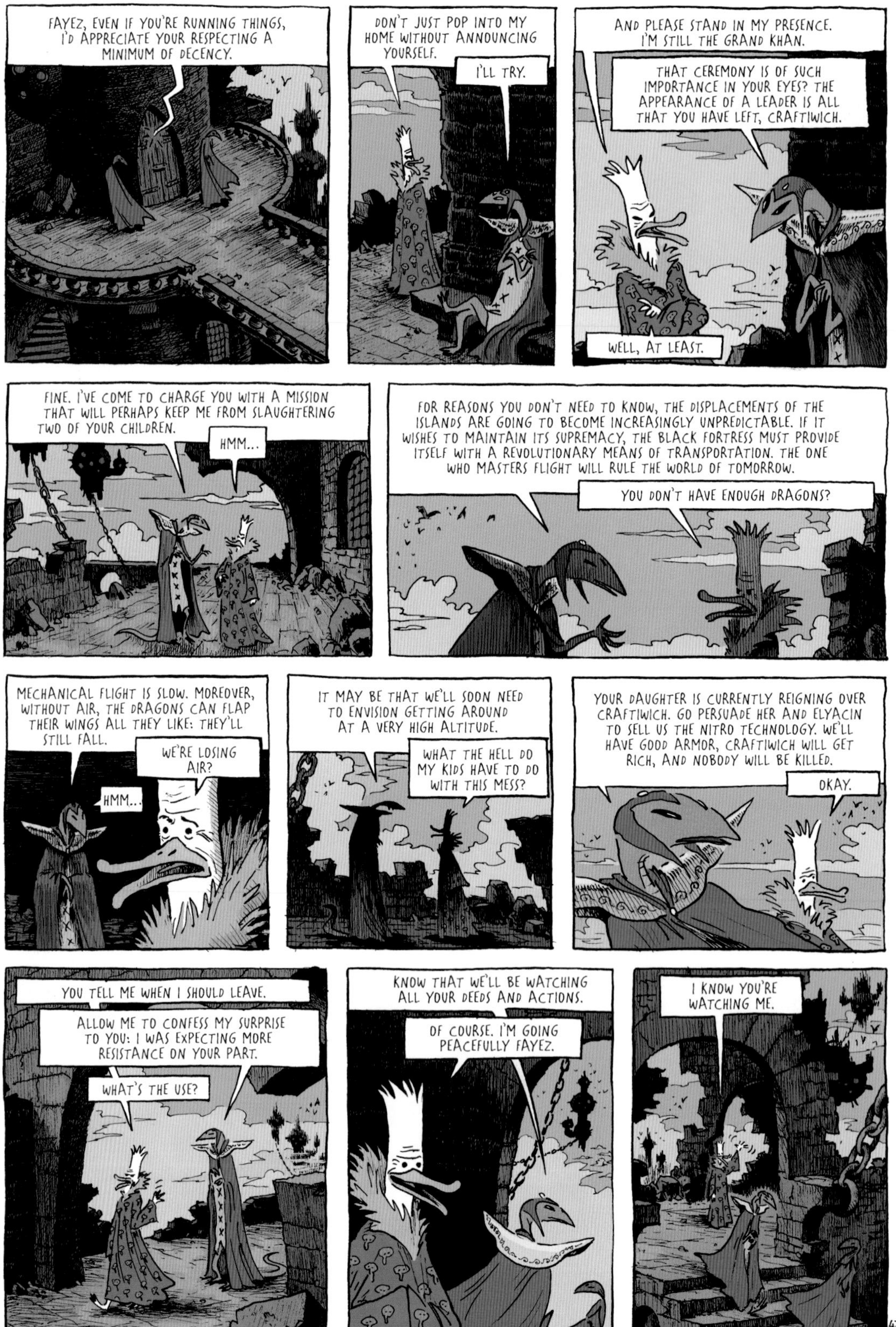
FAYEZ, EVEN IF YOU'RE RUNNING THINGS, I'D APPRECIATE YOUR RESPECTING A MINIMUM OF DECENCY.
DON'T JUST POP INTO MY HOME WITHOUT ANNOUNCING YOURSELF.
I'LL TRY.
AND PLEASE STAND IN MY PRESENCE. I'M STILL THE GRAND KHAN.
THAT CEREMONY IS OF SUCH IMPORTANCE IN YOUR EYES? THE APPEARANCE OF A LEADER IS ALL THAT YOU HAVE LEFT, CRAFTIWICH.
WELL, AT LEAST.
FINE. I'VE COME TO CHARGE YOU WITH A MISSION THAT WILL PERHAPS KEEP ME FROM SLAUGHTERING TWO OF YOUR CHILDREN.
HMM...
FOR REASONS YOU DON'T NEED TO KNOW, THE DISPLACEMENTS OF THE ISLANDS ARE GOING TO BECOME INCREASINGLY UNPREDICTABLE. IF IT WISHES TO MAINTAIN ITS SUPREMACY, THE BLACK FORTRESS MUST PROVIDE ITSELF WITH A REVOLUTIONARY MEANS OF TRANSPORTATION. THE ONE WHO MASTERS FLIGHT WILL RULE THE WORLD OF TOMORROW.
YOU DON'T HAVE ENOUGH DRAGONS?
MECHANICAL FLIGHT IS SLOW. MOREOVER, WITHOUT AIR, THE DRAGONS CAN FLAP THEIR WINGS ALL THEY LIKE: THEY'LL STILL FALL.
WE'RE LOSING AIR?
HMM...
IT MAY BE THAT WE'LL SOON NEED TO ENVISION GETTING AROUND AT A VERY HIGH ALTITUDE.
WHAT THE HELL DO MY KIDS HAVE TO DO WITH THIS MESS?
YOUR DAUGHTER IS CURRENTLY REIGNING OVER CRAFTIWICH. GO PERSUADE HER AND ELYACIN TO SELL US THE NITRO TECHNOLOGY. WE'LL HAVE GOOD ARMOR, CRAFTIWICH WILL GET RICH, AND NOBODY WILL BE KILLED.
OKAY.
YOU TELL ME WHEN I SHOULD LEAVE.
ALLOW ME TO CONFESS MY SURPRISE TO YOU: I WAS EXPECTING MORE RESISTANCE ON YOUR PART.
WHAT'S THE USE?
KNOW THAT WE'LL BE WATCHING ALL YOUR DEEDS AND ACTIONS.
OF COURSE. I'M GOING PEACEFULLY FAYEZ.
I KNOW YOU'RE WATCHING ME.

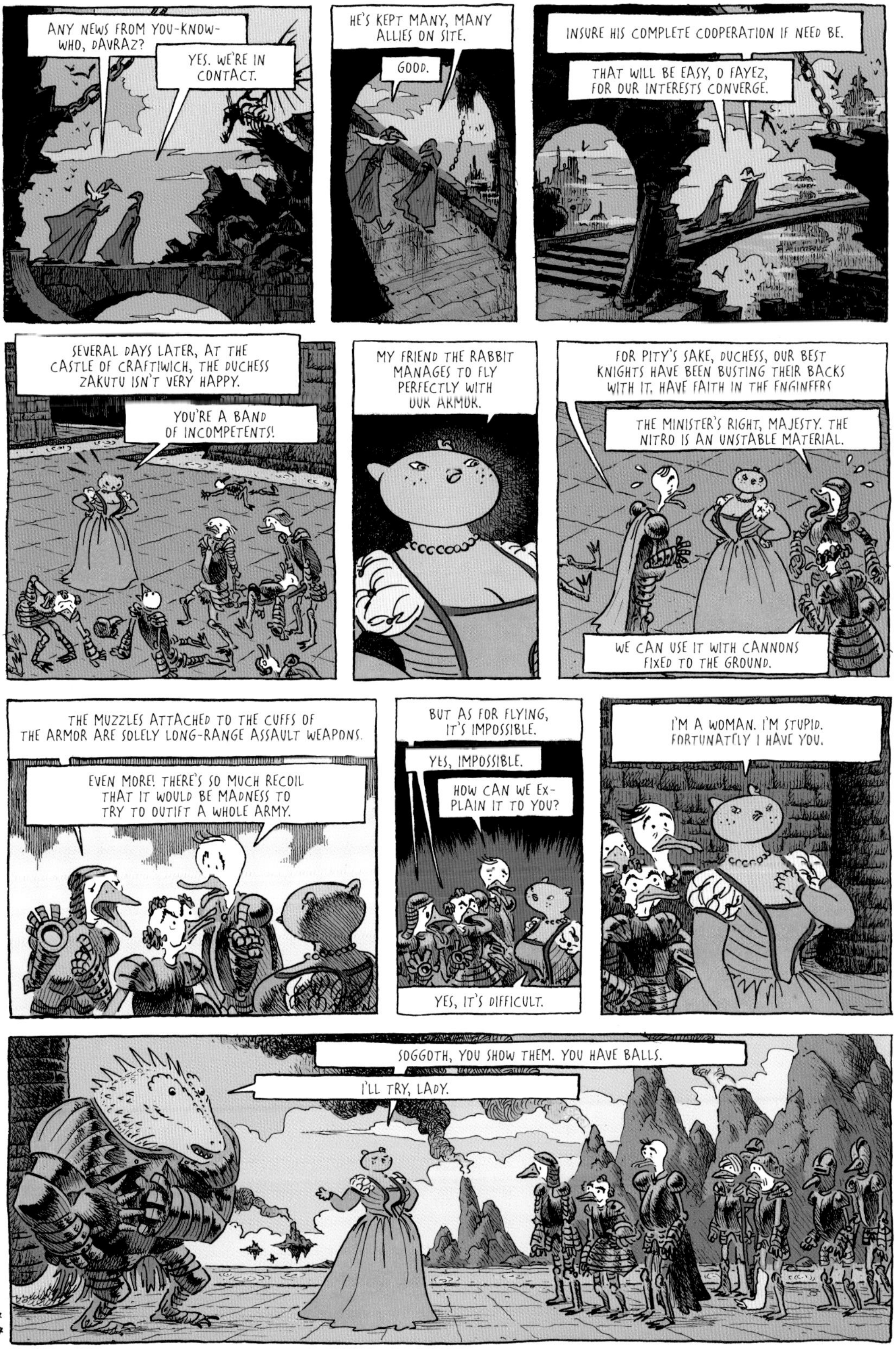

ANY NEWS FROM YOU-KNOW-WHO, DAVRAZ?
YES. WE'RE IN CONTACT.
HE'S KEPT MANY, MANY ALLIES ON SITE.
GOOD.
INSURE HIS COMPLETE COOPERATION IF NEED BE.
THAT WILL BE EASY, O FAYEZ, FOR OUR INTERESTS CONVERGE.
SEVERAL DAYS LATER, AT THE CASTLE OF CRAFTIWICH, THE DUCHESS ZAKUTU ISN'T VERY HAPPY.
YOU'RE A BAND OF INCOMPETENTS!
MY FRIEND THE RABBIT MANAGES TO FLY PERFECTLY WITH OUR ARMOR.
FOR PITY'S SAKE, DUCHESS, OUR BEST KNIGHTS HAVE BEEN BUSTING THEIR BACKS WITH IT. HAVE FAITH IN THE ENGINEERS.
THE MINISTER'S RIGHT, MAJESTY. THE NITRO IS AN UNSTABLE MATERIAL.
WE CAN USE IT WITH CANNONS FIXED TO THE GROUND.
THE MUZZLES ATTACHED TO THE CUFFS OF THE ARMOR ARE SOLELY LONG-RANGE ASSAULT WEAPONS.
EVEN MORE! THERE'S SO MUCH RECOIL THAT IT WOULD BE MADNESS TO TRY TO OUTIFT A WHOLE ARMY.
BUT AS FOR FLYING, IT'S IMPOSSIBLE.
YES, IMPOSSIBLE.
HOW CAN WE EXPLAIN IT TO YOU?
YES, IT'S DIFFICULT.
I'M A WOMAN. I'M STUPID. FORTUNATELY I HAVE YOU.
SOGGOTH, YOU SHOW THEM. YOU HAVE BALLS.
I'LL TRY, LADY.

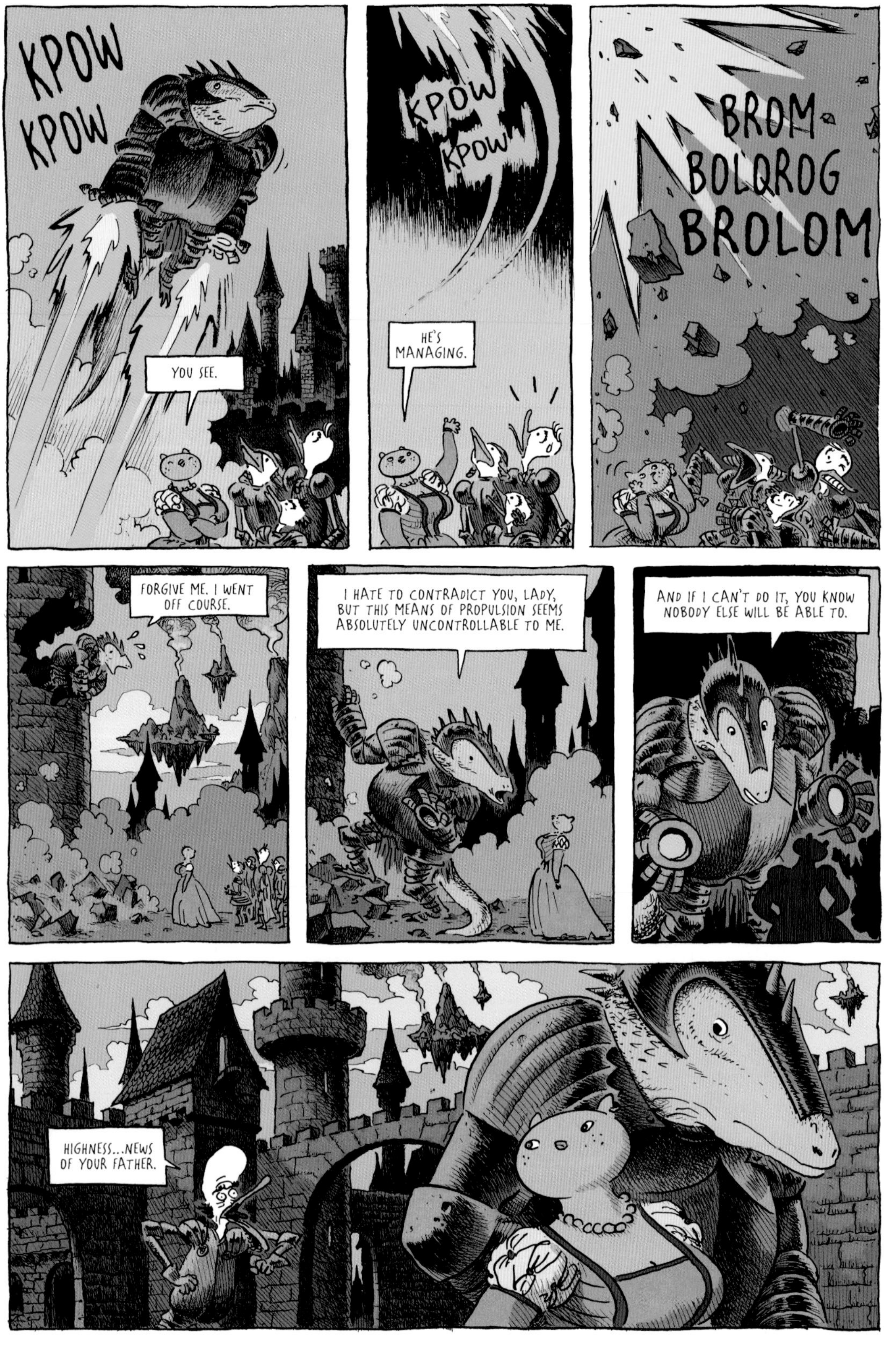
KPOW
KPOW
YOU SEE.
KPOW
KPOW
HE'S MANAGING.
BROM
BOLQROG
BROLOM
FORGIVE ME. I WENT OFF COURSE.
I HATE TO CONTRADICT YOU, LADY, BUT THIS MEANS OF PROPULSION SEEMS ABSOLUTELY UNCONTROLLABLE TO ME.
AND IF I CAN'T DO IT, YOU KNOW NOBODY ELSE WILL BE ABLE TO.
HIGHNESS...NEWS OF YOUR FATHER.

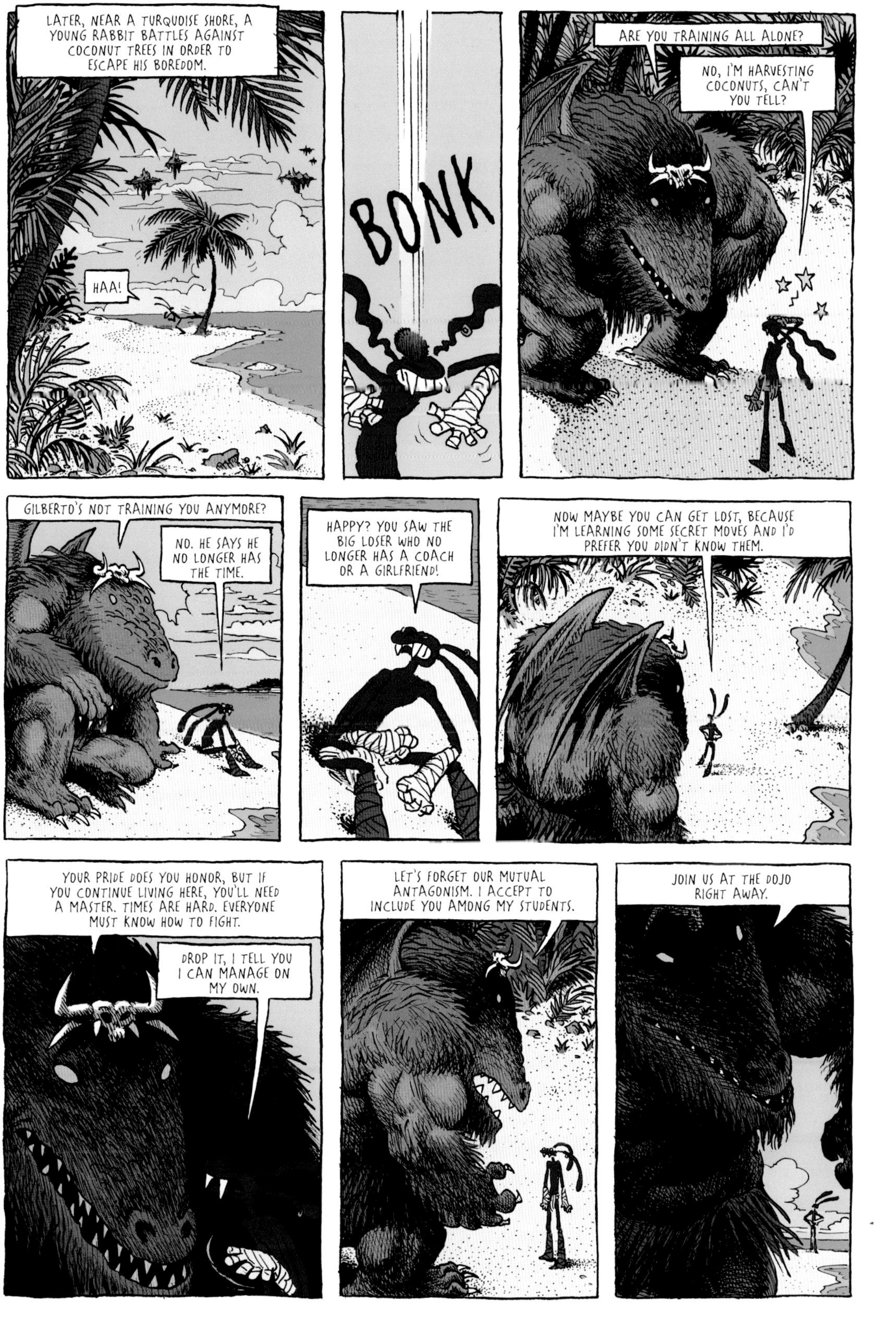
LATER, NEAR A TURQUOISE SHORE, A YOUNG RABBIT BATTLES AGAINST COCONUT TREES IN ORDER TO ESCAPE HIS BOREDOM.
HAA!
BONK
ARE YOU TRAINING ALL ALONE?
NO, I'M HARVESTING COCONUTS, CAN'T YOU TELL?
GILBERTO'S NOT TRAINING YOU ANYMORE?
NO. HE SAYS HE NO LONGER HAS THE TIME.
HAPPY? YOU SAW THE BIG LOSER WHO NO LONGER HAS A COACH OR A GIRLFRIEND!
NOW MAYBE YOU CAN GET LOST, BECAUSE I'M LEARNING SOME SECRET MOVES AND I'D PREFER YOU DIDN'T KNOW THEM.
YOUR PRIDE DOES YOU HONOR, BUT IF YOU CONTINUE LIVING HERE, YOU'LL NEED A MASTER. TIMES ARE HARD. EVERYONE MUST KNOW HOW TO FIGHT.
DROP IT, I TELL YOU I CAN MANAGE ON MY OWN.
LET'S FORGET OUR MUTUAL ANTAGONISM. I ACCEPT TO INCLUDE YOU AMONG MY STUDENTS.
JOIN US AT THE DOJO RIGHT AWAY.

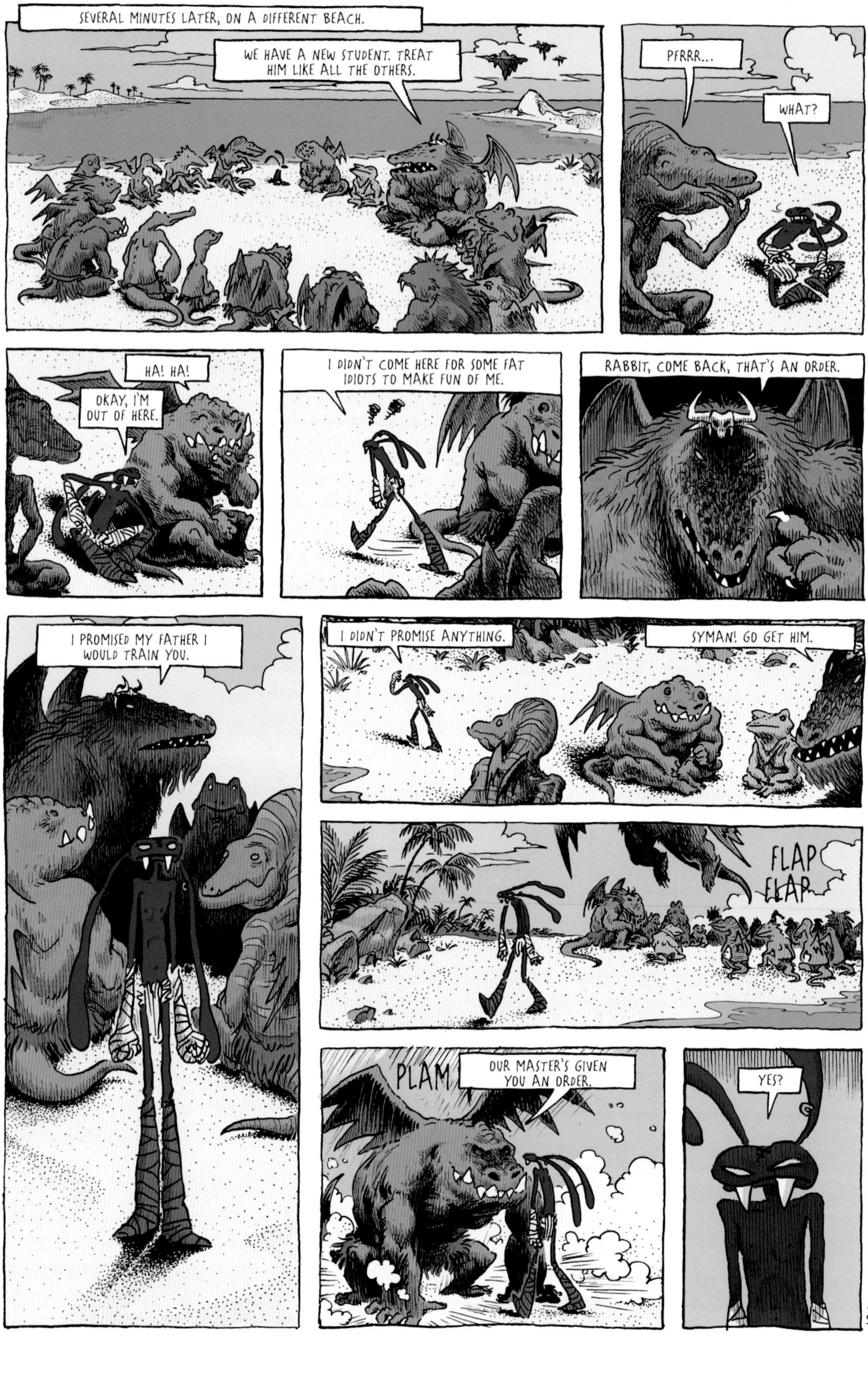
SEVERAL MINUTES LATER, ON A DIFFERENT BEACH.
WE HAVE A NEW STUDENT. TREAT HIM LIKE ALL THE OTHERS.
PFRRR...
WHAT?
HA! HA!
OKAY, I'M OUT OF HERE.
I DIDN'T COME HERE FOR SOME FAT IDIOTS TO MAKE FUN OF ME.
RABBIT, COME BACK, THAT'S AN ORDER.
I PROMISED MY FATHER I WOULD TRAIN YOU.
I DIDN'T PROMISE ANYTHING.
SYMAN! GO GET HIM.
FLAP
FLAP
PLAM
OUR MASTER'S GIVEN YOU AN ORDER.
YES?

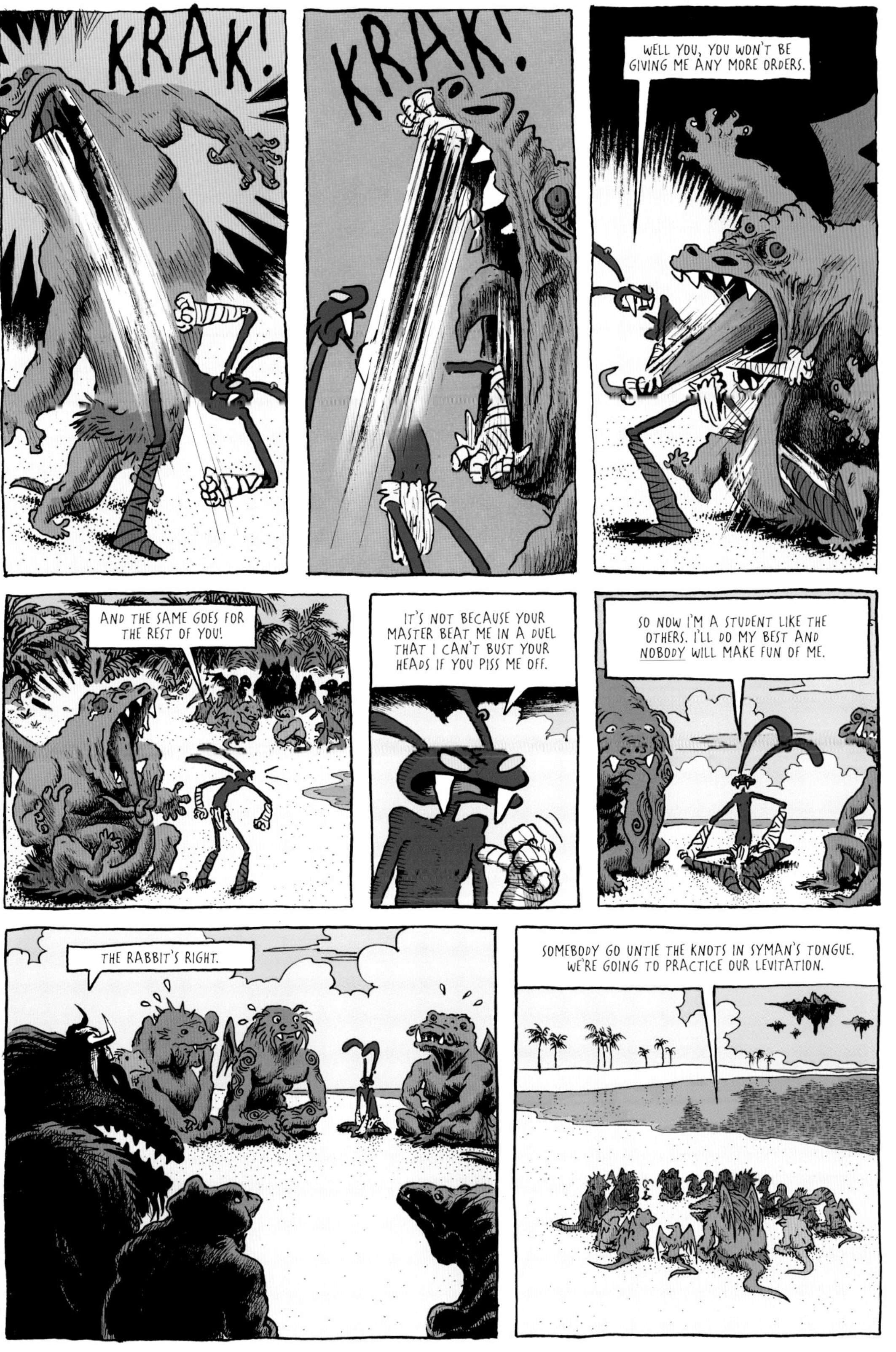
KRAK!
KRAK!
WELL YOU, YOU WON'T BE GIVING ME ANY MORE ORDERS.
AND THE SAME GOES FOR THE REST OF YOU!
IT'S NOT BECAUSE YOUR MASTER BEAT ME IN A DUEL THAT I CAN'T BUST YOUR HEADS IF YOU PISS ME OFF.
SO NOW I'M A STUDENT LIKE THE OTHERS. I'LL DO MY BEST AND NOBODY WILL MAKE FUN OF ME.
THE RABBIT'S RIGHT.
SOMEBODY GO UNTIE THE KNOTS IN SYMAN'S TONGUE. WE'RE GOING TO PRACTICE OUR LEVITATION.

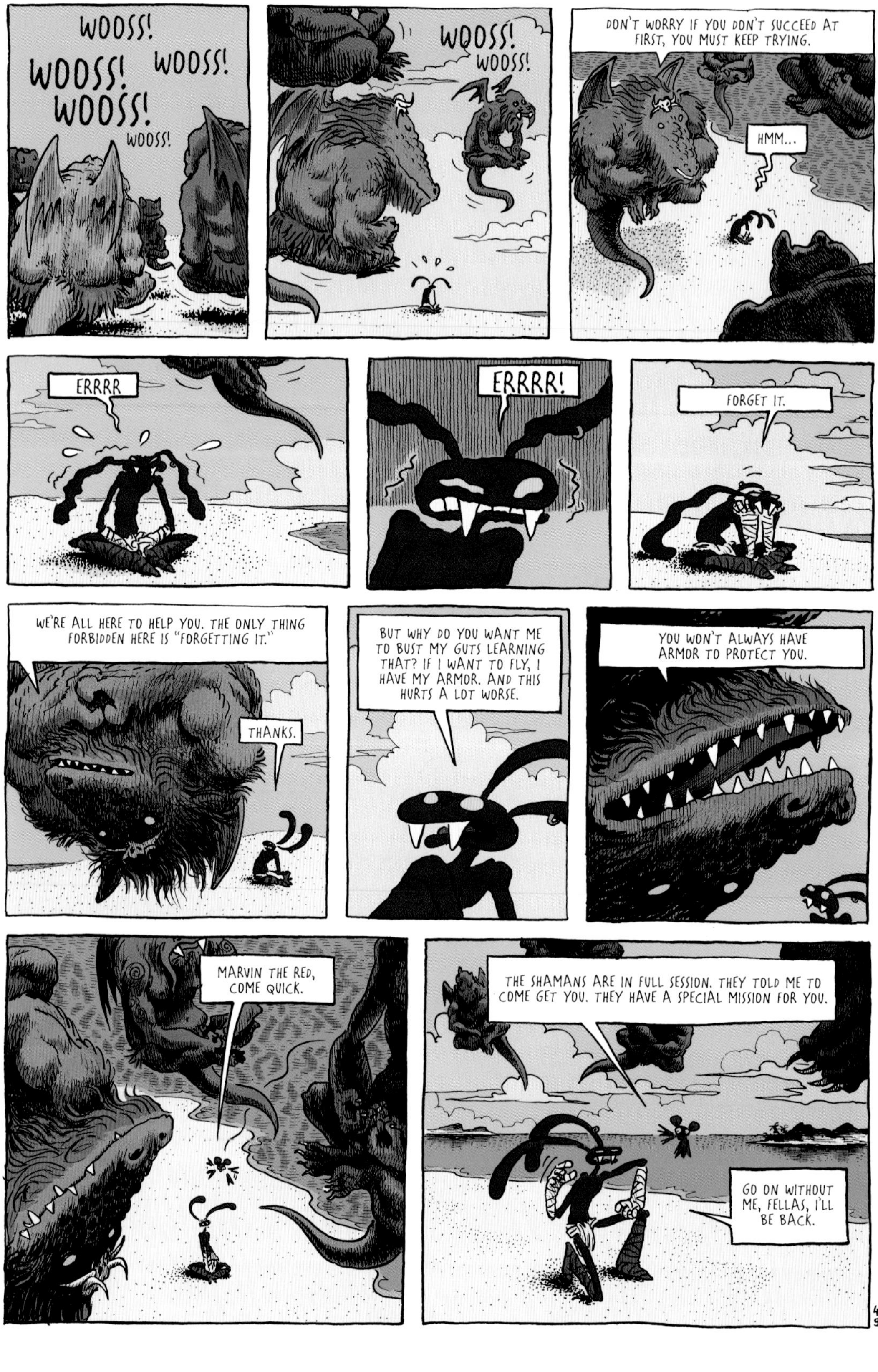
WOOSS! WOOSS! WOOSS! WOOSS! WOOSS!
WOOSS! WOOSS!
DON'T WORRY IF YOU DON'T SUCCEED AT FIRST, YOU MUST KEEP TRYING.
HMM...
ERRRR
ERRRR!
FORGET IT.
WE'RE ALL HERE TO HELP YOU. THE ONLY THING FORBIDDEN HERE IS "FORGETTING IT."
THANKS.
BUT WHY DO YOU WANT ME TO BUST MY GUTS LEARNING THAT? IF I WANT TO FLY, I HAVE MY ARMOR. AND THIS HURTS A LOT WORSE.
YOU WON'T ALWAYS HAVE ARMOR TO PROTECT YOU.
MARVIN THE RED, COME QUICK.
THE SHAMANS ARE IN FULL SESSION. THEY TOLD ME TO COME GET YOU. THEY HAVE A SPECIAL MISSION FOR YOU.
GO ON WITHOUT ME, FELLAS, I'LL BE BACK.

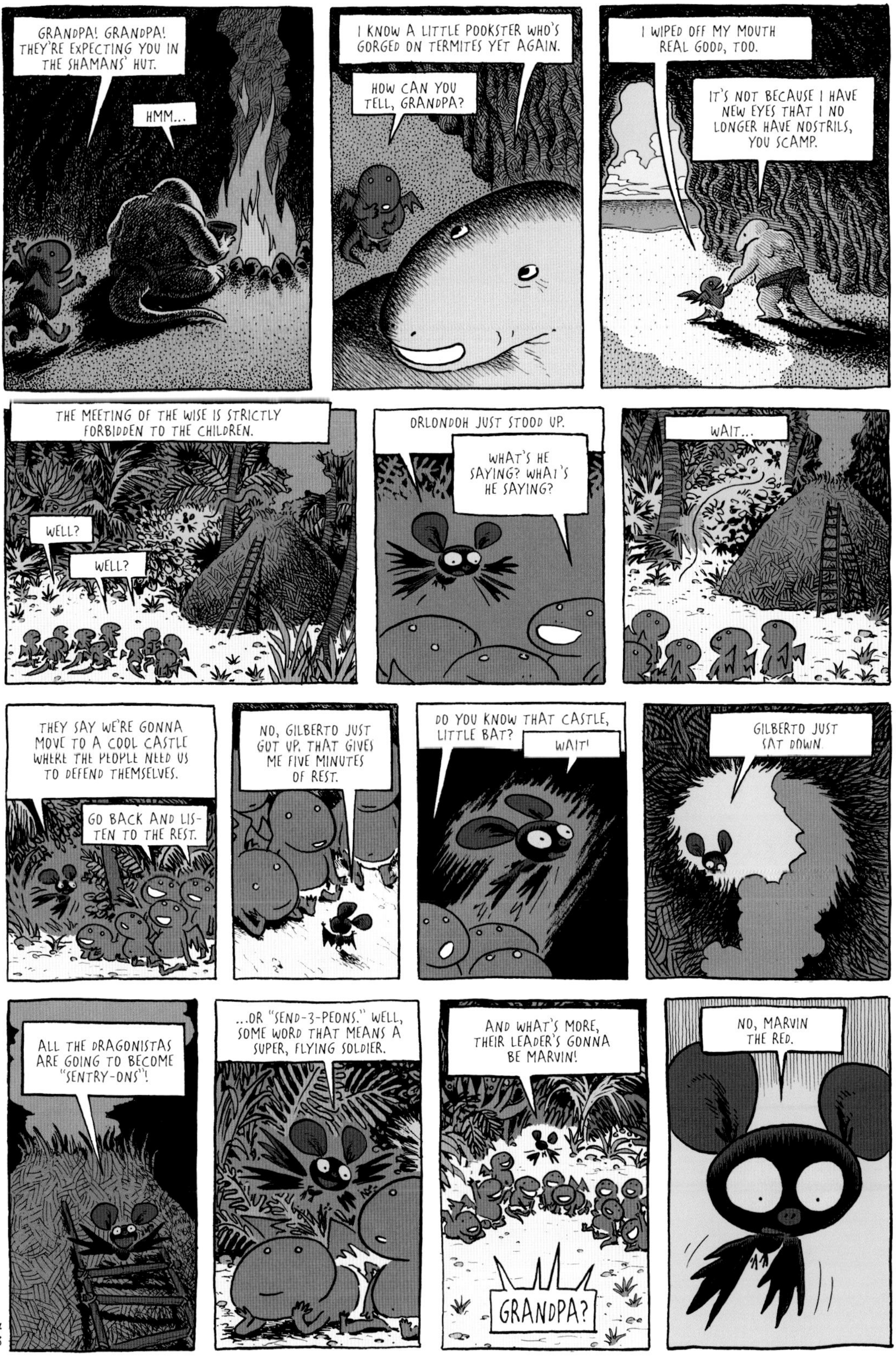

GRANDPA! GRANDPA! THEY'RE EXPECTING YOU IN THE SHAMANS' HUT.
HMM...
I KNOW A LITTLE POOKSTER WHO'S GORGED ON TERMITES YET AGAIN.
HOW CAN YOU TELL, GRANDPA?
I WIPED OFF MY MOUTH REAL GOOD, TOO.
IT'S NOT BECAUSE I HAVE NEW EYES THAT I NO LONGER HAVE NOSTRILS, YOU SCAMP.
THE MEETING OF THE WISE IS STRICTLY FORBIDDEN TO THE CHILDREN.
WELL?
WELL?
ORLONDOH JUST STOOD UP.
WHAT'S HE SAYING? WHAT'S HE SAYING?
WAIT...
THEY SAY WE'RE GONNA MOVE TO A COOL CASTLE WHERE THE PEOPLE NEED US TO DEFEND THEMSELVES.
GO BACK AND LISTEN TO THE REST.
NO, GILBERTO JUST GOT UP. THAT GIVES ME FIVE MINUTES OF REST.
DO YOU KNOW THAT CASTLE, LITTLE BAT?
WAIT!
GILBERTO JUST SAT DOWN.
ALL THE DRAGONISTAS ARE GOING TO BECOME "SENTRY-ONS"!
...OR "SEND-3-PEONS." WELL, SOME WORD THAT MEANS A SUPER, FLYING SOLDIER.
AND WHAT'S MORE, THEIR LEADER'S GONNA BE MARVIN!
GRANDPA?
NO, MARVIN THE RED.

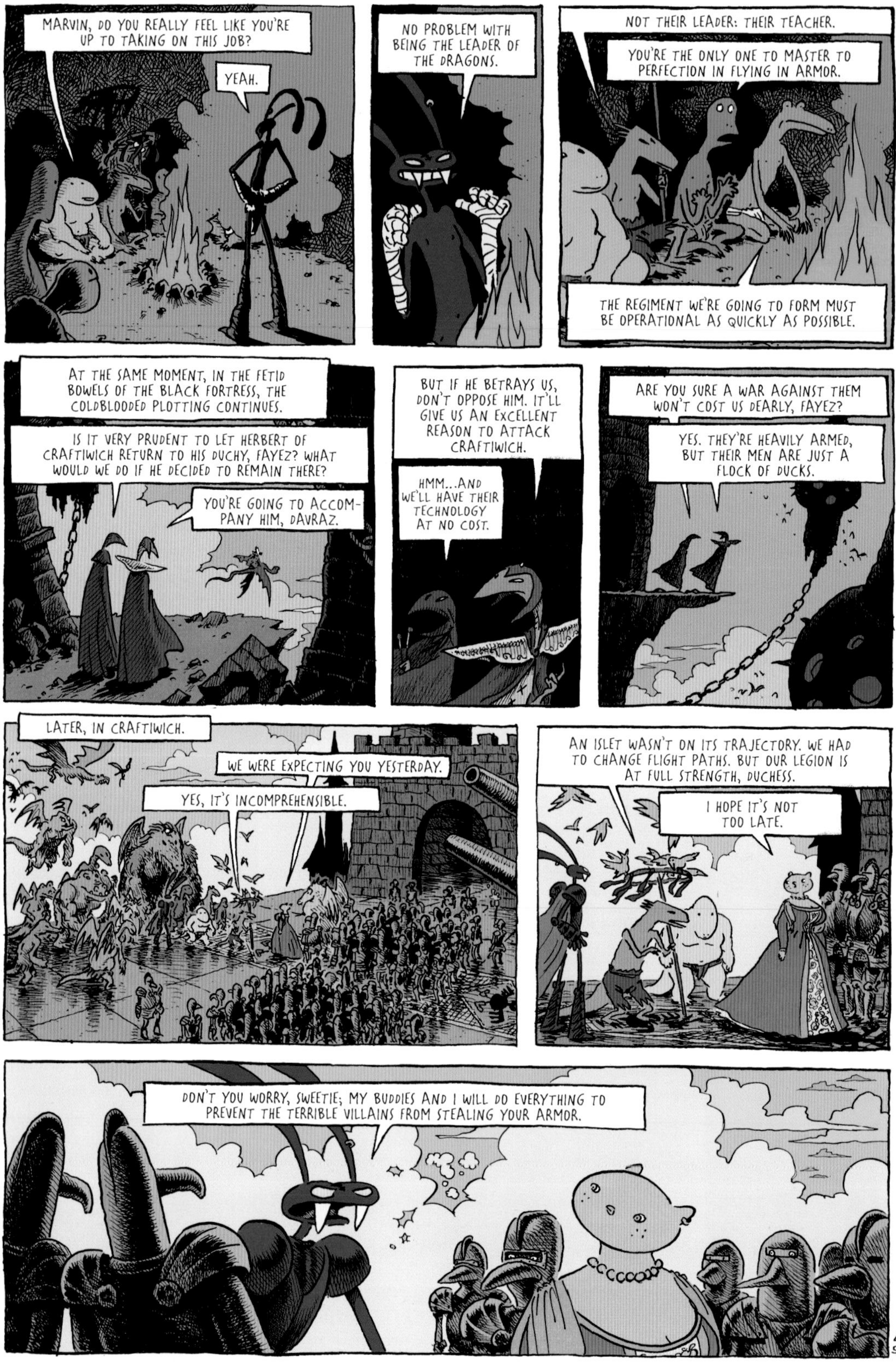

MARVIN, DO YOU REALLY FEEL LIKE YOU'RE UP TO TAKING ON THIS JOB?
YEAH.
NO PROBLEM WITH BEING THE LEADER OF THE DRAGONS.
NOT THEIR LEADER: THEIR TEACHER.
YOU'RE THE ONLY ONE TO MASTER TO PERFECTION IN FLYING IN ARMOR.
THE REGIMENT WE'RE GOING TO FORM MUST BE OPERATIONAL AS QUICKLY AS POSSIBLE.
AT THE SAME MOMENT, IN THE FETID BOWELS OF THE BLACK FORTRESS, THE COLDBLOODED PLOTTING CONTINUES.
IS IT VERY PRUDENT TO LET HERBERT OF CRAFTIWICH RETURN TO HIS DUCHY, FAYEZ? WHAT WOULD WE DO IF HE DECIDED TO REMAIN THERE?
YOU'RE GOING TO ACCOMPANY HIM, DAVRAZ.
BUT IF HE BETRAYS US, DON'T OPPOSE HIM. IT'LL GIVE US AN EXCELLENT REASON TO ATTACK CRAFTIWICH.
HMM...AND WE'LL HAVE THEIR TECHNOLOGY AT NO COST.
ARE YOU SURE A WAR AGAINST THEM WON'T COST US DEARLY, FAYEZ?
YES. THEY'RE HEAVILY ARMED, BUT THEIR MEN ARE JUST A FLOCK OF DUCKS.
LATER, IN CRAFTIWICH.
WE WERE EXPECTING YOU YESTERDAY.
YES, IT'S INCOMPREHENSIBLE.
AN ISLET WASN'T ON ITS TRAJECTORY. WE HAD TO CHANGE FLIGHT PATHS. BUT OUR LEGION IS AT FULL STRENGTH, DUCHESS.
I HOPE IT'S NOT TOO LATE.
DON'T YOU WORRY, SWEETIE; MY BUDDIES AND I WILL DO EVERYTHING TO PREVENT THE TERRIBLE VILLAINS FROM STEALING YOUR ARMOR.

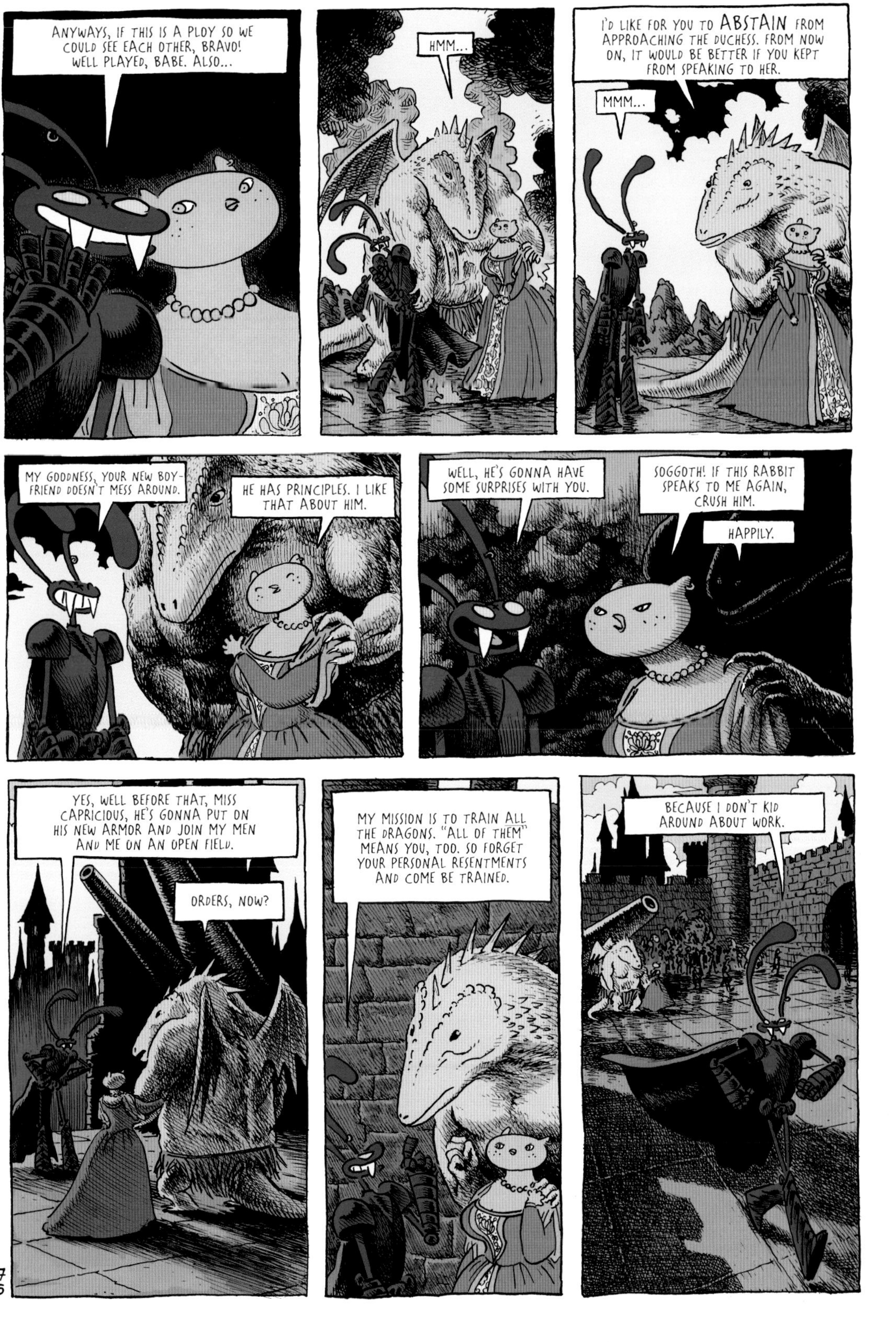
ANYWAYS, IF THIS IS A PLOY SO WE COULD SEE EACH OTHER, BRAVO! WELL PLAYED, BABE. ALSO...
HMM...
I'D LIKE FOR YOU TO ABSTAIN FROM APPROACHING THE DUCHESS. FROM NOW ON, IT WOULD BE BETTER IF YOU KEPT FROM SPEAKING TO HER.
MMM...
MY GOODNESS, YOUR NEW BOY-FRIEND DOESN'T MESS AROUND.
HE HAS PRINCIPLES. I LIKE THAT ABOUT HIM.
WELL, HE'S GONNA HAVE SOME SURPRISES WITH YOU.
SOGGOTH! IF THIS RABBIT SPEAKS TO ME AGAIN, CRUSH HIM.
HAPPILY.
YES, WELL BEFORE THAT, MISS CAPRICIOUS, HE'S GONNA PUT ON HIS NEW ARMOR AND JOIN MY MEN AND ME ON AN OPEN FIELD.
ORDERS, NOW?
MY MISSION IS TO TRAIN ALL THE DRAGONS. "ALL OF THEM" MEANS YOU, TOO. SO FORGET YOUR PERSONAL RESENTMENTS AND COME BE TRAINED.
BECAUSE I DON'T KID AROUND ABOUT WORK.

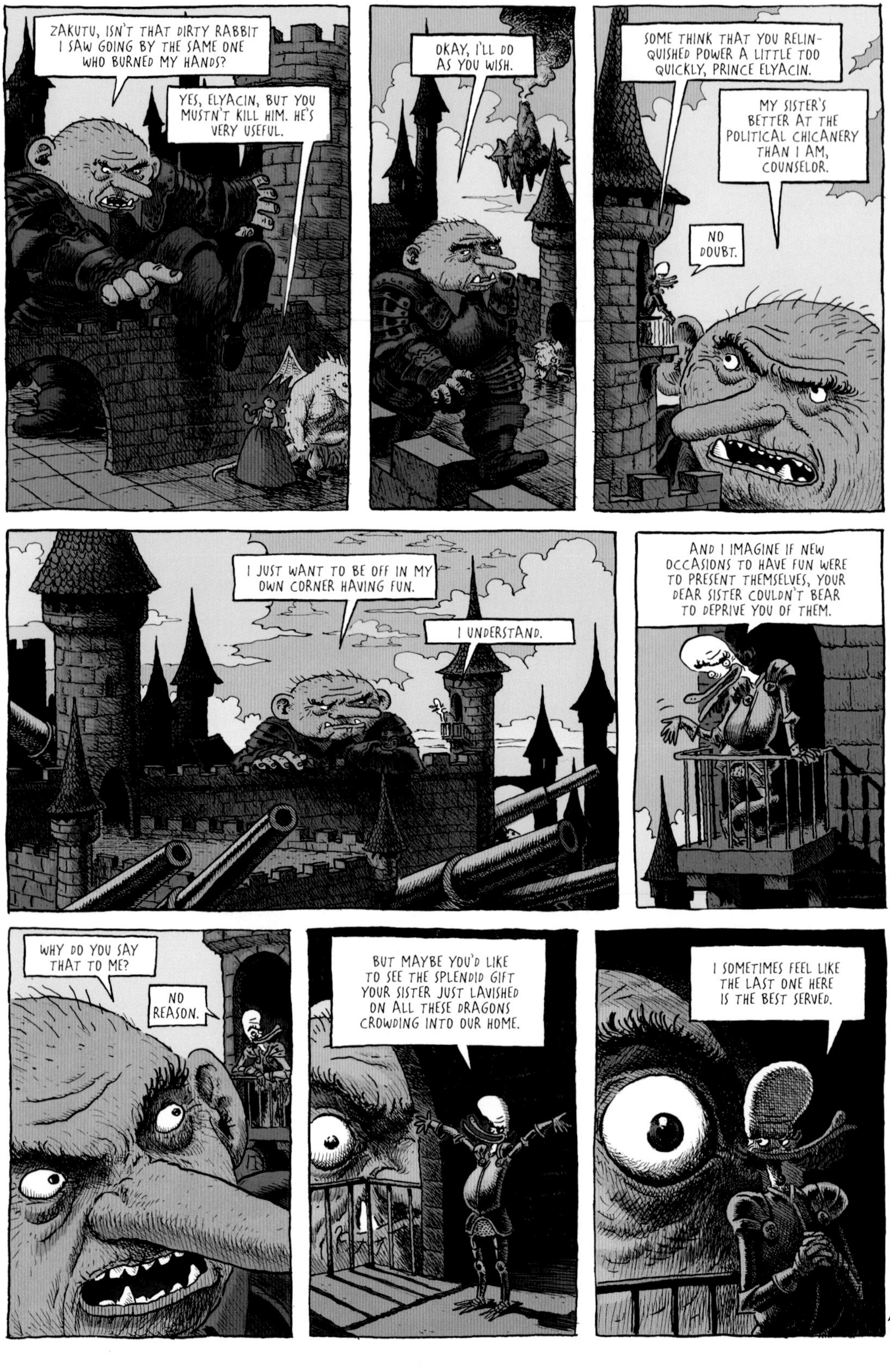
ZAKUTU, ISN'T THAT DIRTY RABBIT I SAW GOING BY THE SAME ONE WHO BURNED MY HANDS?
YES, ELYACIN, BUT YOU MUSTN'T KILL HIM. HE'S VERY USEFUL.
OKAY, I'LL DO AS YOU WISH.
SOME THINK THAT YOU RELINQUISHED POWER A LITTLE TOO QUICKLY, PRINCE ELYACIN.
MY SISTER'S BETTER AT THE POLITICAL CHICANERY THAN I AM, COUNSELOR.
NO DOUBT.
I JUST WANT TO BE OFF IN MY OWN CORNER HAVING FUN.
I UNDERSTAND.
AND I IMAGINE IF NEW OCCASIONS TO HAVE FUN WERE TO PRESENT THEMSELVES, YOUR DEAR SISTER COULDN'T BEAR TO DEPRIVE YOU OF THEM.
WHY DO YOU SAY THAT TO ME?
NO REASON.
BUT MAYBE YOU'D LIKE TO SEE THE SPLENDID GIFT YOUR SISTER JUST LAVISHED ON ALL THESE DRAGONS CROWDING INTO OUR HOME.
I SOMETIMES FEEL LIKE THE LAST ONE HERE IS THE BEST SERVED.

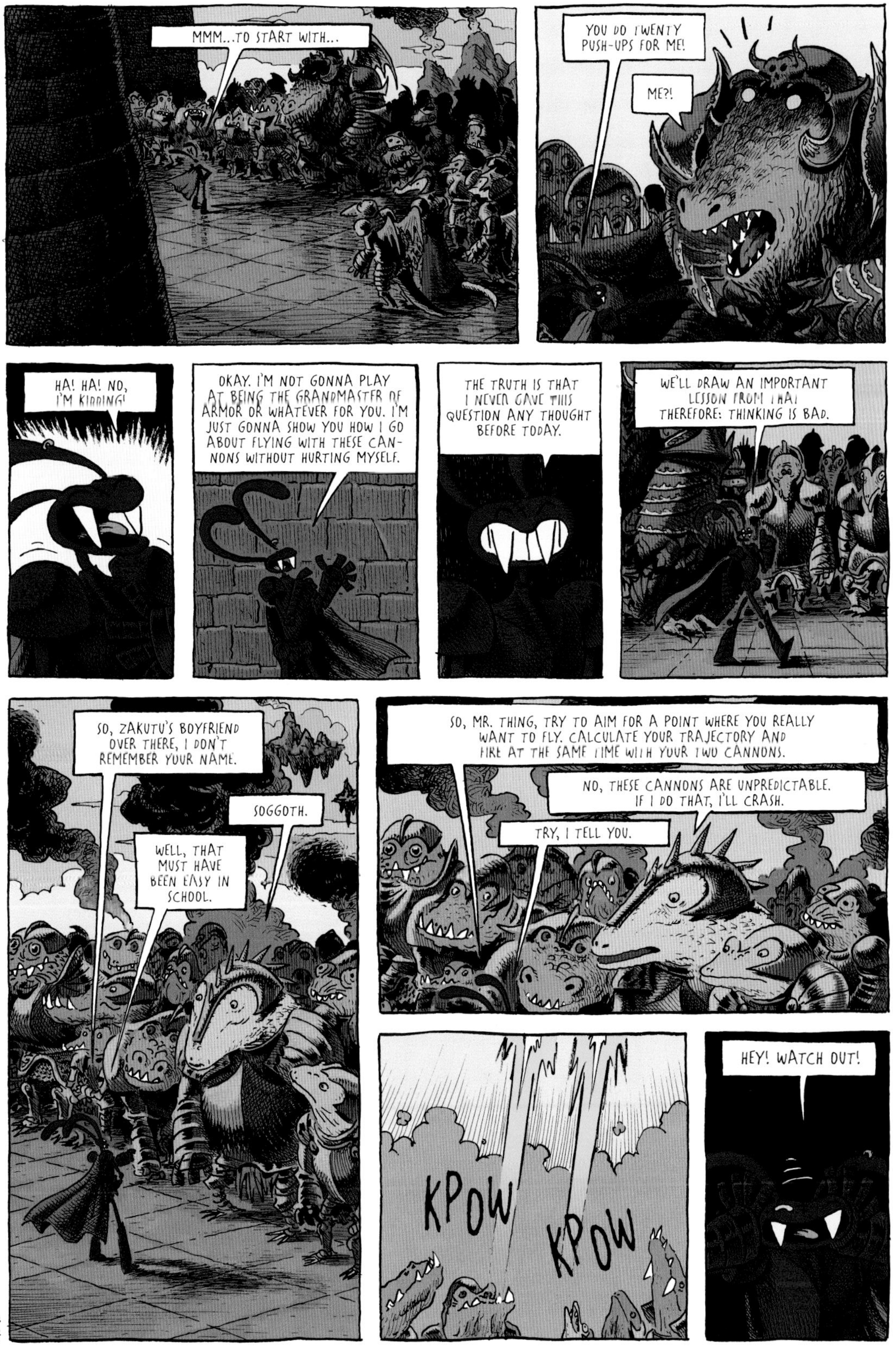
MMM...TO START WITH...
YOU DO TWENTY PUSH-UPS FOR ME!
ME?!
HA! HA! NO, I'M KIDDING!
OKAY. I'M NOT GONNA PLAY AT BEING THE GRANDMASTER OF ARMOR OR WHATEVER FOR YOU. I'M JUST GONNA SHOW YOU HOW I GO ABOUT FLYING WITH THESE CANNONS WITHOUT HURTING MYSELF.
THE TRUTH IS THAT I NEVER GAVE THIS QUESTION ANY THOUGHT BEFORE TODAY.
WE'LL DRAW AN IMPORTANT LESSON FROM THAT THEREFORE: THINKING IS BAD.
SO, ZAKUTU'S BOYFRIEND OVER THERE, I DON'T REMEMBER YOUR NAME.
SOGGOTH.
WELL, THAT MUST HAVE BEEN EASY IN SCHOOL.
SO, MR. THING, TRY TO AIM FOR A POINT WHERE YOU REALLY WANT TO FLY. CALCULATE YOUR TRAJECTORY AND FIRE AT THE SAME TIME WITH YOUR TWO CANNONS.
NO, THESE CANNONS ARE UNPREDICTABLE. IF I DO THAT, I'LL CRASH.
TRY, I TELL YOU.
KPOW
KPOW
HEY! WATCH OUT!

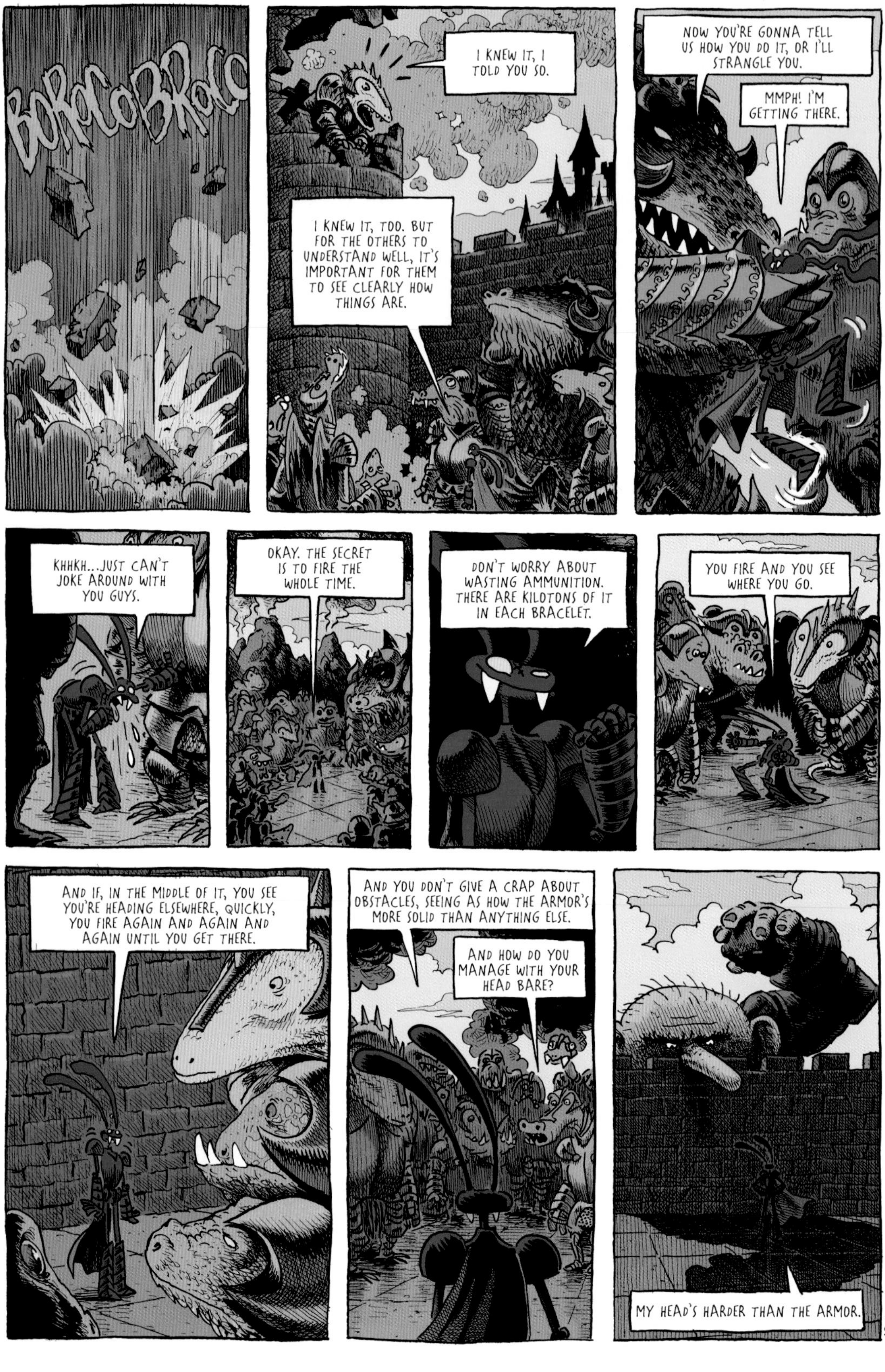
BORCOBROC
I KNEW IT, I TOLD YOU SO.
I KNEW IT, TOO. BUT FOR THE OTHERS TO UNDERSTAND WELL, IT'S IMPORTANT FOR THEM TO SEE CLEARLY HOW THINGS ARE.
NOW YOU'RE GONNA TELL US HOW YOU DO IT, OR I'LL STRANGLE YOU.
MMPH! I'M GETTING THERE.
KHHKH...JUST CAN'T JOKE AROUND WITH YOU GUYS.
OKAY. THE SECRET IS TO FIRE THE WHOLE TIME.
DON'T WORRY ABOUT WASTING AMMUNITION. THERE ARE KILOTONS OF IT IN EACH BRACELET.
YOU FIRE AND YOU SEE WHERE YOU GO.
AND IF, IN THE MIDDLE OF IT, YOU SEE YOU'RE HEADING ELSEWHERE, QUICKLY, YOU FIRE AGAIN AND AGAIN AND AGAIN UNTIL YOU GET THERE.
AND YOU DON'T GIVE A CRAP ABOUT OBSTACLES, SEEING AS HOW THE ARMOR'S MORE SOLID THAN ANYTHING ELSE.
AND HOW DO YOU MANAGE WITH YOUR HEAD BARE?
MY HEAD'S HARDER THAN THE ARMOR.

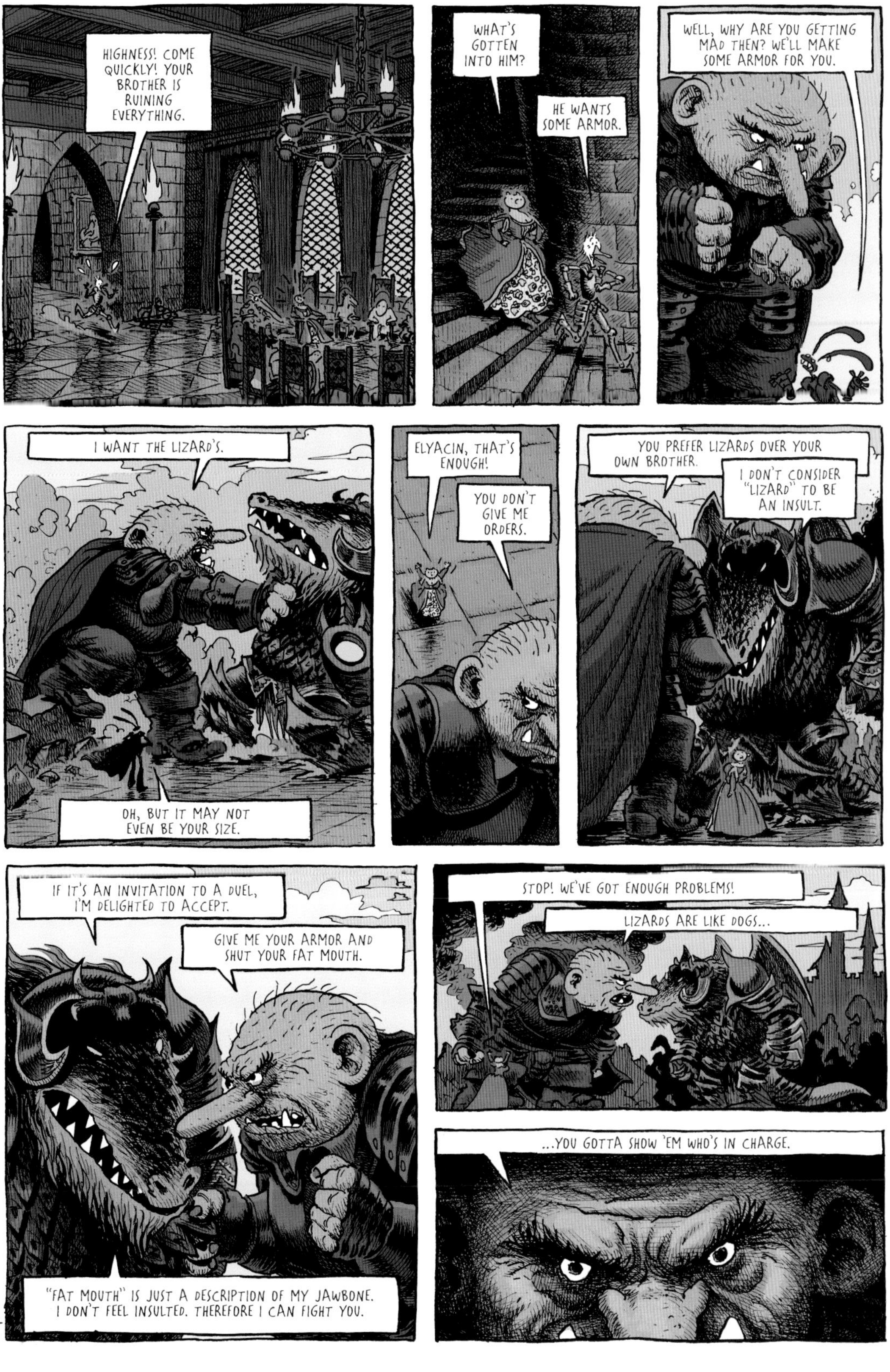

HIGHNESS! COME QUICKLY! YOUR BROTHER IS RUINING EVERYTHING.
WHAT'S GOTTEN INTO HIM?
HE WANTS SOME ARMOR.
WELL, WHY ARE YOU GETTING MAD THEN? WE'LL MAKE SOME ARMOR FOR YOU.
I WANT THE LIZARD'S.
OH, BUT IT MAY NOT EVEN BE YOUR SIZE.
ELYACIN, THAT'S ENOUGH!
YOU DON'T GIVE ME ORDERS.
YOU PREFER LIZARDS OVER YOUR OWN BROTHER.
I DON'T CONSIDER "LIZARD" TO BE AN INSULT.
IF IT'S AN INVITATION TO A DUEL, I'M DELIGHTED TO ACCEPT.
GIVE ME YOUR ARMOR AND SHUT YOUR FAT MOUTH.
"FAT MOUTH" IS JUST A DESCRIPTION OF MY JAWBONE. I DON'T FEEL INSULTED. THEREFORE I CAN FIGHT YOU.
STOP! WE'VE GOT ENOUGH PROBLEMS!
LIZARDS ARE LIKE DOGS...
...YOU GOTTA SHOW 'EM WHO'S IN CHARGE.

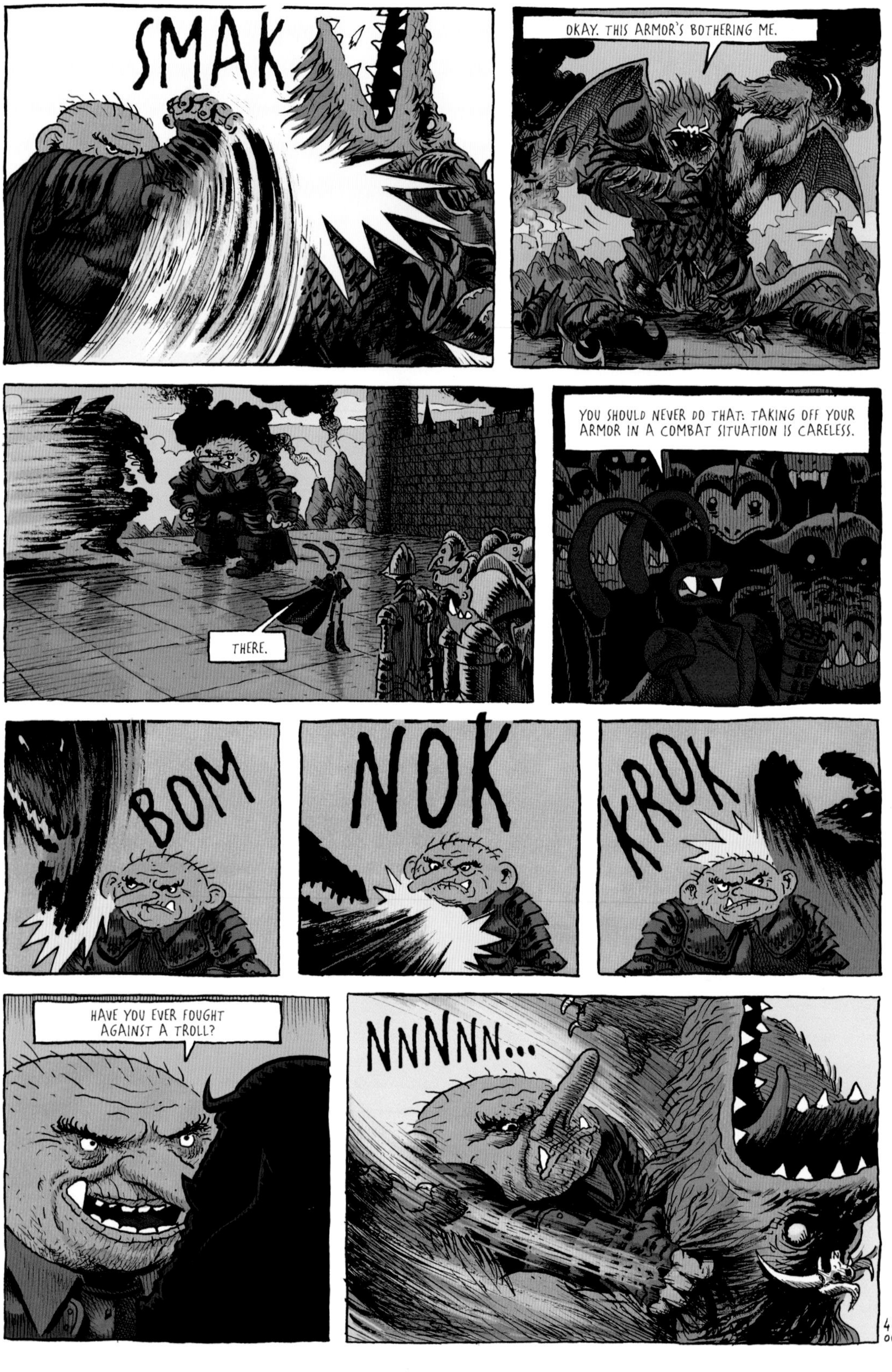
SMAK
OKAY. THIS ARMOR'S BOTHERING ME.
THERE.
YOU SHOULD NEVER DO THAT: TAKING OFF YOUR ARMOR IN A COMBAT SITUATION IS CARELESS.
BOM
NOK
KROK
HAVE YOU EVER FOUGHT AGAINST A TROLL?
NNNNN...

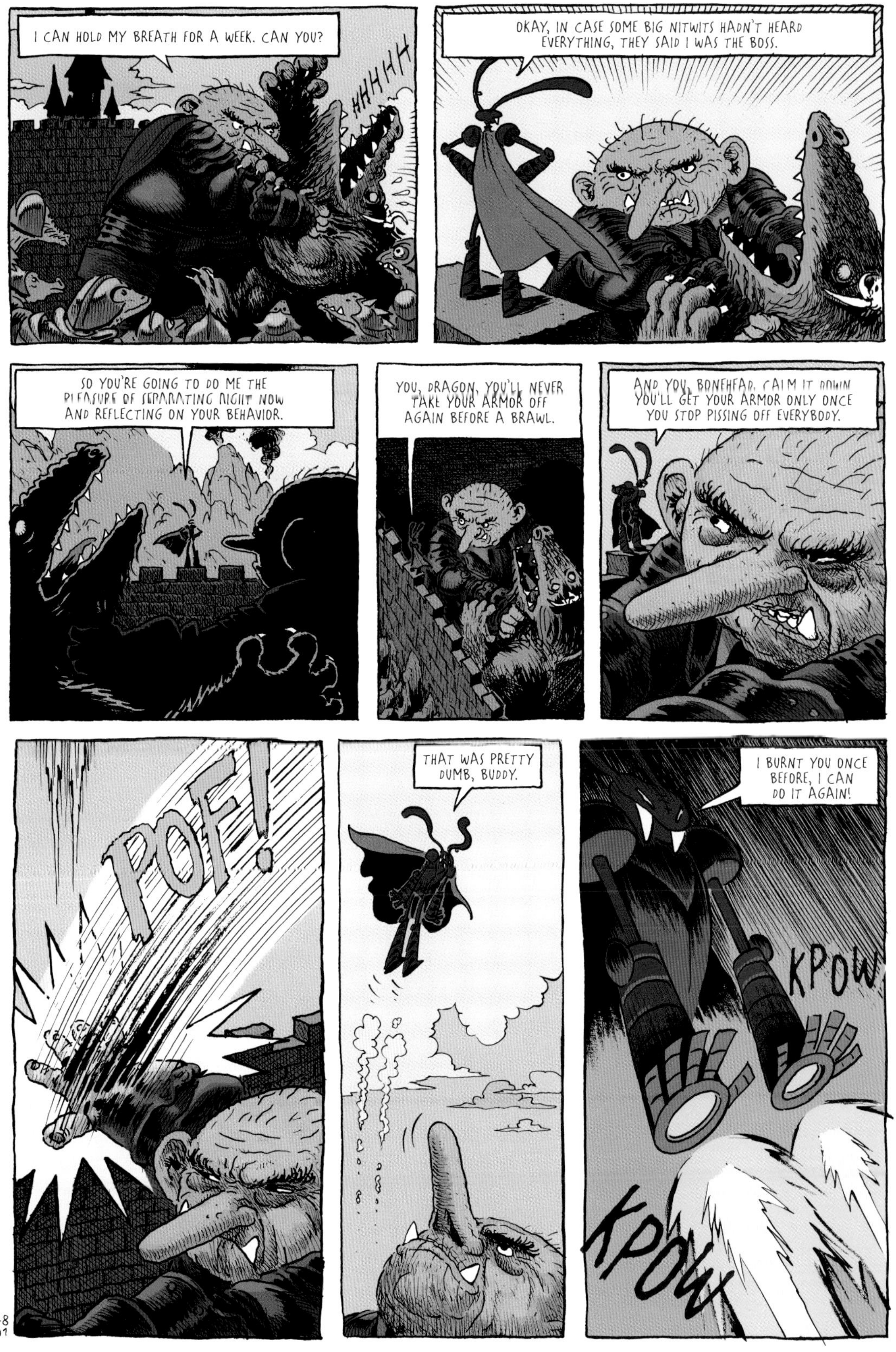

I CAN HOLD MY BREATH FOR A WEEK. CAN YOU?
HHHHHH
OKAY, IN CASE SOME BIG NITWITS HADN'T HEARD EVERYTHING, THEY SAID I WAS THE BOSS.
SO YOU'RE GOING TO DO ME THE PLEASURE OF SEPARATING RIGHT NOW AND REFLECTING ON YOUR BEHAVIOR.
YOU, DRAGON, YOU'LL NEVER TAKE YOUR ARMOR OFF AGAIN BEFORE A BRAWL.
AND YOU, BONEHEAD, CALM IT DOWN. YOU'LL GET YOUR ARMOR ONLY ONCE YOU STOP PISSING OFF EVERYBODY.
POF!
THAT WAS PRETTY DUMB, BUDDY.
I BURNT YOU ONCE BEFORE, I CAN DO IT AGAIN!
KPOW
KPOW

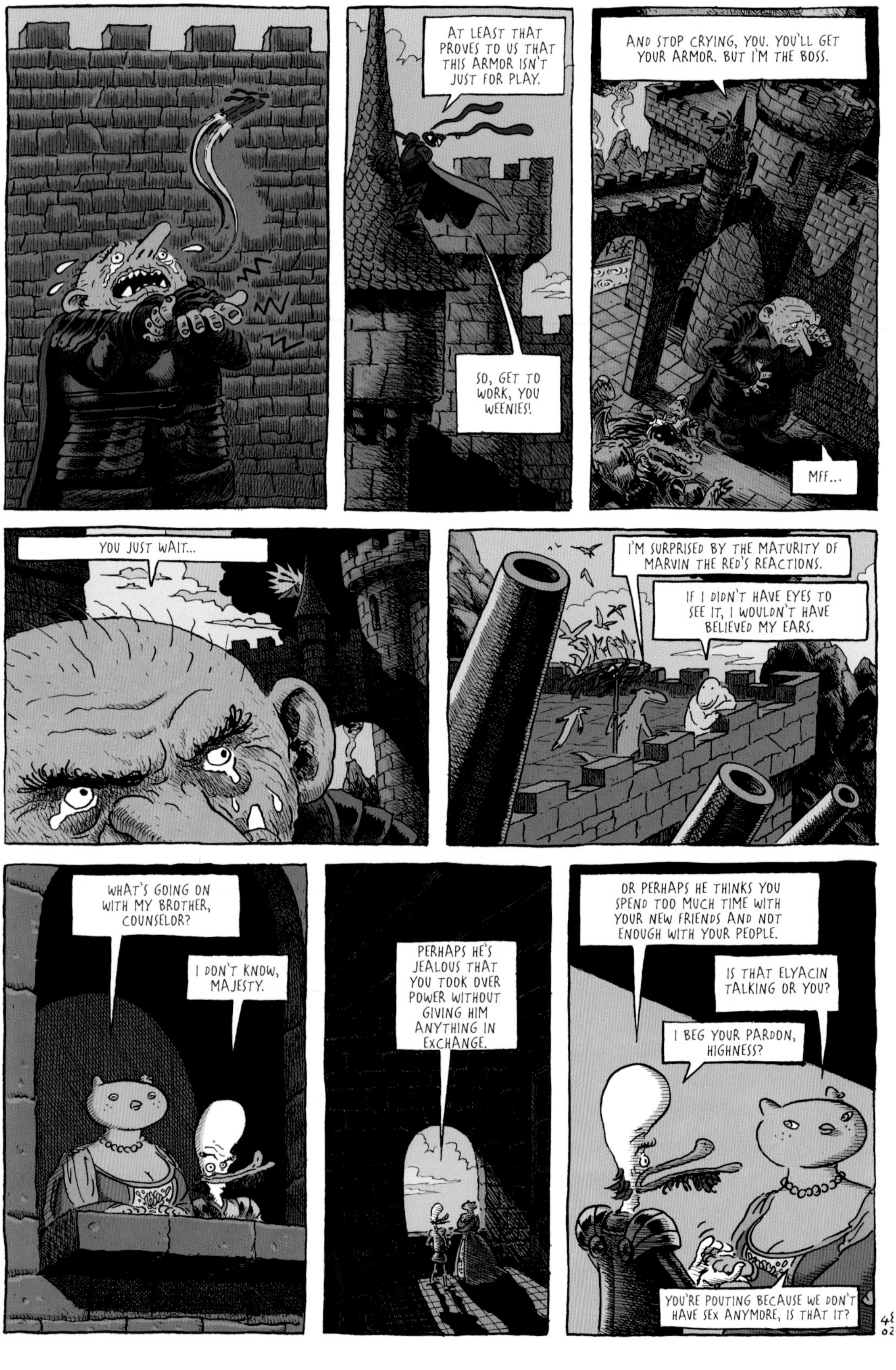
AT LEAST THAT PROVES TO US THAT THIS ARMOR ISN'T JUST FOR PLAY.
SO, GET TO WORK, YOU WEENIES!
AND STOP CRYING, YOU. YOU'LL GET YOUR ARMOR. BUT I'M THE BOSS.
MFF...
YOU JUST WAIT...
I'M SURPRISED BY THE MATURITY OF MARVIN THE RED'S REACTIONS.
IF I DIDN'T HAVE EYES TO SEE IT, I WOULDN'T HAVE BELIEVED MY EARS.
WHAT'S GOING ON WITH MY BROTHER, COUNSELOR?
I DON'T KNOW, MAJESTY.
PERHAPS HE'S JEALOUS THAT YOU TOOK OVER POWER WITHOUT GIVING HIM ANYTHING IN EXCHANGE.
OR PERHAPS HE THINKS YOU SPEND TOO MUCH TIME WITH YOUR NEW FRIENDS AND NOT ENOUGH WITH YOUR PEOPLE.
IS THAT ELYACIN TALKING OR YOU?
I BEG YOUR PARDON, HIGHNESS?
YOU'RE POUTING BECAUSE WE DON'T HAVE SEX ANYMORE, IS THAT IT?

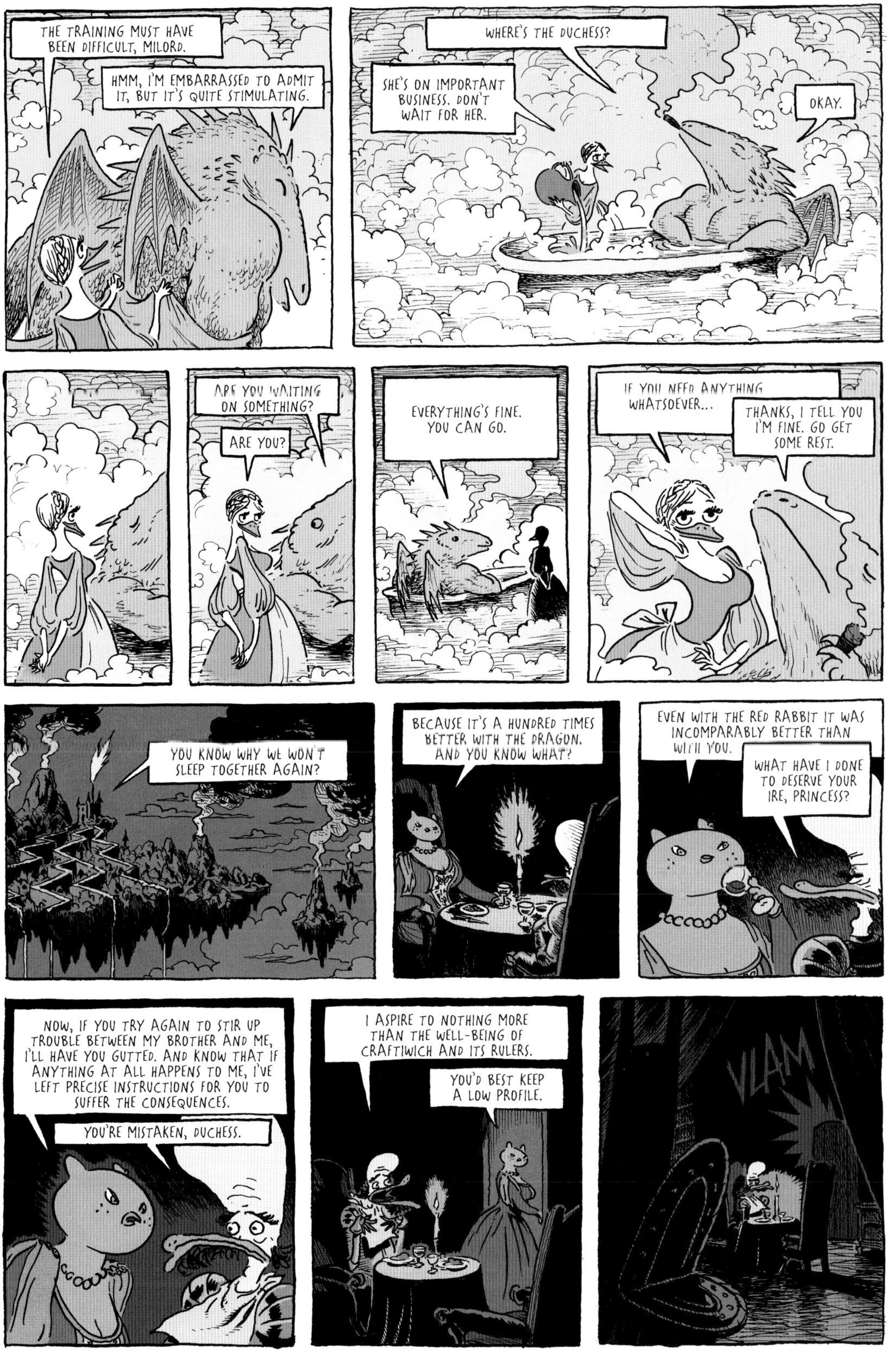
THE TRAINING MUST HAVE BEEN DIFFICULT, MILORD.
HMM, I'M EMBARRASSED TO ADMIT IT, BUT IT'S QUITE STIMULATING.
WHERE'S THE DUCHESS?
SHE'S ON IMPORTANT BUSINESS. DON'T WAIT FOR HER.
OKAY.
ARE YOU WAITING ON SOMETHING?
ARE YOU?
EVERYTHING'S FINE. YOU CAN GO.
IF YOU NEED ANYTHING WHATSOEVER...
THANKS, I TELL YOU I'M FINE. GO GET SOME REST.
YOU KNOW WHY WE WON'T SLEEP TOGETHER AGAIN?
BECAUSE IT'S A HUNDRED TIMES BETTER WITH THE DRAGON. AND YOU KNOW WHAT?
EVEN WITH THE RED RABBIT IT WAS INCOMPARABLY BETTER THAN WITH YOU.
WHAT HAVE I DONE TO DESERVE YOUR IRE, PRINCESS?
NOW, IF YOU TRY AGAIN TO STIR UP TROUBLE BETWEEN MY BROTHER AND ME, I'LL HAVE YOU GUTTED. AND KNOW THAT IF ANYTHING AT ALL HAPPENS TO ME, I'VE LEFT PRECISE INSTRUCTIONS FOR YOU TO SUFFER THE CONSEQUENCES.
YOU'RE MISTAKEN, DUCHESS.
I ASPIRE TO NOTHING MORE THAN THE WELL-BEING OF CRAFTIWICH AND ITS RULERS.
YOU'D BEST KEEP A LOW PROFILE.
VLAM

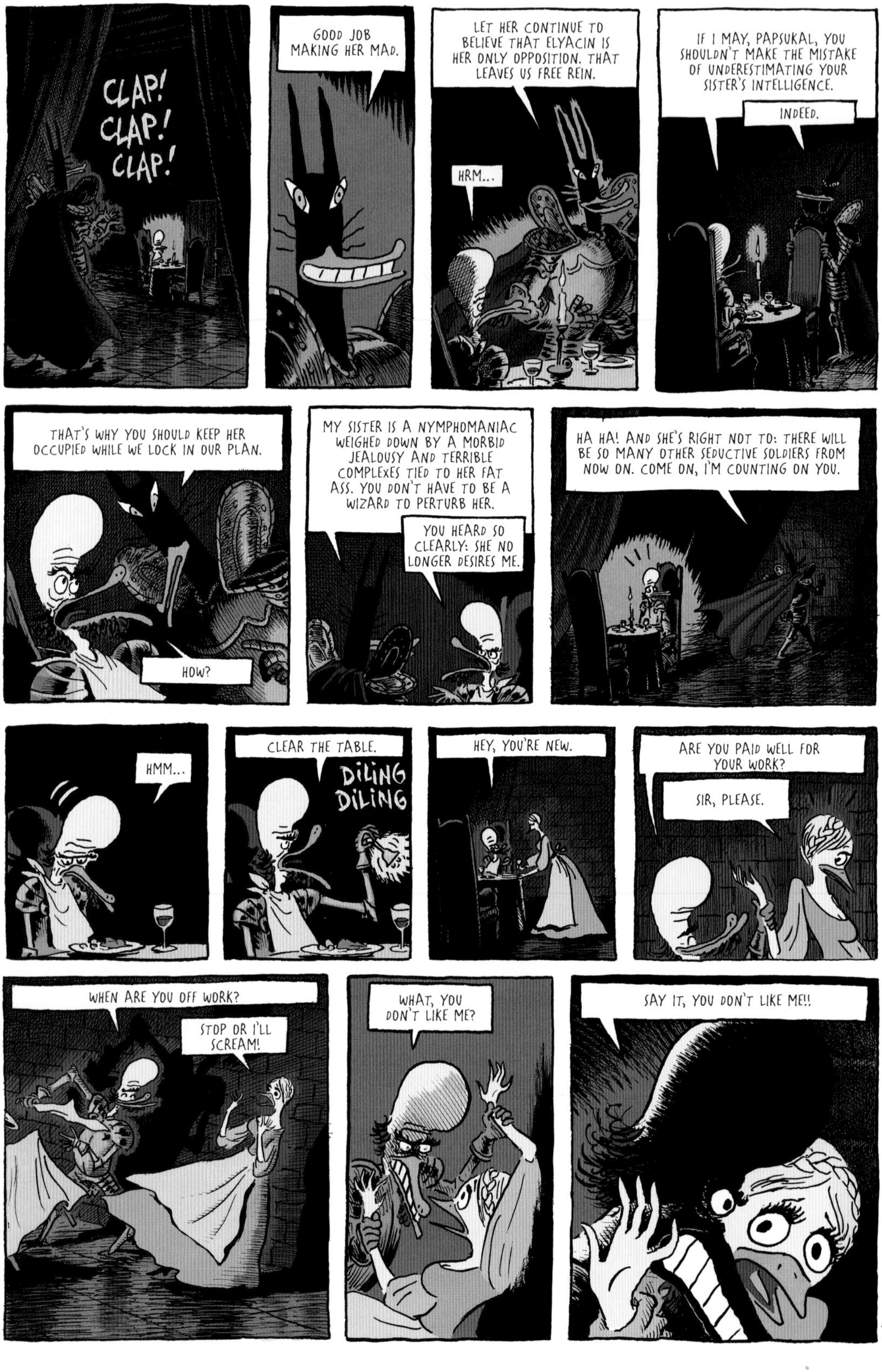
CLAP! CLAP! CLAP!
GOOD JOB MAKING HER MAD.
LET HER CONTINUE TO BELIEVE THAT ELYACIN IS HER ONLY OPPOSITION. THAT LEAVES US FREE REIN.
HRM...
IF I MAY, PAPSUKAL, YOU SHOULDN'T MAKE THE MISTAKE OF UNDERESTIMATING YOUR SISTER'S INTELLIGENCE.
INDEED.
THAT'S WHY YOU SHOULD KEEP HER OCCUPIED WHILE WE LOCK IN OUR PLAN.
HOW?
MY SISTER IS A NYMPHOMANIAC WEIGHED DOWN BY A MORBID JEALOUSY AND TERRIBLE COMPLEXES TIED TO HER FAT ASS. YOU DON'T HAVE TO BE A WIZARD TO PERTURB HER.
YOU HEARD SO CLEARLY: SHE NO LONGER DESIRES ME.
HA HA! AND SHE'S RIGHT NOT TO: THERE WILL BE SO MANY OTHER SEDUCTIVE SOLDIERS FROM NOW ON. COME ON, I'M COUNTING ON YOU.
HMM...
CLEAR THE TABLE.
DILING DILING
HEY, YOU'RE NEW.
ARE YOU PAID WELL FOR YOUR WORK?
SIR, PLEASE.
WHEN ARE YOU OFF WORK?
STOP OR I'LL SCREAM!
WHAT, YOU DON'T LIKE ME?
SAY IT, YOU DON'T LIKE ME!!

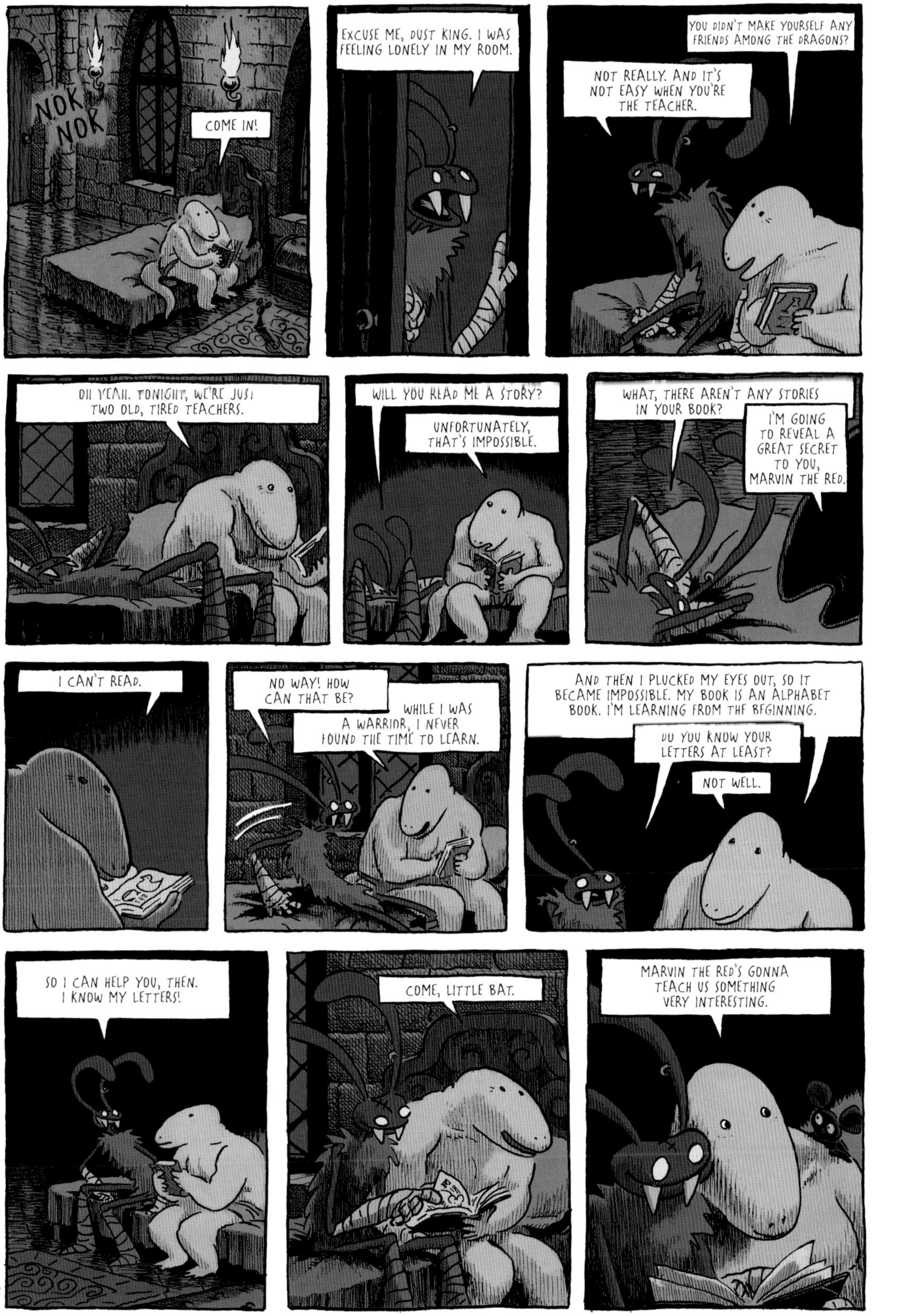

NOK NOK
COME IN!
EXCUSE ME, DUST KING. I WAS FEELING LONELY IN MY ROOM.
YOU DIDN'T MAKE YOURSELF ANY FRIENDS AMONG THE DRAGONS?
NOT REALLY. AND IT'S NOT EASY WHEN YOU'RE THE TEACHER.
OH YEAH. TONIGHT, WE'RE JUST TWO OLD, TIRED TEACHERS.
WILL YOU READ ME A STORY?
UNFORTUNATELY, THAT'S IMPOSSIBLE.
WHAT, THERE AREN'T ANY STORIES IN YOUR BOOK?
I'M GOING TO REVEAL A GREAT SECRET TO YOU, MARVIN THE RED.
I CAN'T READ.
NO WAY! HOW CAN THAT BE?
WHILE I WAS A WARRIOR, I NEVER FOUND THE TIME TO LEARN.
AND THEN I PLUCKED MY EYES OUT, SO IT BECAME IMPOSSIBLE. MY BOOK IS AN ALPHABET BOOK. I'M LEARNING FROM THE BEGINNING.
DO YOU KNOW YOUR LETTERS AT LEAST?
NOT WELL.
SO I CAN HELP YOU, THEN. I KNOW MY LETTERS!
COME, LITTLE BAT.
MARVIN THE RED'S GONNA TEACH US SOMETHING VERY INTERESTING.

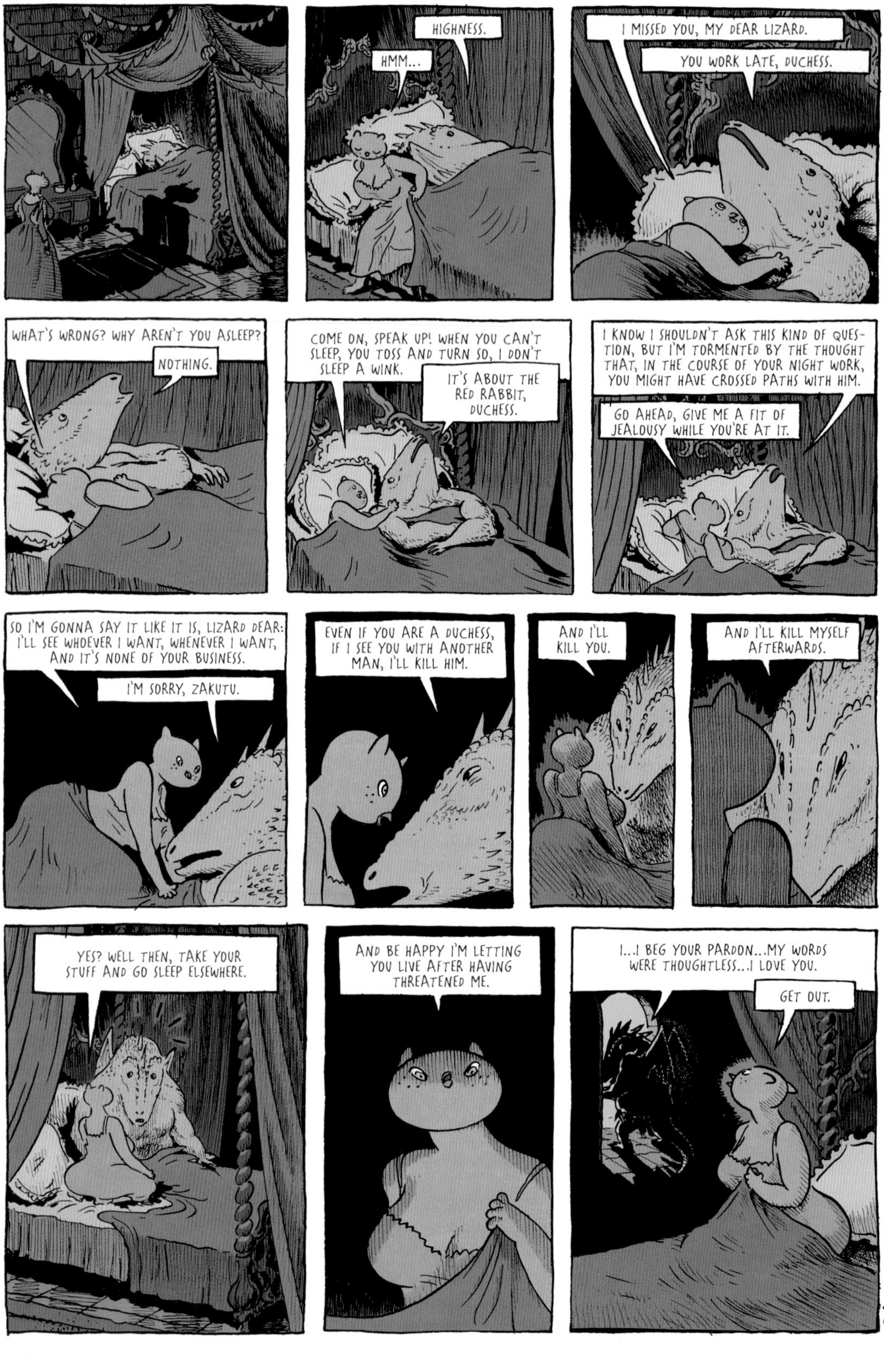
HMM...
HIGHNESS.
I MISSED YOU, MY DEAR LIZARD.
YOU WORK LATE, DUCHESS.
WHAT'S WRONG? WHY AREN'T YOU ASLEEP?
NOTHING.
COME ON, SPEAK UP! WHEN YOU CAN'T SLEEP, YOU TOSS AND TURN SO, I DON'T SLEEP A WINK.
IT'S ABOUT THE RED RABBIT, DUCHESS.
I KNOW I SHOULDN'T ASK THIS KIND OF QUESTION, BUT I'M TORMENTED BY THE THOUGHT THAT, IN THE COURSE OF YOUR NIGHT WORK, YOU MIGHT HAVE CROSSED PATHS WITH HIM.
GO AHEAD, GIVE ME A FIT OF JEALOUSY WHILE YOU'RE AT IT.
SO I'M GONNA SAY IT LIKE IT IS, LIZARD DEAR: I'LL SEE WHOEVER I WANT, WHENEVER I WANT, AND IT'S NONE OF YOUR BUSINESS.
I'M SORRY, ZAKUTU.
EVEN IF YOU ARE A DUCHESS, IF I SEE YOU WITH ANOTHER MAN, I'LL KILL HIM.
AND I'LL KILL YOU.
AND I'LL KILL MYSELF AFTERWARDS.
YES? WELL THEN, TAKE YOUR STUFF AND GO SLEEP ELSEWHERE.
AND BE HAPPY I'M LETTING YOU LIVE AFTER HAVING THREATENED ME.
I...I BEG YOUR PARDON...MY WORDS WERE THOUGHTLESS...I LOVE YOU.
GET OUT.

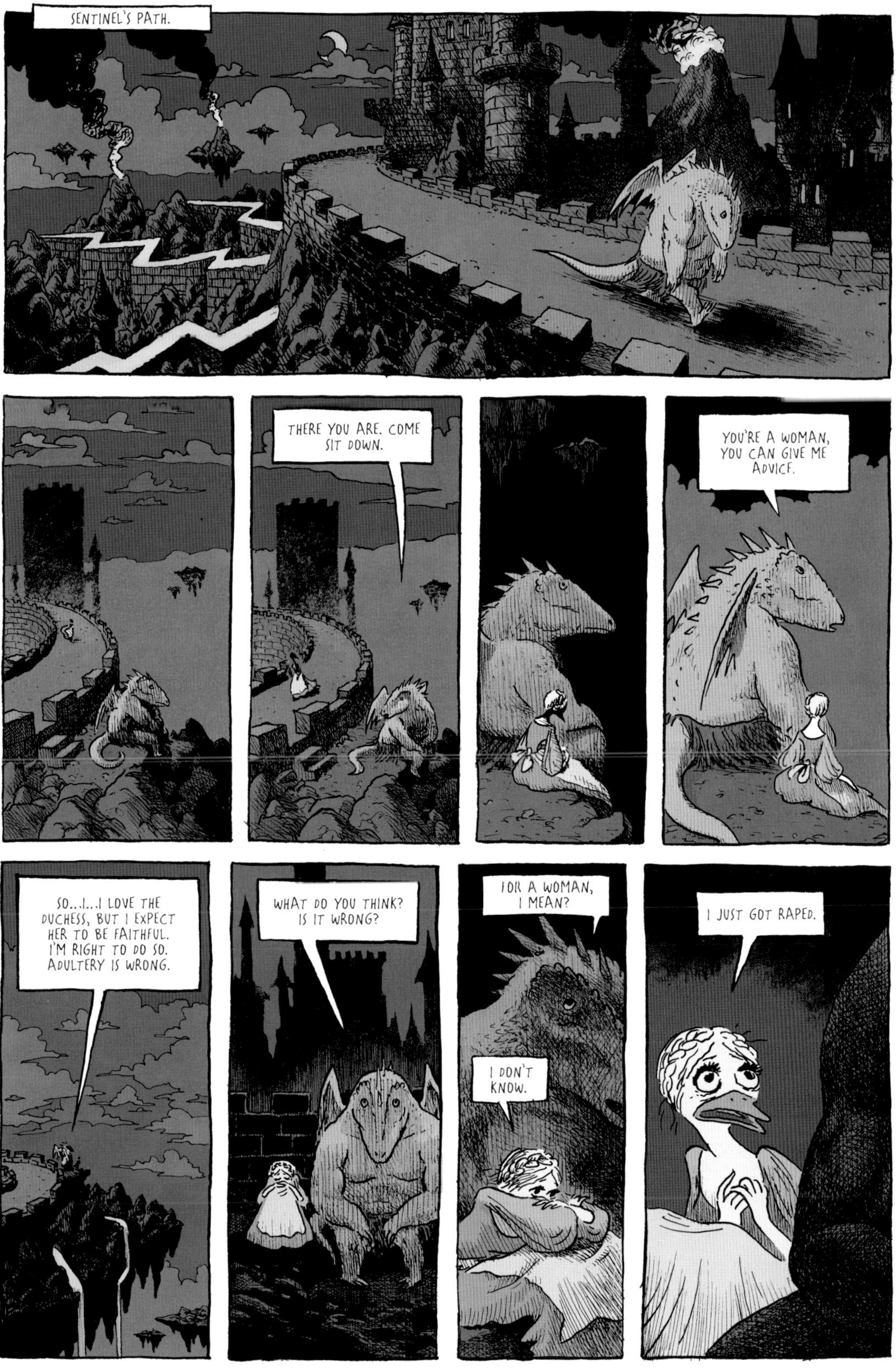
SENTINEL'S PATH.
THERE YOU ARE. COME SIT DOWN.
YOU'RE A WOMAN, YOU CAN GIVE ME ADVICE.
SO...I...I LOVE THE DUCHESS, BUT I EXPECT HER TO BE FAITHFUL. I'M RIGHT TO DO SO. ADULTERY IS WRONG.
WHAT DO YOU THINK? IS IT WRONG?
FOR A WOMAN, I MEAN?
I DON'T KNOW.
I JUST GOT RAPED.

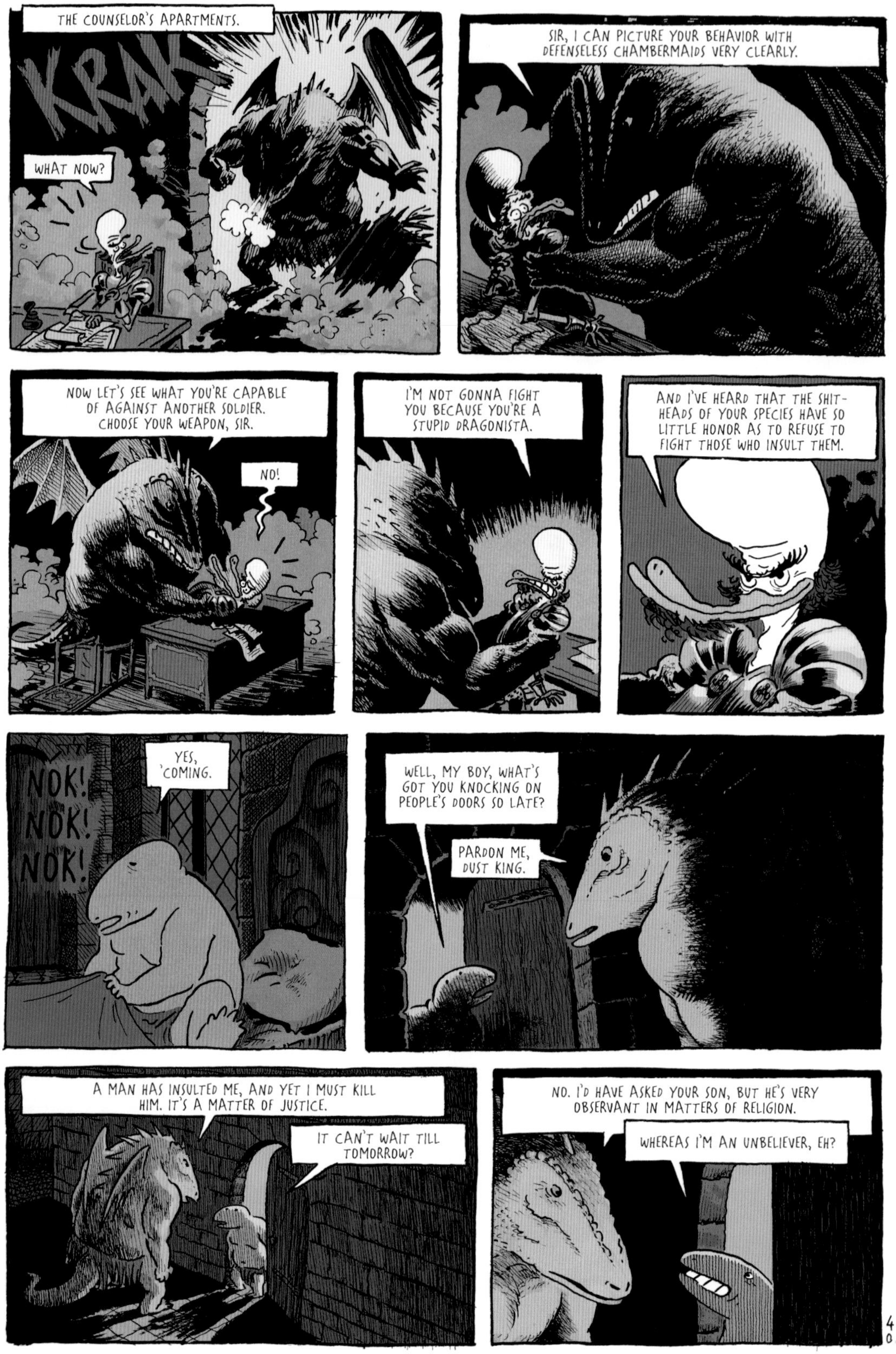
THE COUNSELOR'S APARTMENTS.
KRAK
WHAT NOW?
SIR, I CAN PICTURE YOUR BEHAVIOR WITH DEFENSELESS CHAMBERMAIDS VERY CLEARLY.
NOW LET'S SEE WHAT YOU'RE CAPABLE OF AGAINST ANOTHER SOLDIER. CHOOSE YOUR WEAPON, SIR.
NO!
I'M NOT GONNA FIGHT YOU BECAUSE YOU'RE A STUPID DRAGONISTA.
AND I'VE HEARD THAT THE SHIT-HEADS OF YOUR SPECIES HAVE SO LITTLE HONOR AS TO REFUSE TO FIGHT THOSE WHO INSULT THEM.
NOK! NOK! NOK!
YES, 'COMING.
WELL, MY BOY, WHAT'S GOT YOU KNOCKING ON PEOPLE'S DOORS SO LATE?
PARDON ME, DUST KING.
A MAN HAS INSULTED ME, AND YET I MUST KILL HIM. IT'S A MATTER OF JUSTICE.
IT CAN'T WAIT TILL TOMORROW?
NO. I'D HAVE ASKED YOUR SON, BUT HE'S VERY OBSERVANT IN MATTERS OF RELIGION.
WHEREAS I'M AN UNBELIEVER, EH?

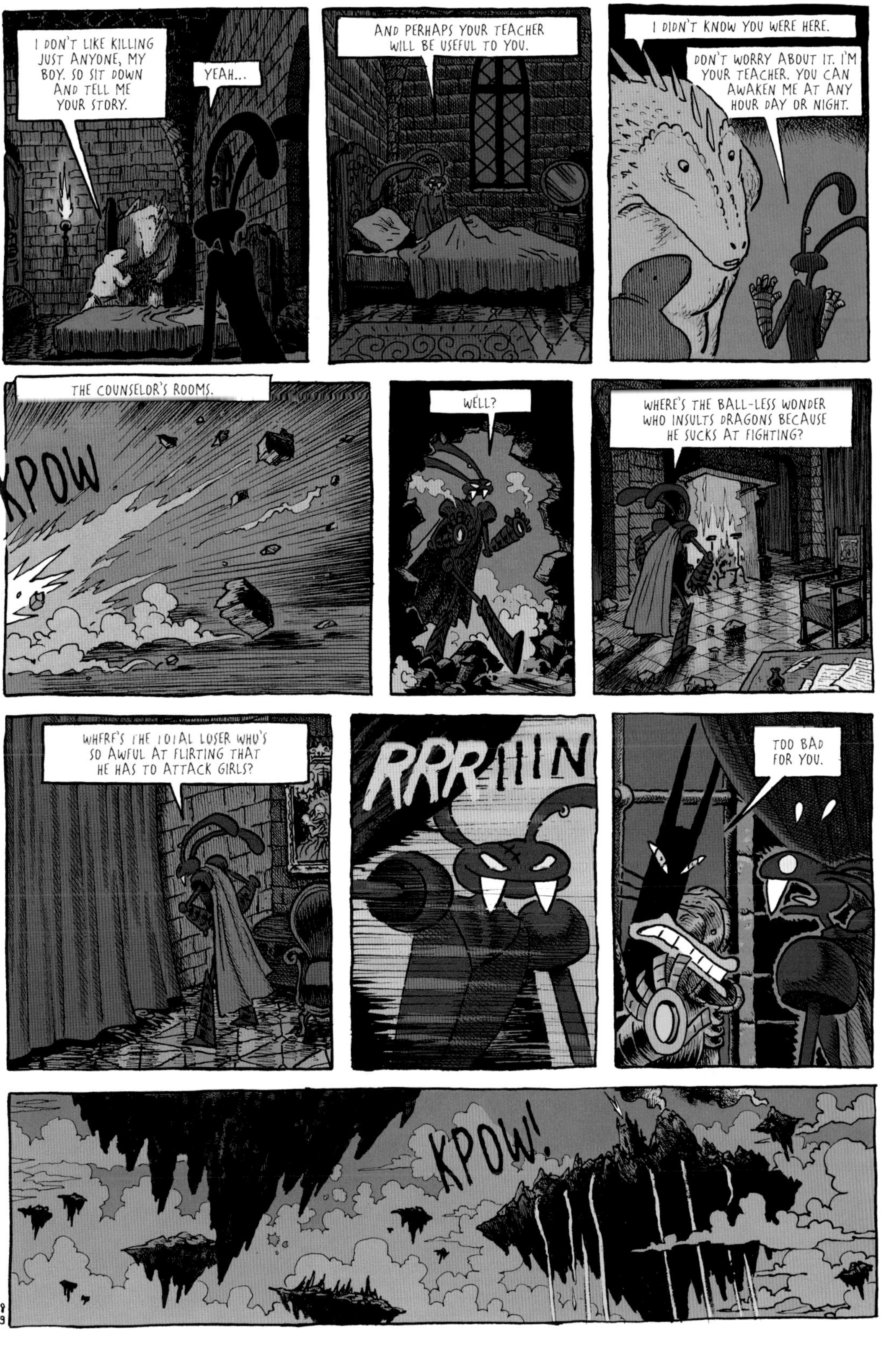

I DON'T LIKE KILLING JUST ANYONE, MY BOY. SO SIT DOWN AND TELL ME YOUR STORY.
YEAH...
AND PERHAPS YOUR TEACHER WILL BE USEFUL TO YOU.
I DIDN'T KNOW YOU WERE HERE.
DON'T WORRY ABOUT IT. I'M YOUR TEACHER. YOU CAN AWAKEN ME AT ANY HOUR DAY OR NIGHT.
THE COUNSELOR'S ROOMS.
KPOW
WELL?
WHERE'S THE BALL-LESS WONDER WHO INSULTS DRAGONS BECAUSE HE SUCKS AT FIGHTING?
WHERE'S THE TOTAL LOSER WHO'S SO AWFUL AT FLIRTING THAT HE HAS TO ATTACK GIRLS?
RRRIIIN
TOO BAD FOR YOU.
KPOW!

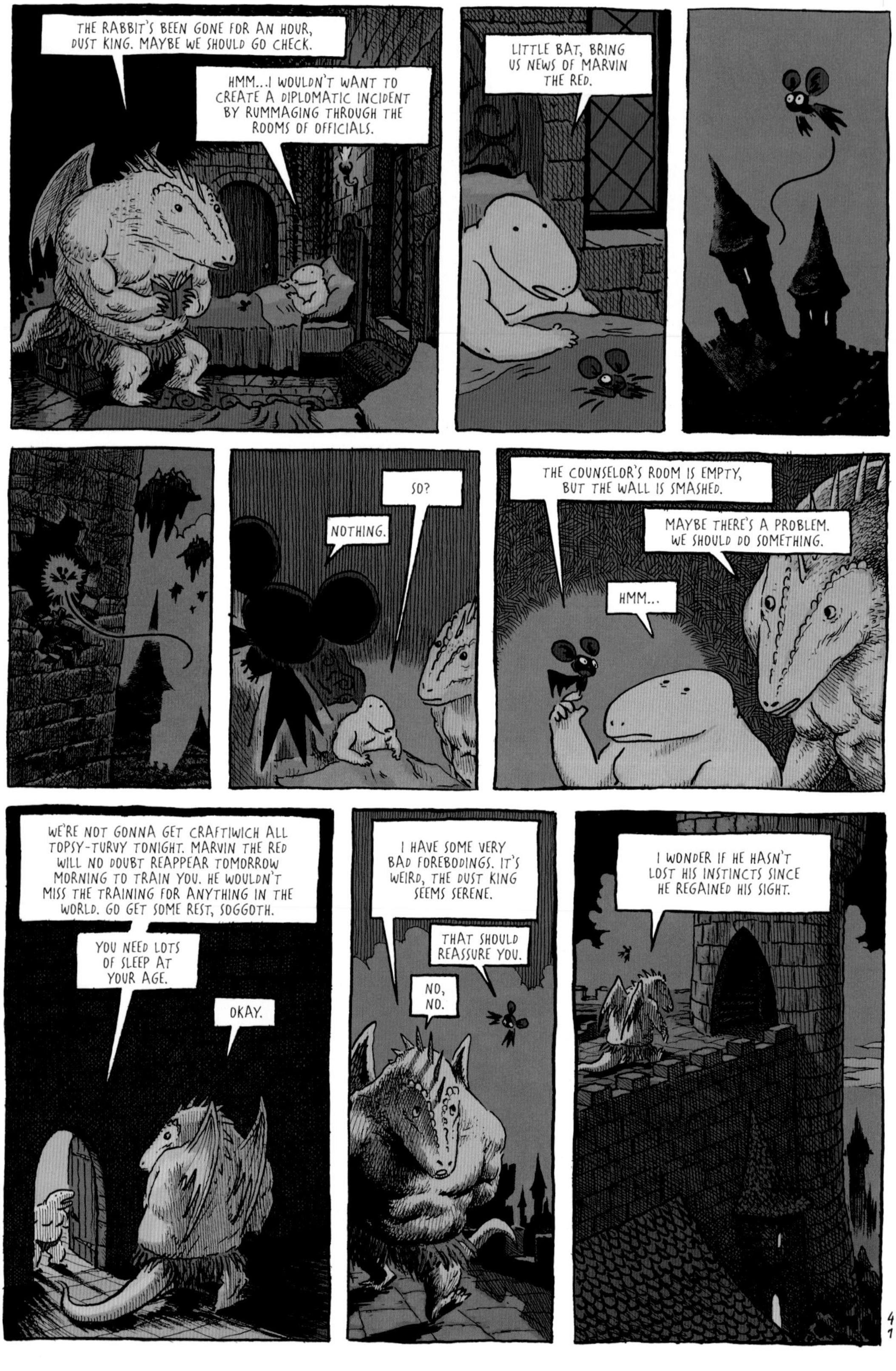
THE RABBIT'S BEEN GONE FOR AN HOUR, DUST KING. MAYBE WE SHOULD GO CHECK.
HMM...I WOULDN'T WANT TO CREATE A DIPLOMATIC INCIDENT BY RUMMAGING THROUGH THE ROOMS OF OFFICIALS.
LITTLE BAT, BRING US NEWS OF MARVIN THE RED.
SO?
NOTHING.
THE COUNSELOR'S ROOM IS EMPTY, BUT THE WALL IS SMASHED.
MAYBE THERE'S A PROBLEM. WE SHOULD DO SOMETHING.
HMM...
WE'RE NOT GONNA GET CRAFTIWICH ALL TOPSY-TURVY TONIGHT. MARVIN THE RED WILL NO DOUBT REAPPEAR TOMORROW MORNING TO TRAIN YOU. HE WOULDN'T MISS THE TRAINING FOR ANYTHING IN THE WORLD. GO GET SOME REST, SOGGOTH.
YOU NEED LOTS OF SLEEP AT YOUR AGE.
OKAY.
I HAVE SOME VERY BAD FOREBODINGS. IT'S WEIRD, THE DUST KING SEEMS SERENE.
THAT SHOULD REASSURE YOU.
NO, NO.
I WONDER IF HE HASN'T LOST HIS INSTINCTS SINCE HE REGAINED HIS SIGHT.

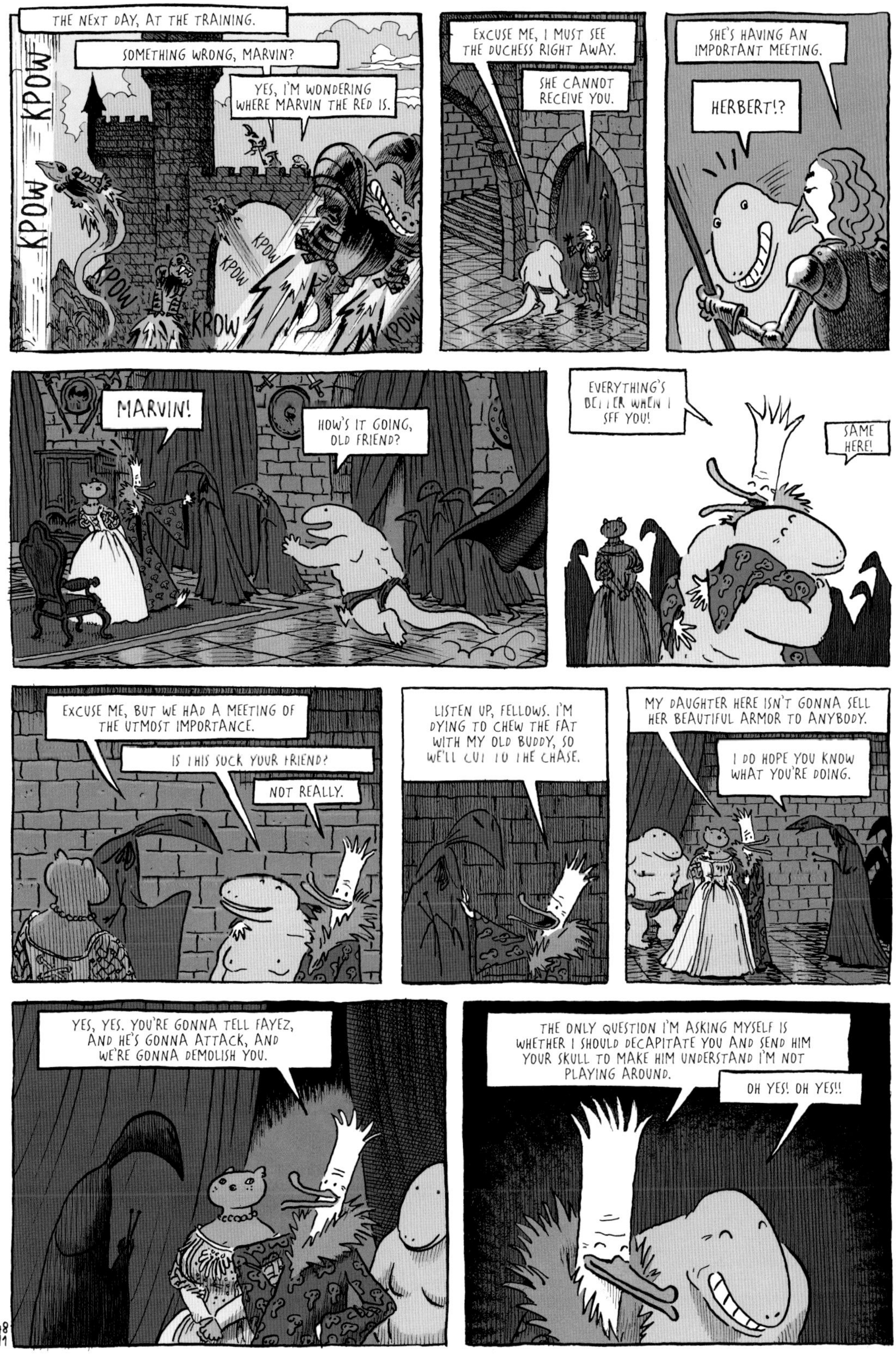

THE NEXT DAY, AT THE TRAINING.
SOMETHING WRONG, MARVIN?
YES, I'M WONDERING WHERE MARVIN THE RED IS.
KPOW KPOW
KPOW
KPOW
KPOW
KPOW
KROW
KPOW
EXCUSE ME, I MUST SEE THE DUCHESS RIGHT AWAY.
SHE CANNOT RECEIVE YOU.
SHE'S HAVING AN IMPORTANT MEETING.
HERBERT!?
MARVIN!
HOW'S IT GOING, OLD FRIEND?
EVERYTHING'S BETTER WHEN I SEE YOU!
SAME HERE!
EXCUSE ME, BUT WE HAD A MEETING OF THE UTMOST IMPORTANCE.
IS THIS SUCK YOUR FRIEND?
NOT REALLY.
LISTEN UP, FELLOWS. I'M DYING TO CHEW THE FAT WITH MY OLD BUDDY, SO WE'LL CUT TO THE CHASE.
MY DAUGHTER HERE ISN'T GONNA SELL HER BEAUTIFUL ARMOR TO ANYBODY.
I DO HOPE YOU KNOW WHAT YOU'RE DOING.
YES, YES. YOU'RE GONNA TELL FAYEZ, AND HE'S GONNA ATTACK, AND WE'RE GONNA DEMOLISH YOU.
THE ONLY QUESTION I'M ASKING MYSELF IS WHETHER I SHOULD DECAPITATE YOU AND SEND HIM YOUR SKULL TO MAKE HIM UNDERSTAND I'M NOT PLAYING AROUND.
OH YES! OH YES!!

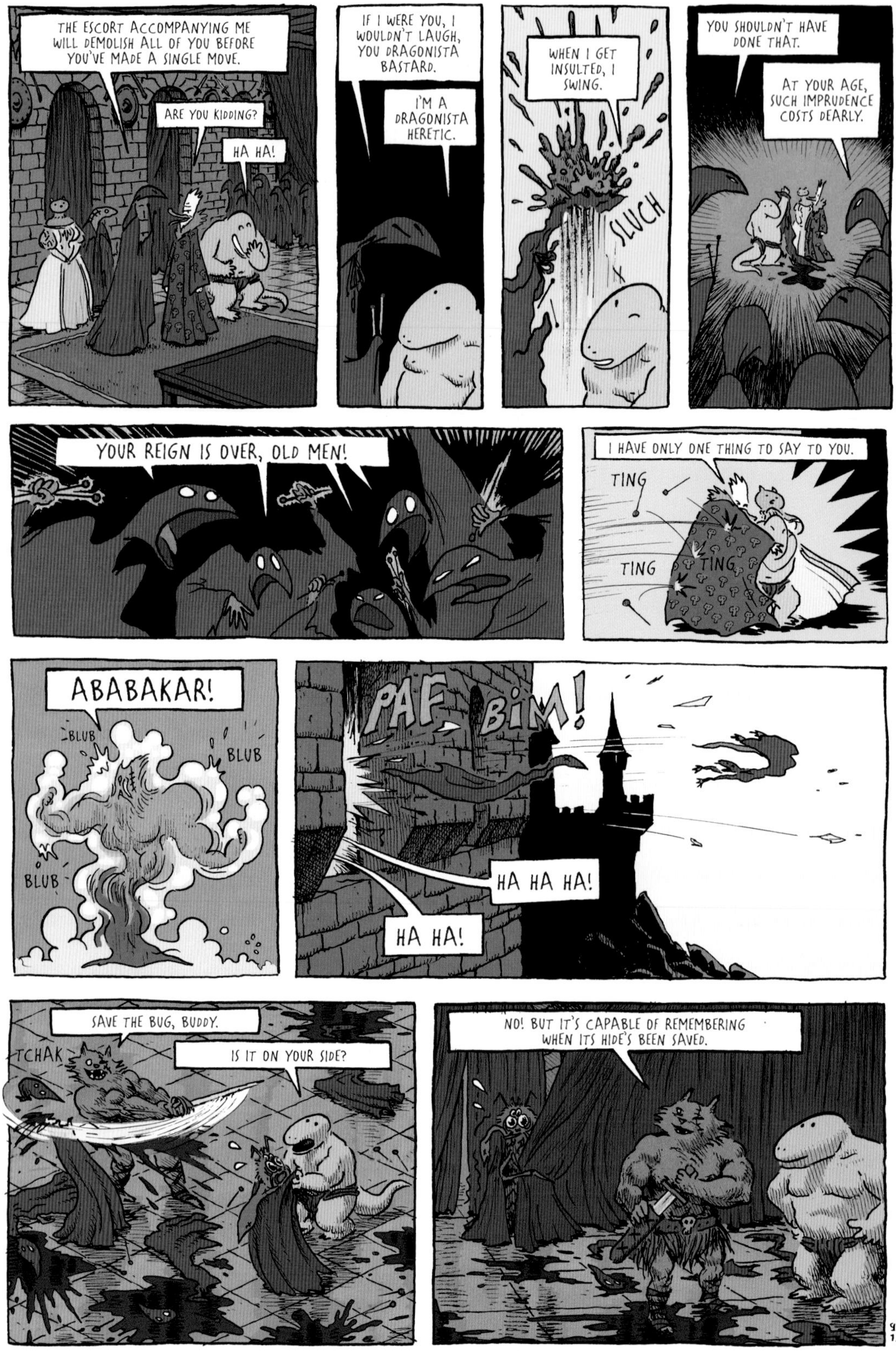

THE ESCORT ACCOMPANYING ME WILL DEMOLISH ALL OF YOU BEFORE YOU'VE MADE A SINGLE MOVE.
ARE YOU KIDDING?
HA HA!
IF I WERE YOU, I WOULDN'T LAUGH, YOU DRAGONISTA BASTARD.
I'M A DRAGONISTA HERETIC.
WHEN I GET INSULTED, I SWING.
SLUCH
YOU SHOULDN'T HAVE DONE THAT.
AT YOUR AGE, SUCH IMPRUDENCE COSTS DEARLY.
YOUR REIGN IS OVER, OLD MEN!
I HAVE ONLY ONE THING TO SAY TO YOU.
TING
TING
TING
ABABAKAR!
BLUB
BLUB
BLUB
PAF
BIM!
HA HA HA!
HA HA!
SAVE THE BUG, BUDDY.
TCHAK
IS IT ON YOUR SIDE?
NO! BUT IT'S CAPABLE OF REMEMBERING WHEN ITS HIDE'S BEEN SAVED.

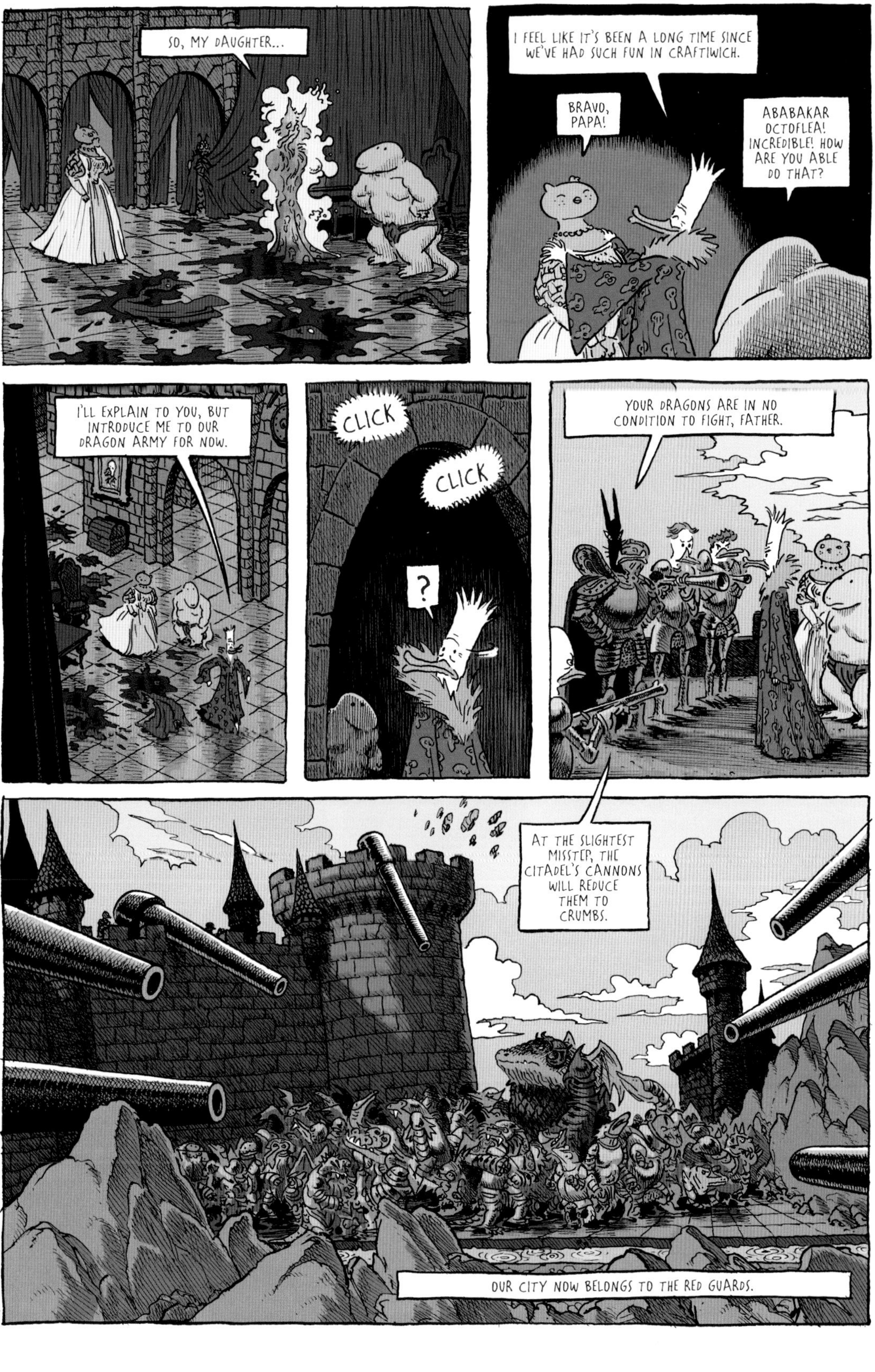

SO, MY DAUGHTER...
I FEEL LIKE IT'S BEEN A LONG TIME SINCE WE'VE HAD SUCH FUN IN CRAFTIWICH.
BRAVO, PAPA!
ABABAKAR OCTOFLEA! INCREDIBLE! HOW ARE YOU ABLE DO THAT?
I'LL EXPLAIN TO YOU, BUT INTRODUCE ME TO OUR DRAGON ARMY FOR NOW.
CLICK
CLICK
?
YOUR DRAGONS ARE IN NO CONDITION TO FIGHT, FATHER.
AT THE SLIGHTEST MISSTEP, THE CITADEL'S CANNONS WILL REDUCE THEM TO CRUMBS.
OUR CITY NOW BELONGS TO THE RED GUARDS.

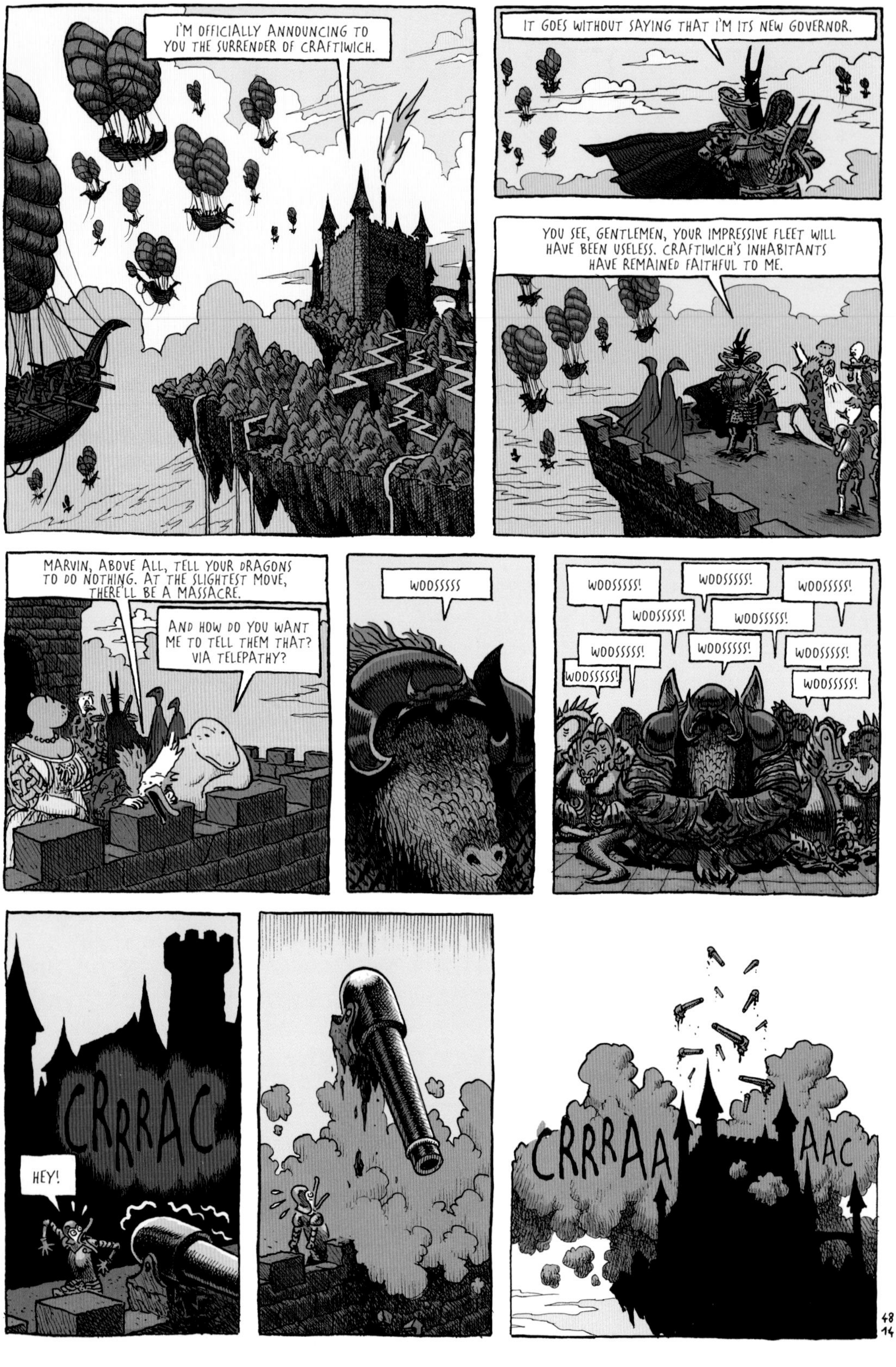

I'M OFFICIALLY ANNOUNCING TO YOU THE SURRENDER OF CRAFTIWICH.
IT GOES WITHOUT SAYING THAT I'M ITS NEW GOVERNOR.
YOU SEE, GENTLEMEN, YOUR IMPRESSIVE FLEET WILL HAVE BEEN USELESS. CRAFTIWICH'S INHABITANTS HAVE REMAINED FAITHFUL TO ME.
MARVIN, ABOVE ALL, TELL YOUR DRAGONS TO DO NOTHING. AT THE SLIGHTEST MOVE, THERE'LL BE A MASSACRE.
AND HOW DO YOU WANT ME TO TELL THEM THAT? VIA TELEPATHY?
WOOSSSSS
WOOSSSSS!
WOOSSSSS!
WOOSSSSS!
WOOSSSSS!
WOOSSSSS!
WOOSSSSS!
WOOSSSSS!
WOOSSSSS!
WOOSSSSS!
WOOSSSSS!
CRRRAC
HEY!
CRRRAA
AAC

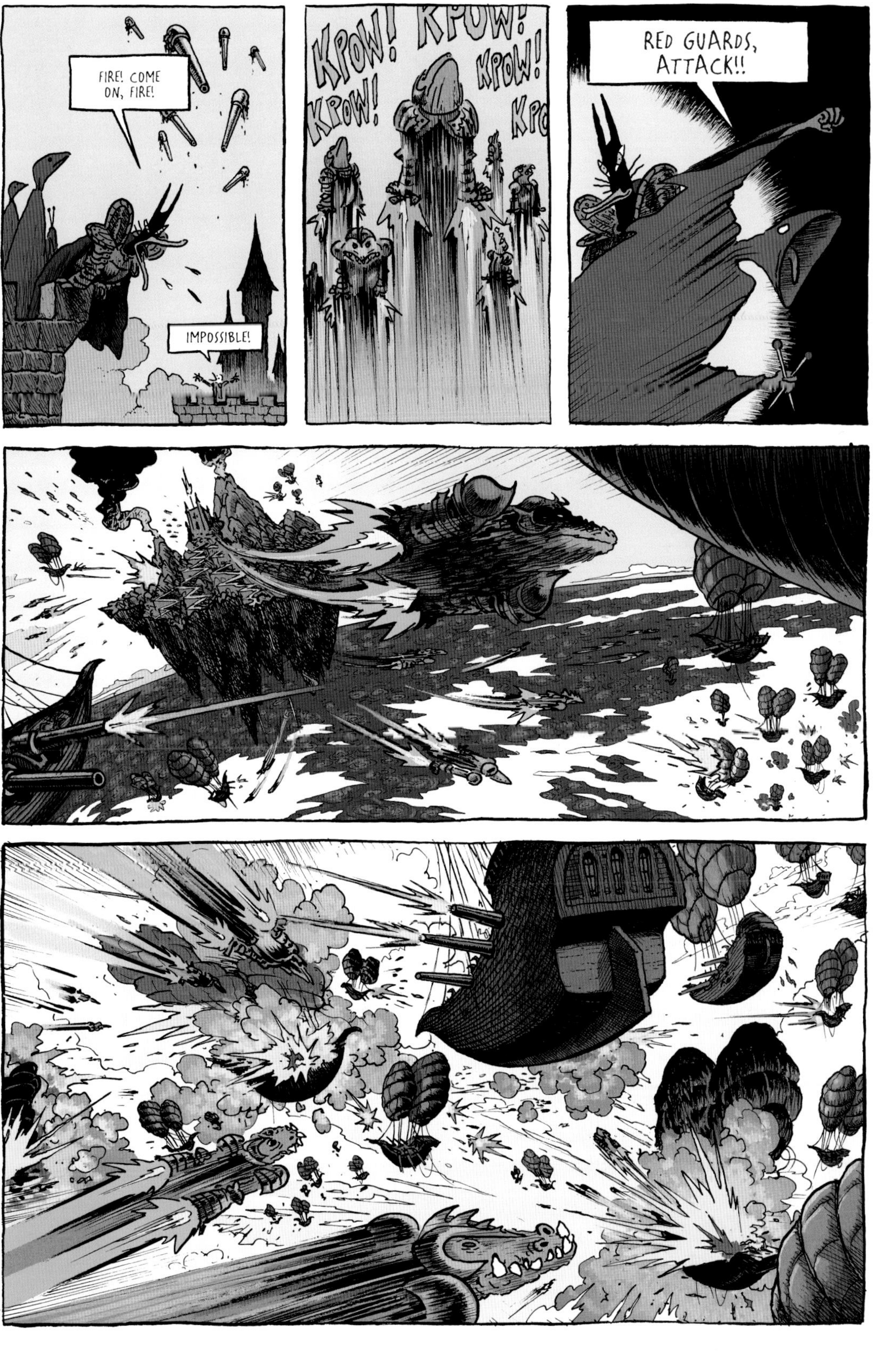
FIRE! COME ON, FIRE!
IMPOSSIBLE!
KPOW! KPOW!
KPOW!
KPOW!
KPO
RED GUARDS, ATTACK!!

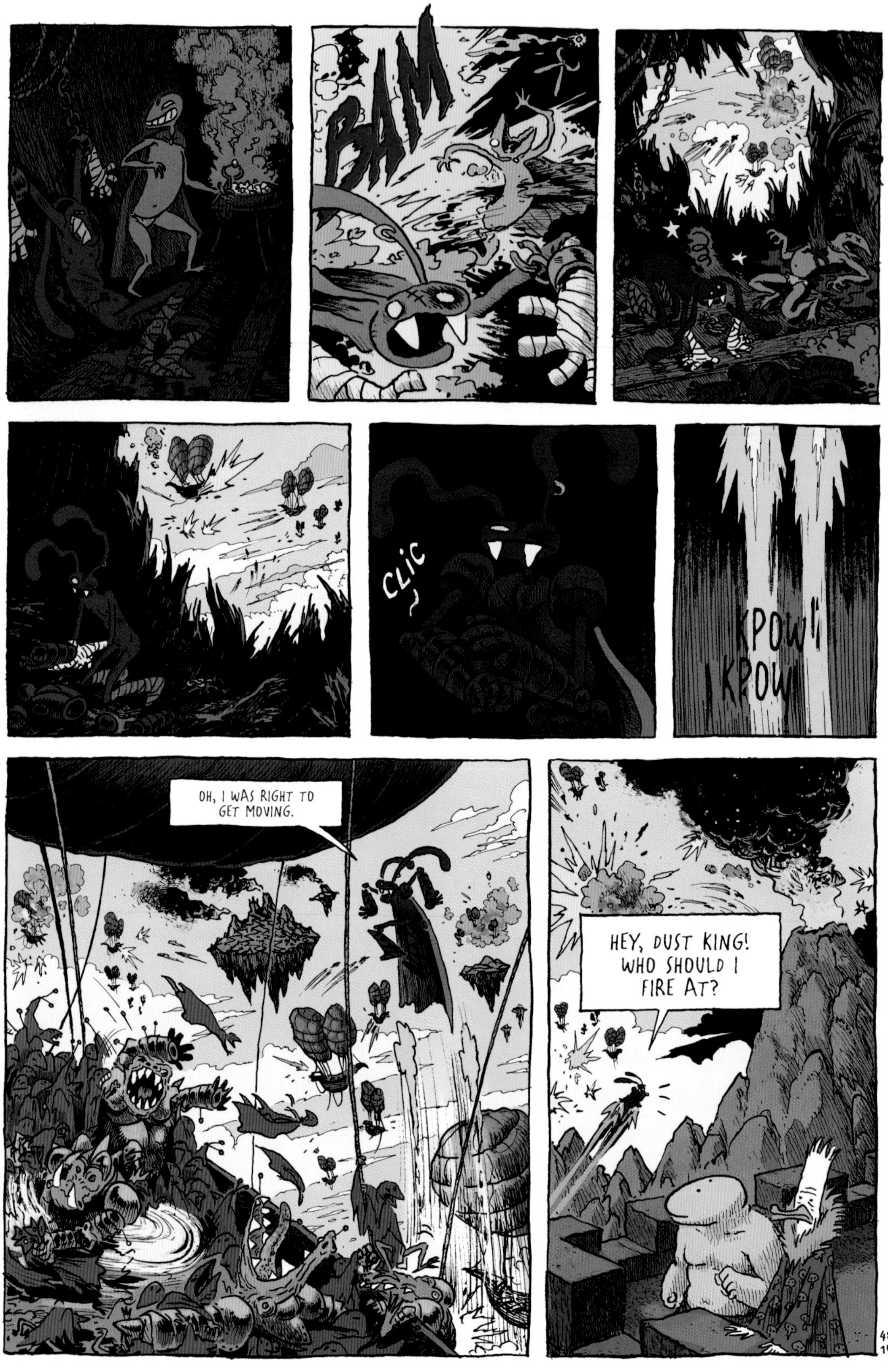
BAM
CLIC
KPOW
KPOW
OH, I WAS RIGHT TO GET MOVING.
HEY, DUST KING! WHO SHOULD I FIRE AT?

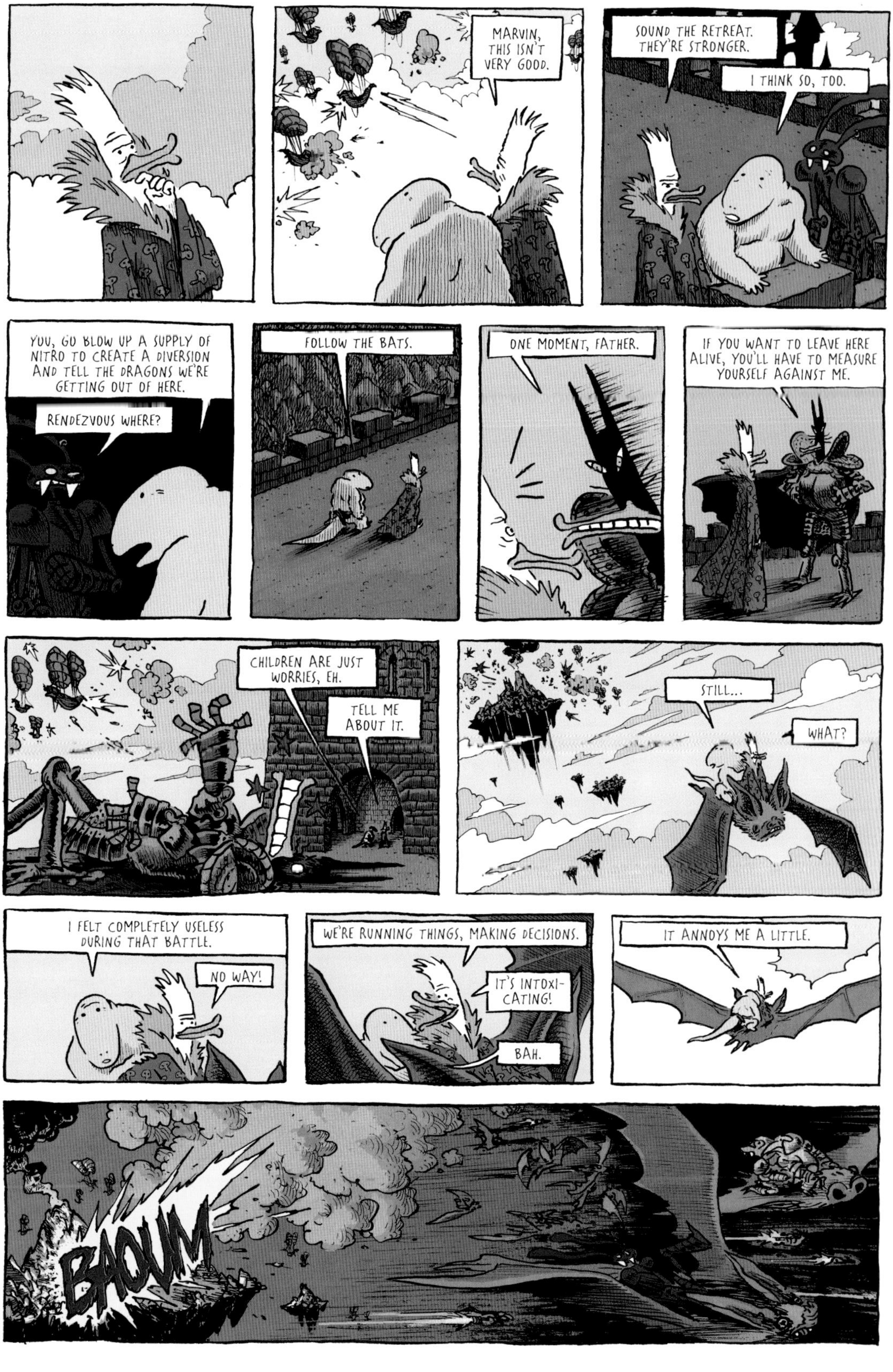

MARVIN, THIS ISN'T VERY GOOD.
SOUND THE RETREAT. THEY'RE STRONGER.
I THINK SO, TOO.
YOU, GO BLOW UP A SUPPLY OF NITRO TO CREATE A DIVERSION AND TELL THE DRAGONS WE'RE GETTING OUT OF HERE.
RENDEZVOUS WHERE?
FOLLOW THE BATS.
ONE MOMENT, FATHER.
IF YOU WANT TO LEAVE HERE ALIVE, YOU'LL HAVE TO MEASURE YOURSELF AGAINST ME.
CHILDREN ARE JUST WORRIES, EH.
TELL ME ABOUT IT.
STILL...
WHAT?
I FELT COMPLETELY USELESS DURING THAT BATTLE.
NO WAY!
WE'RE RUNNING THINGS, MAKING DECISIONS.
IT'S INTOXI-CATING!
BAH.
IT ANNOYS ME A LITTLE.
BAOUM

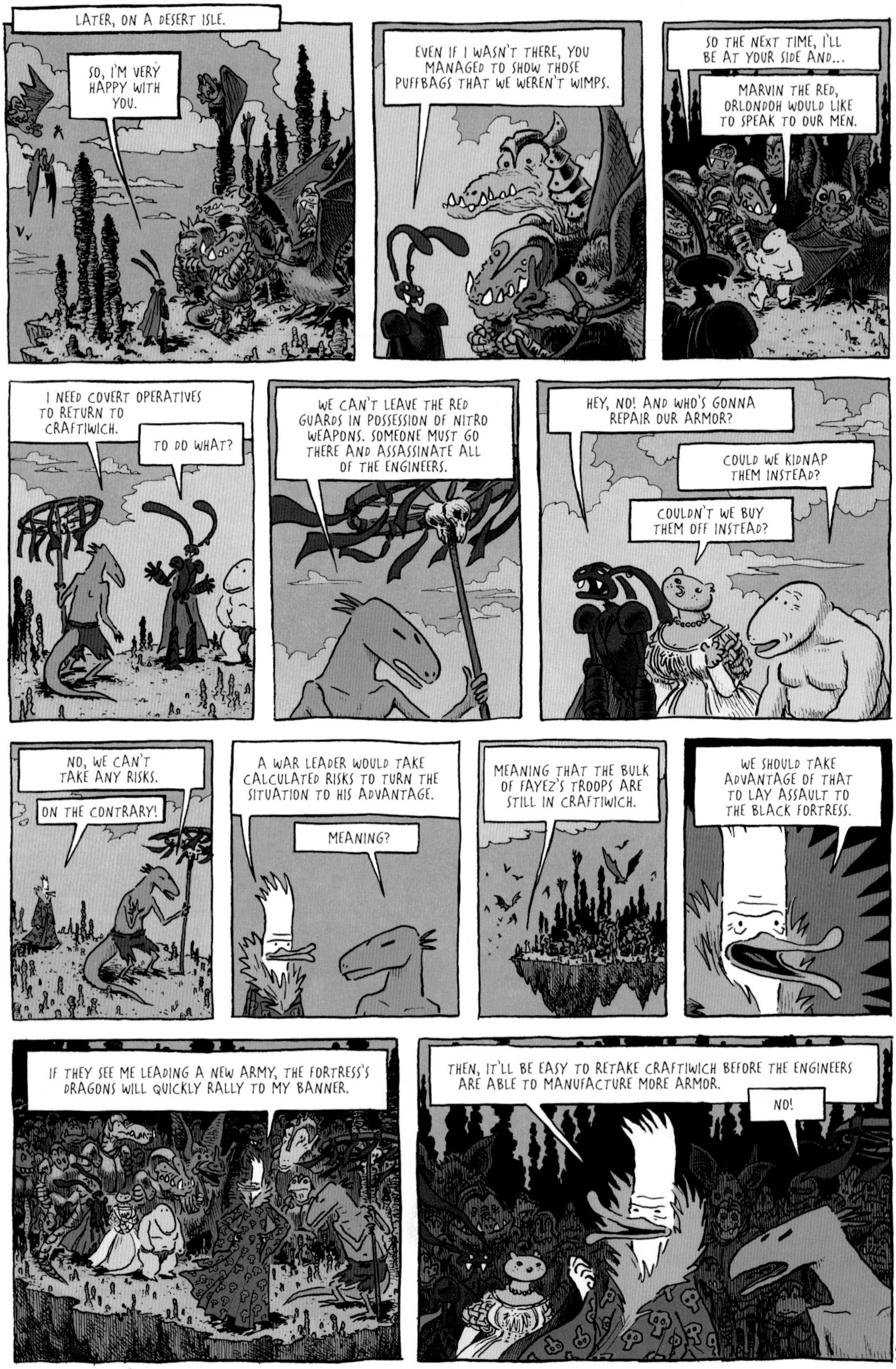
LATER, ON A DESERT ISLE.
SO, I'M VERY HAPPY WITH YOU.
EVEN IF I WASN'T THERE, YOU MANAGED TO SHOW THOSE PUFFBAGS THAT WE WEREN'T WIMPS.
SO THE NEXT TIME, I'LL BE AT YOUR SIDE AND...
MARVIN THE RED, ORLONDOH WOULD LIKE TO SPEAK TO OUR MEN.
I NEED COVERT OPERATIVES TO RETURN TO CRAFTIWICH.
TO DO WHAT?
WE CAN'T LEAVE THE RED GUARDS IN POSSESSION OF NITRO WEAPONS. SOMEONE MUST GO THERE AND ASSASSINATE ALL OF THE ENGINEERS.
HEY, NO! AND WHO'S GONNA REPAIR OUR ARMOR?
COULD WE KIDNAP THEM INSTEAD?
COULDN'T WE BUY THEM OFF INSTEAD?
NO, WE CAN'T TAKE ANY RISKS.
ON THE CONTRARY!
A WAR LEADER WOULD TAKE CALCULATED RISKS TO TURN THE SITUATION TO HIS ADVANTAGE.
MEANING?
MEANING THAT THE BULK OF FAYEZ'S TROOPS ARE STILL IN CRAFTIWICH.
WE SHOULD TAKE ADVANTAGE OF THAT TO LAY ASSAULT TO THE BLACK FORTRESS.
IF THEY SEE ME LEADING A NEW ARMY, THE FORTRESS'S DRAGONS WILL QUICKLY RALLY TO MY BANNER.
THEN, IT'LL BE EASY TO RETAKE CRAFTIWICH BEFORE THE ENGINEERS ARE ABLE TO MANUFACTURE MORE ARMOR.
NO!

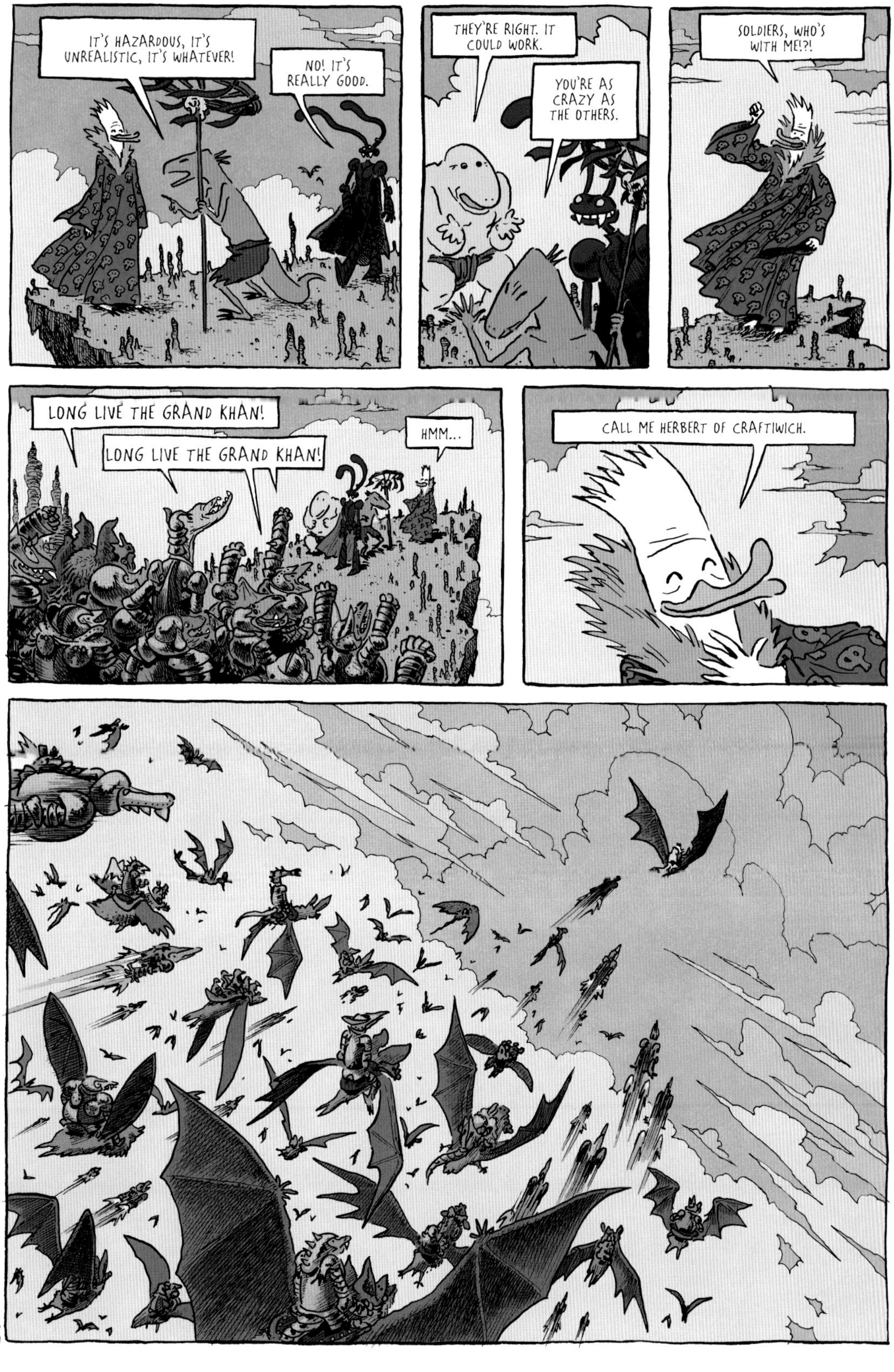

IT'S HAZARDOUS, IT'S UNREALISTIC, IT'S WHATEVER!
NO! IT'S REALLY GOOD.
THEY'RE RIGHT. IT COULD WORK.
YOU'RE AS CRAZY AS THE OTHERS.
SOLDIERS, WHO'S WITH ME!?!
LONG LIVE THE GRAND KHAN!
LONG LIVE THE GRAND KHAN!
HMM...
CALL ME HERBERT OF CRAFTIWICH.

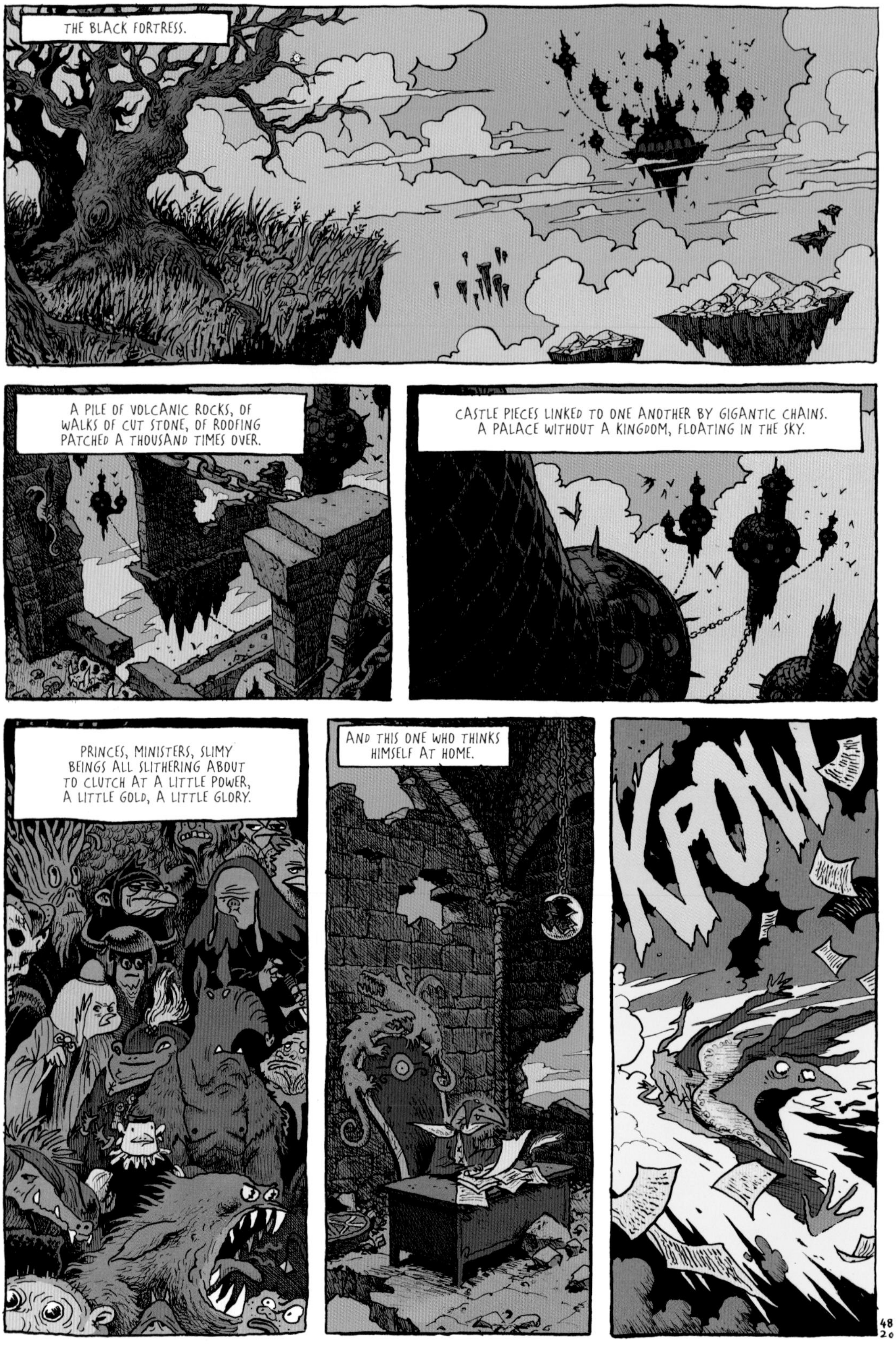
THE BLACK FORTRESS.
A PILE OF VOLCANIC ROCKS, OF WALKS OF CUT STONE, OF ROOFING PATCHED A THOUSAND TIMES OVER.
CASTLE PIECES LINKED TO ONE ANOTHER BY GIGANTIC CHAINS. A PALACE WITHOUT A KINGDOM, FLOATING IN THE SKY.
PRINCES, MINISTERS, SLIMY BEINGS ALL SLITHERING ABOUT TO CLUTCH AT A LITTLE POWER, A LITTLE GOLD, A LITTLE GLORY.
AND THIS ONE WHO THINKS HIMSELF AT HOME.
KPOW

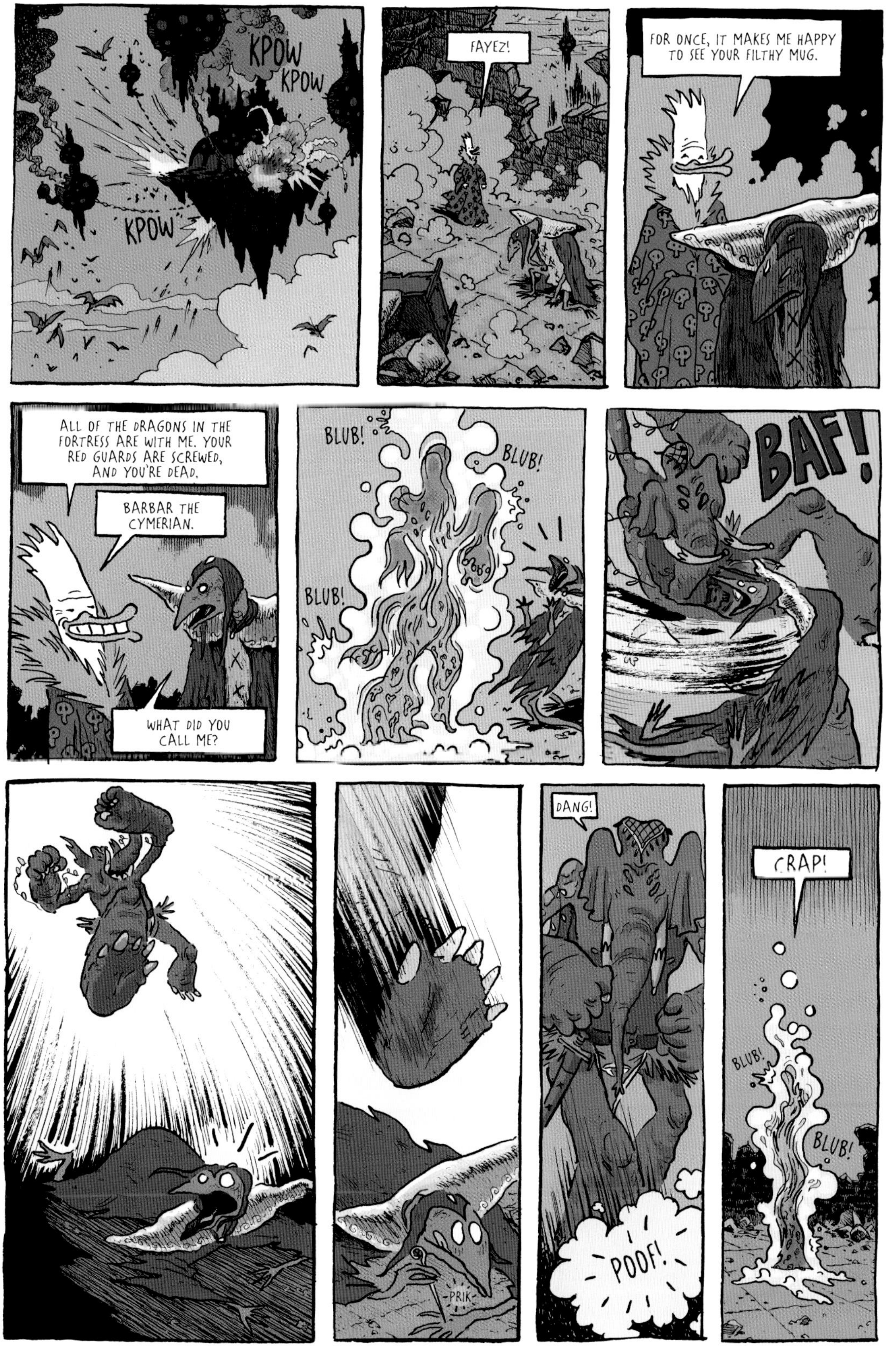
KPOW
KPOW
KPOW
FAYEZ!
FOR ONCE, IT MAKES ME HAPPY TO SEE YOUR FILTHY MUG.
ALL OF THE DRAGONS IN THE FORTRESS ARE WITH ME. YOUR RED GUARDS ARE SCREWED, AND YOU'RE DEAD.
BARBAR THE CYMERIAN.
WHAT DID YOU CALL ME?
BLUB!
BLUB!
BLUB!
BAF!
PRIK
DANG!
POOF!
CRAP!
BLUB!
BLUB!

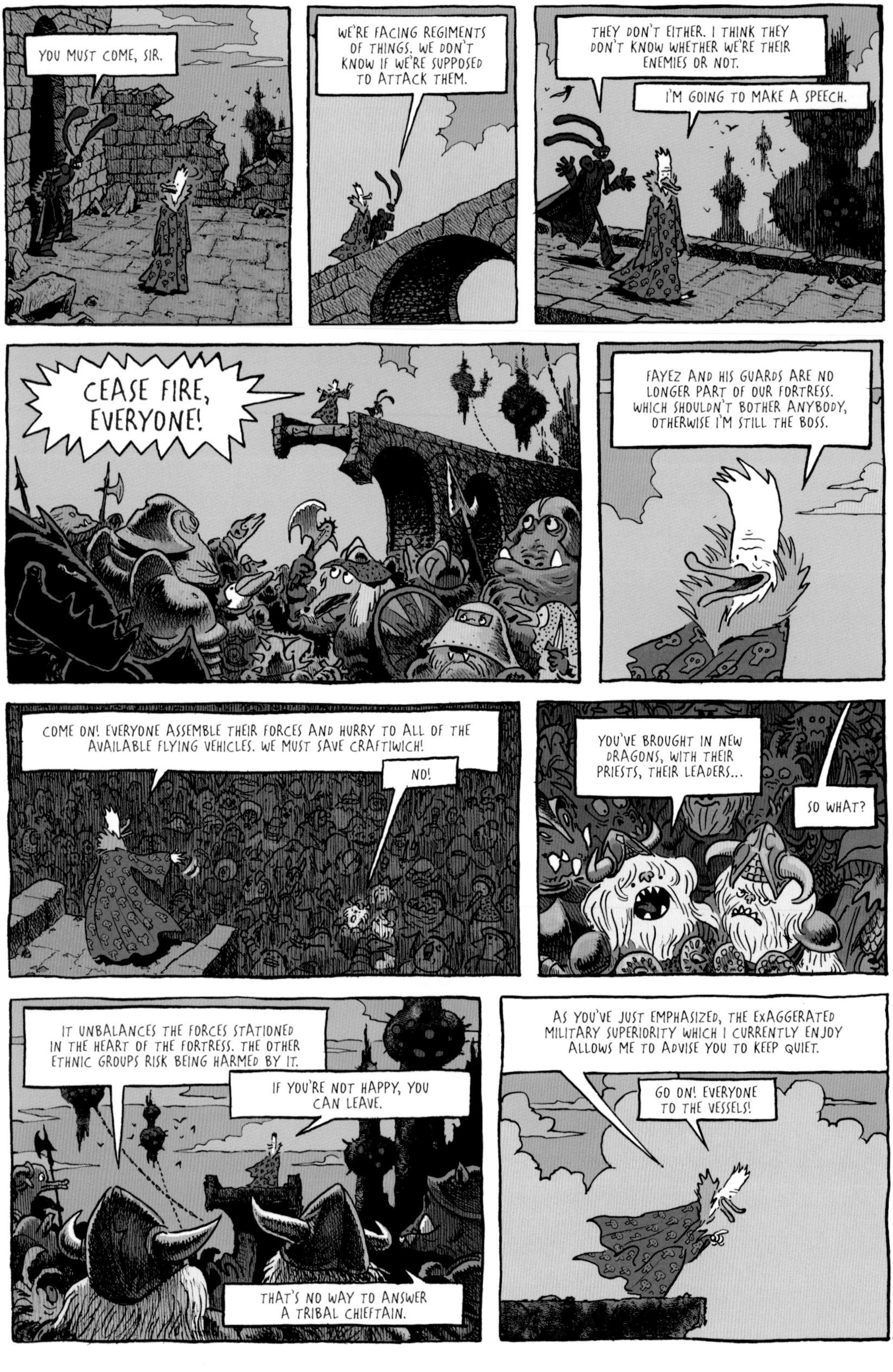
YOU MUST COME, SIR.
WE'RE FACING REGIMENTS OF THINGS. WE DON'T KNOW IF WE'RE SUPPOSED TO ATTACK THEM.
THEY DON'T EITHER. I THINK THEY DON'T KNOW WHETHER WE'RE THEIR ENEMIES OR NOT.
I'M GOING TO MAKE A SPEECH.
CEASE FIRE, EVERYONE!
FAYEZ AND HIS GUARDS ARE NO LONGER PART OF OUR FORTRESS. WHICH SHOULDN'T BOTHER ANYBODY, OTHERWISE I'M STILL THE BOSS.
COME ON! EVERYONE ASSEMBLE THEIR FORCES AND HURRY TO ALL OF THE AVAILABLE FLYING VEHICLES. WE MUST SAVE CRAFTIWICH!
NO!
YOU'VE BROUGHT IN NEW DRAGONS, WITH THEIR PRIESTS, THEIR LEADERS...
SO WHAT?
IT UNBALANCES THE FORCES STATIONED IN THE HEART OF THE FORTRESS. THE OTHER ETHNIC GROUPS RISK BEING HARMED BY IT.
IF YOU'RE NOT HAPPY, YOU CAN LEAVE.
THAT'S NO WAY TO ANSWER A TRIBAL CHIEFTAIN.
AS YOU'VE JUST EMPHASIZED, THE EXAGGERATED MILITARY SUPERIORITY WHICH I CURRENTLY ENJOY ALLOWS ME TO ADVISE YOU TO KEEP QUIET.
GO ON! EVERYONE TO THE VESSELS!

ALL THE DRAGONS OF THE FORTRESS.

I WONDER WHERE FAYEZ HAS ESCAPED TO.

NO BIG DEAL.

ALL THE CENTURIONS IN THEIR NEW ARMOR.

WITH WHAT I'M BRINGING TO HIM, HE CAN DO NOTHING.

AND YOUR SONS?

THE WHOLE MOTLEY FLOTILLA OF THE HUNDRED TRIBES INHABITING THE AREA.

WHAT WILL YOU DO WITH THEM ONCE YOU'VE REGAINED POWER?

I DON'T KNOW.

HEADING TOWARDS CRAFTIWICH.

IF I LEAVE THEM FREE, THEY WON'T CEASE TRYING TO WIN BACK THE DUCHY. I CAN'T KILL THEM. I CAN'T SEE MYSELF IMPRISONING THEM. I'M MAYBE GOING TO NAME THEM AS MINISTERS IN THE FORTRESS. THEY'LL HAVE ELEVATED RANKS, AND I'LL BE ABLE TO KEEP AN EYE ON THEM.

AND I THOUGHT I HAD A PROBLEM CHILD.

GRAND KHAN, WE'RE AT CRAFTIWICH.

WHAT ARE YOU TALKING ABOUT? WE'RE FLOATING IN THE MIDDLE OF THE STRATOSPHERE!

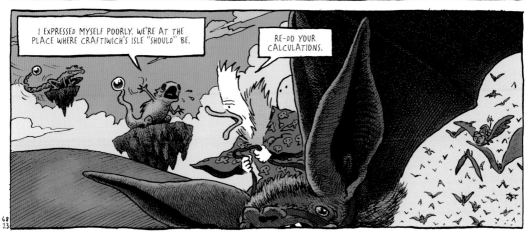

I EXPRESSED MYSELF POORLY. WE'RE AT THE PLACE WHERE CRAFTIWICH'S ISLE "SHOULD" BE.

RE-DO YOUR CALCULATIONS.

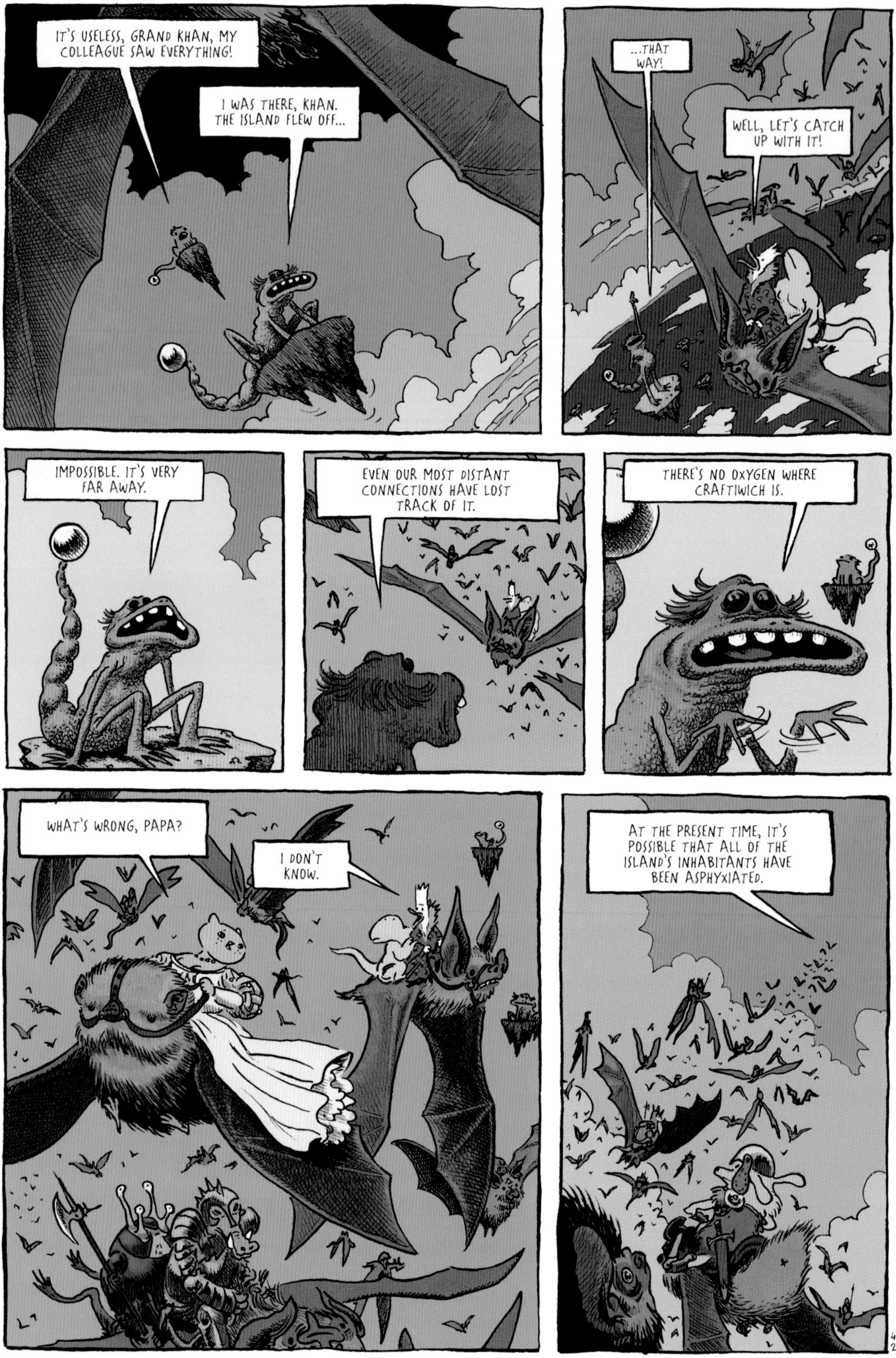

IT'S USELESS, GRAND KHAN, MY COLLEAGUE SAW EVERYTHING!
I WAS THERE, KHAN. THE ISLAND FLEW OFF...
...THAT WAY!
WELL, LET'S CATCH UP WITH IT!
IMPOSSIBLE. IT'S VERY FAR AWAY.
EVEN OUR MOST DISTANT CONNECTIONS HAVE LOST TRACK OF IT.
THERE'S NO OXYGEN WHERE CRAFTIWICH IS.
WHAT'S WRONG, PAPA?
I DON'T KNOW.
AT THE PRESENT TIME, IT'S POSSIBLE THAT ALL OF THE ISLAND'S INHABITANTS HAVE BEEN ASPHYXIATED.

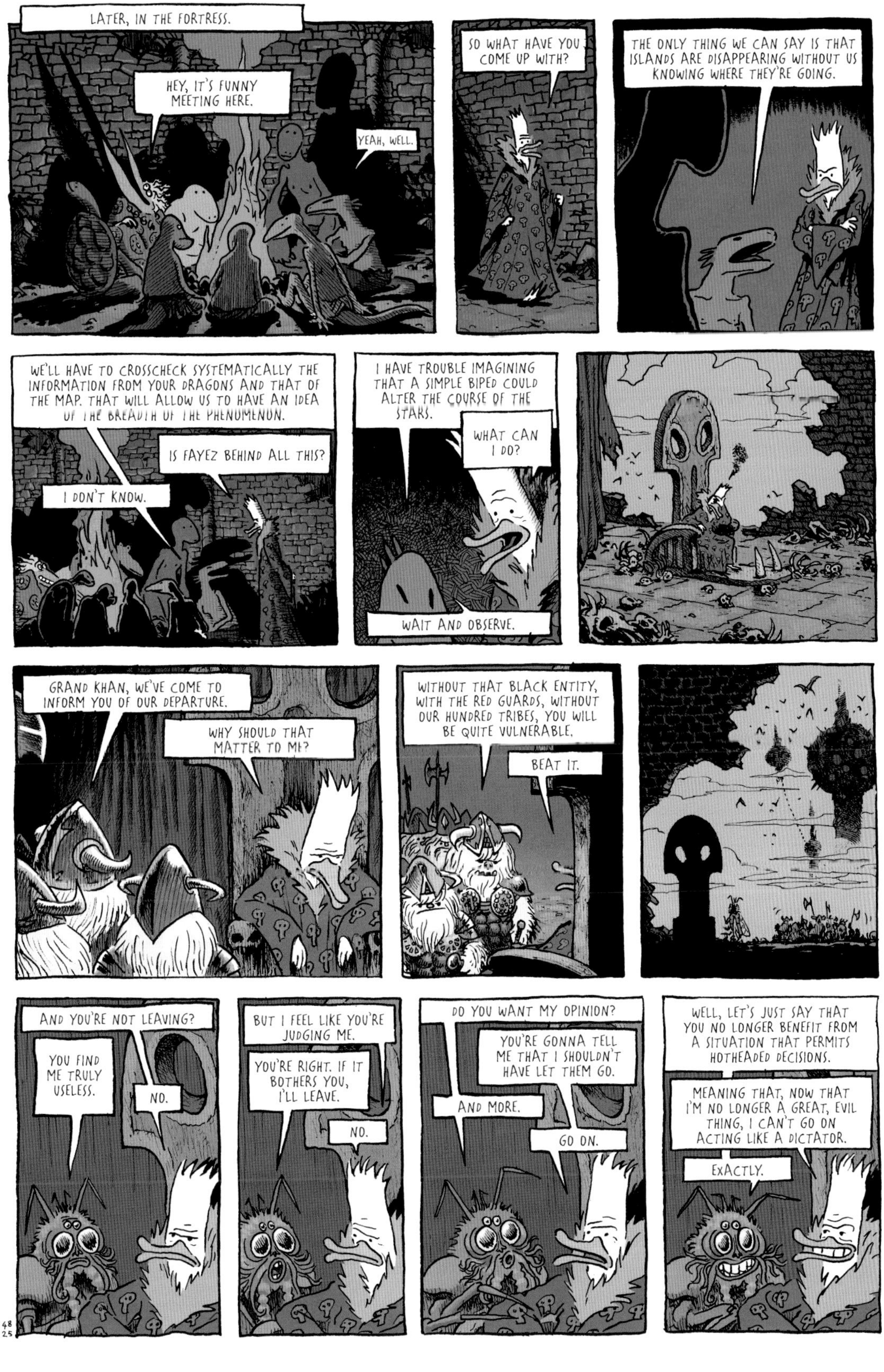
LATER, IN THE FORTRESS.
HEY, IT'S FUNNY MEETING HERE.
YEAH, WELL.
SO WHAT HAVE YOU COME UP WITH?
THE ONLY THING WE CAN SAY IS THAT ISLANDS ARE DISAPPEARING WITHOUT US KNOWING WHERE THEY'RE GOING.
WE'LL HAVE TO CROSSCHECK SYSTEMATICALLY THE INFORMATION FROM YOUR DRAGONS AND THAT OF THE MAP. THAT WILL ALLOW US TO HAVE AN IDEA OF THE BREADTH OF THE PHENOMENON.
IS FAYEZ BEHIND ALL THIS?
I DON'T KNOW.
I HAVE TROUBLE IMAGINING THAT A SIMPLE BIPED COULD ALTER THE COURSE OF THE STARS.
WHAT CAN I DO?
WAIT AND OBSERVE.
GRAND KHAN, WE'VE COME TO INFORM YOU OF OUR DEPARTURE.
WHY SHOULD THAT MATTER TO ME?
WITHOUT THAT BLACK ENTITY, WITH THE RED GUARDS, WITHOUT OUR HUNDRED TRIBES, YOU WILL BE QUITE VULNERABLE.
BEAT IT.
AND YOU'RE NOT LEAVING?
YOU FIND ME TRULY USELESS.
NO.
BUT I FEEL LIKE YOU'RE JUDGING ME.
YOU'RE RIGHT. IF IT BOTHERS YOU, I'LL LEAVE.
NO.
DO YOU WANT MY OPINION?
YOU'RE GONNA TELL ME THAT I SHOULDN'T HAVE LET THEM GO.
AND MORE.
GO ON.
WELL, LET'S JUST SAY THAT YOU NO LONGER BENEFIT FROM A SITUATION THAT PERMITS HOTHEADED DECISIONS.
MEANING THAT, NOW THAT I'M NO LONGER A GREAT, EVIL THING, I CAN'T GO ON ACTING LIKE A DICTATOR.
EXACTLY.

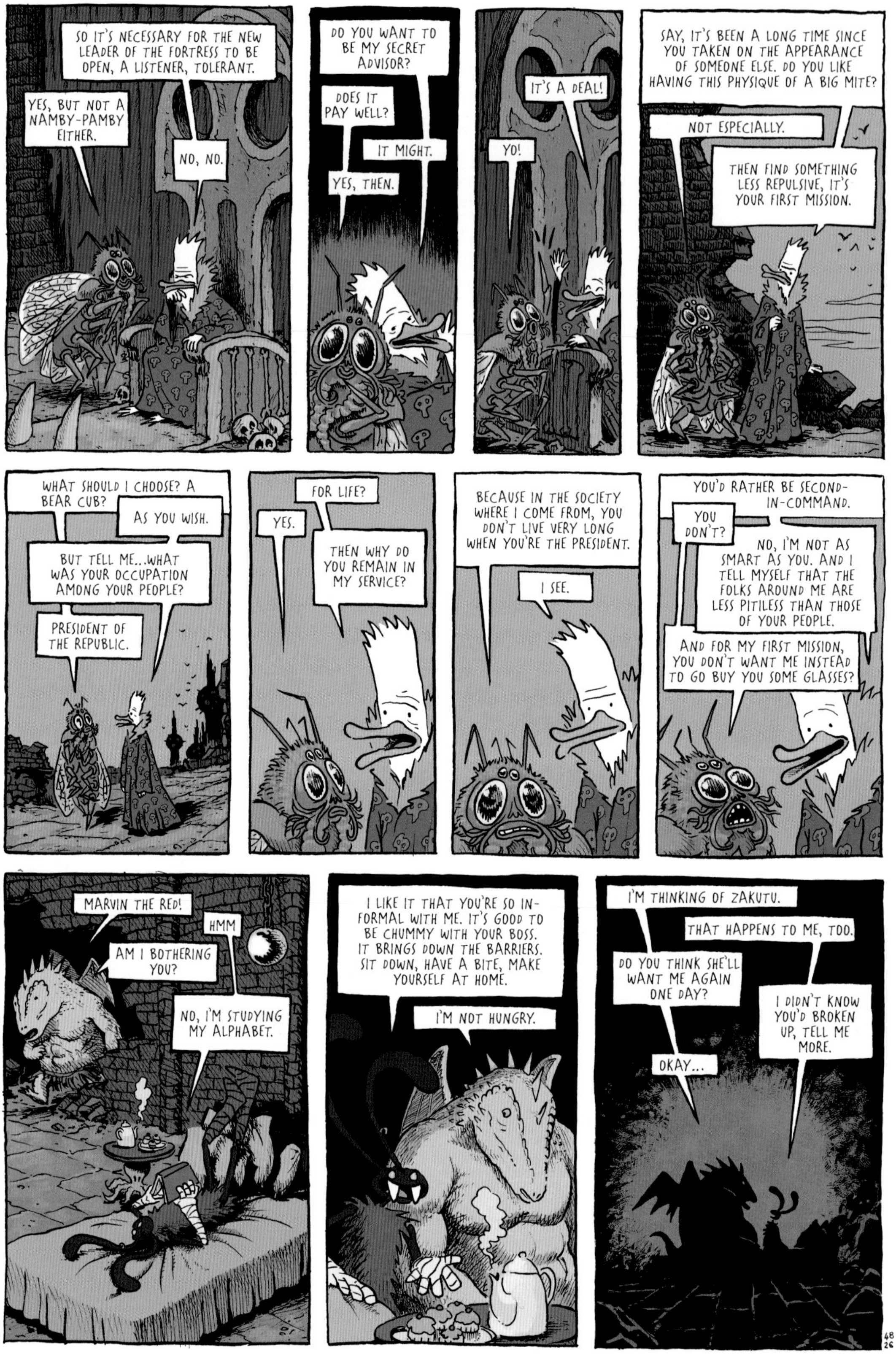
SO IT'S NECESSARY FOR THE NEW LEADER OF THE FORTRESS TO BE OPEN, A LISTENER, TOLERANT.
YES, BUT NOT A NAMBY-PAMBY EITHER.
NO, NO.
DO YOU WANT TO BE MY SECRET ADVISOR?
DOES IT PAY WELL?
IT MIGHT.
YES, THEN.
IT'S A DEAL!
YO!
SAY, IT'S BEEN A LONG TIME SINCE YOU TAKEN ON THE APPEARANCE OF SOMEONE ELSE. DO YOU LIKE HAVING THIS PHYSIQUE OF A BIG MITE?
NOT ESPECIALLY.
THEN FIND SOMETHING LESS REPULSIVE, IT'S YOUR FIRST MISSION.
WHAT SHOULD I CHOOSE? A BEAR CUB?
AS YOU WISH.
BUT TELL ME...WHAT WAS YOUR OCCUPATION AMONG YOUR PEOPLE?
PRESIDENT OF THE REPUBLIC.
FOR LIFE?
YES.
THEN WHY DO YOU REMAIN IN MY SERVICE?
BECAUSE IN THE SOCIETY WHERE I COME FROM, YOU DON'T LIVE VERY LONG WHEN YOU'RE THE PRESIDENT.
I SEE.
YOU'D RATHER BE SECOND-IN-COMMAND.
YOU DON'T?
NO, I'M NOT AS SMART AS YOU. AND I TELL MYSELF THAT THE FOLKS AROUND ME ARE LESS PITILESS THAN THOSE OF YOUR PEOPLE.
AND FOR MY FIRST MISSION, YOU DON'T WANT ME INSTEAD TO GO BUY YOU SOME GLASSES?
MARVIN THE RED!
HMM
AM I BOTHERING YOU?
NO, I'M STUDYING MY ALPHABET.
I LIKE IT THAT YOU'RE SO INFORMAL WITH ME. IT'S GOOD TO BE CHUMMY WITH YOUR BOSS. IT BRINGS DOWN THE BARRIERS. SIT DOWN, HAVE A BITE, MAKE YOURSELF AT HOME.
I'M NOT HUNGRY.
I'M THINKING OF ZAKUTU.
THAT HAPPENS TO ME, TOO.
DO YOU THINK SHE'LL WANT ME AGAIN ONE DAY?
I DIDN'T KNOW YOU'D BROKEN UP, TELL ME MORE.
OKAY...

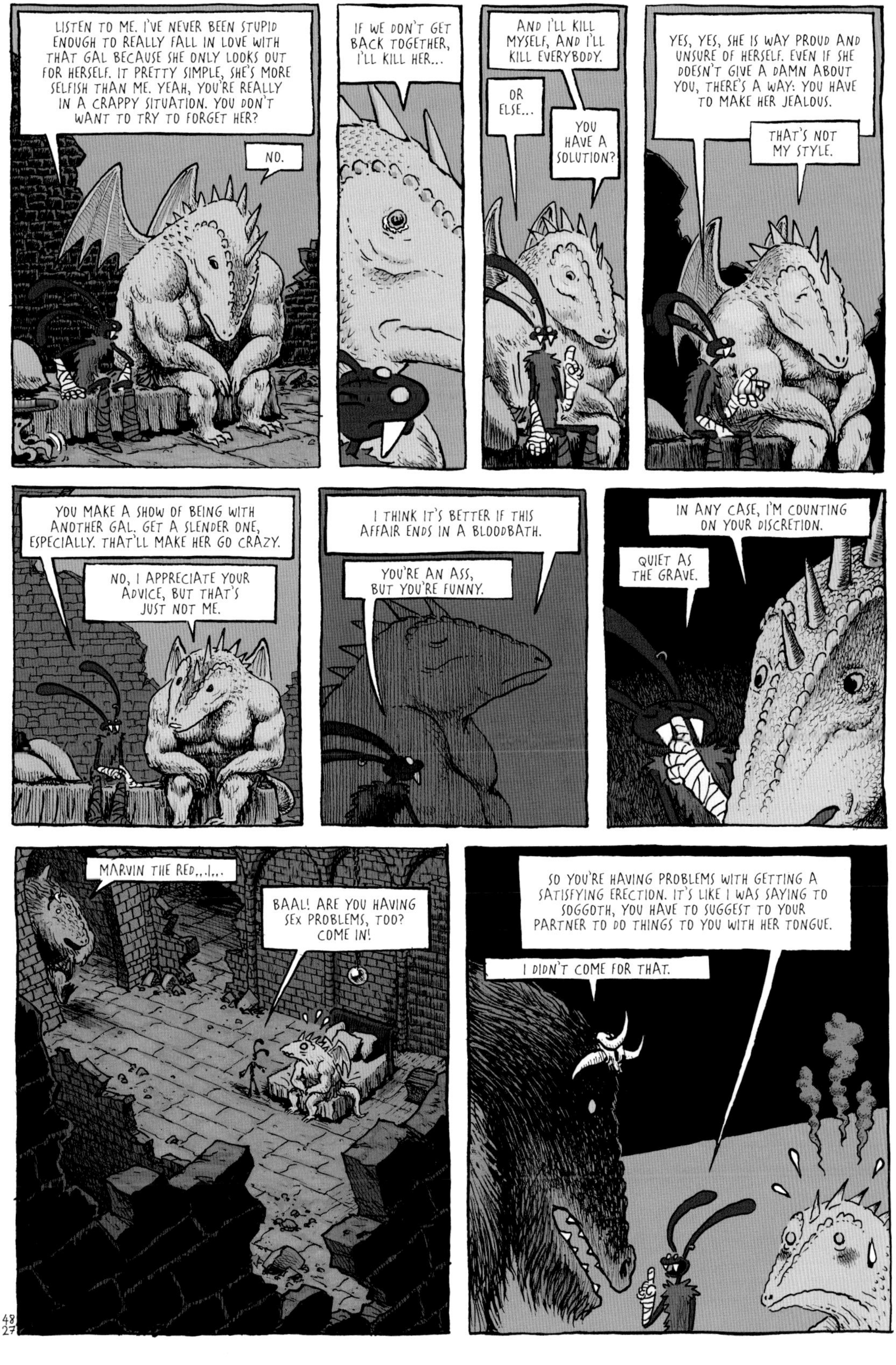
LISTEN TO ME. I'VE NEVER BEEN STUPID ENOUGH TO REALLY FALL IN LOVE WITH THAT GAL BECAUSE SHE ONLY LOOKS OUT FOR HERSELF. IT PRETTY SIMPLE, SHE'S MORE SELFISH THAN ME. YEAH, YOU'RE REALLY IN A CRAPPY SITUATION. YOU DON'T WANT TO TRY TO FORGET HER?
NO.
IF WE DON'T GET BACK TOGETHER, I'LL KILL HER...
AND I'LL KILL MYSELF, AND I'LL KILL EVERYBODY.
OR ELSE...
YOU HAVE A SOLUTION?
YES, YES, SHE IS WAY PROUD AND UNSURE OF HERSELF. EVEN IF SHE DOESN'T GIVE A DAMN ABOUT YOU, THERE'S A WAY: YOU HAVE TO MAKE HER JEALOUS.
THAT'S NOT MY STYLE.
YOU MAKE A SHOW OF BEING WITH ANOTHER GAL. GET A SLENDER ONE, ESPECIALLY. THAT'LL MAKE HER GO CRAZY.
NO, I APPRECIATE YOUR ADVICE, BUT THAT'S JUST NOT ME.
I THINK IT'S BETTER IF THIS AFFAIR ENDS IN A BLOODBATH.
YOU'RE AN ASS, BUT YOU'RE FUNNY.
IN ANY CASE, I'M COUNTING ON YOUR DISCRETION.
QUIET AS THE GRAVE.
MARVIN THE RED,..I...
BAAL! ARE YOU HAVING SEX PROBLEMS, TOO? COME IN!
SO YOU'RE HAVING PROBLEMS WITH GETTING A SATISFYING ERECTION. IT'S LIKE I WAS SAYING TO SOGGOTH, YOU HAVE TO SUGGEST TO YOUR PARTNER TO DO THINGS TO YOU WITH HER TONGUE.
I DIDN'T COME FOR THAT.

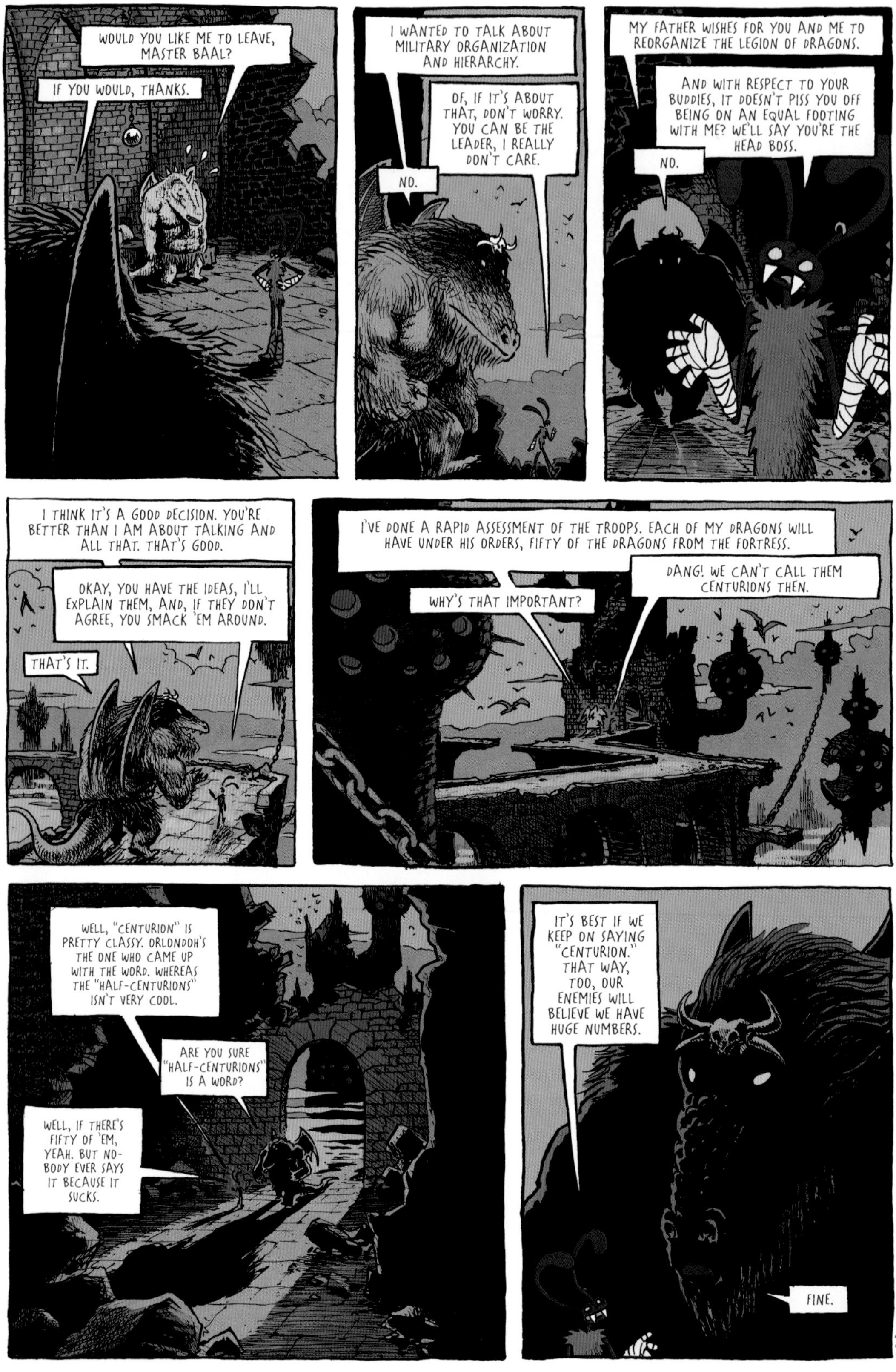
WOULD YOU LIKE ME TO LEAVE, MASTER BAAL?
IF YOU WOULD, THANKS.
I WANTED TO TALK ABOUT MILITARY ORGANIZATION AND HIERARCHY.
OF, IF IT'S ABOUT THAT, DON'T WORRY. YOU CAN BE THE LEADER, I REALLY DON'T CARE.
NO.
MY FATHER WISHES FOR YOU AND ME TO REORGANIZE THE LEGION OF DRAGONS.
AND WITH RESPECT TO YOUR BUDDIES, IT DOESN'T PISS YOU OFF BEING ON AN EQUAL FOOTING WITH ME? WE'LL SAY YOU'RE THE HEAD BOSS.
NO.
I THINK IT'S A GOOD DECISION. YOU'RE BETTER THAN I AM ABOUT TALKING AND ALL THAT. THAT'S GOOD.
OKAY, YOU HAVE THE IDEAS, I'LL EXPLAIN THEM, AND, IF THEY DON'T AGREE, YOU SMACK 'EM AROUND.
THAT'S IT.
I'VE DONE A RAPID ASSESSMENT OF THE TROOPS. EACH OF MY DRAGONS WILL HAVE UNDER HIS ORDERS, FIFTY OF THE DRAGONS FROM THE FORTRESS.
WHY'S THAT IMPORTANT?
DANG! WE CAN'T CALL THEM CENTURIONS THEN.
WELL, "CENTURION" IS PRETTY CLASSY. ORLONDOH'S THE ONE WHO CAME UP WITH THE WORD. WHEREAS THE "HALF-CENTURIONS" ISN'T VERY COOL.
ARE YOU SURE "HALF-CENTURIONS" IS A WORD?
WELL, IF THERE'S FIFTY OF 'EM, YEAH. BUT NOBODY EVER SAYS IT BECAUSE IT SUCKS.
IT'S BEST IF WE KEEP ON SAYING "CENTURION." THAT WAY, TOO, OUR ENEMIES WILL BELIEVE WE HAVE HUGE NUMBERS.
FINE.

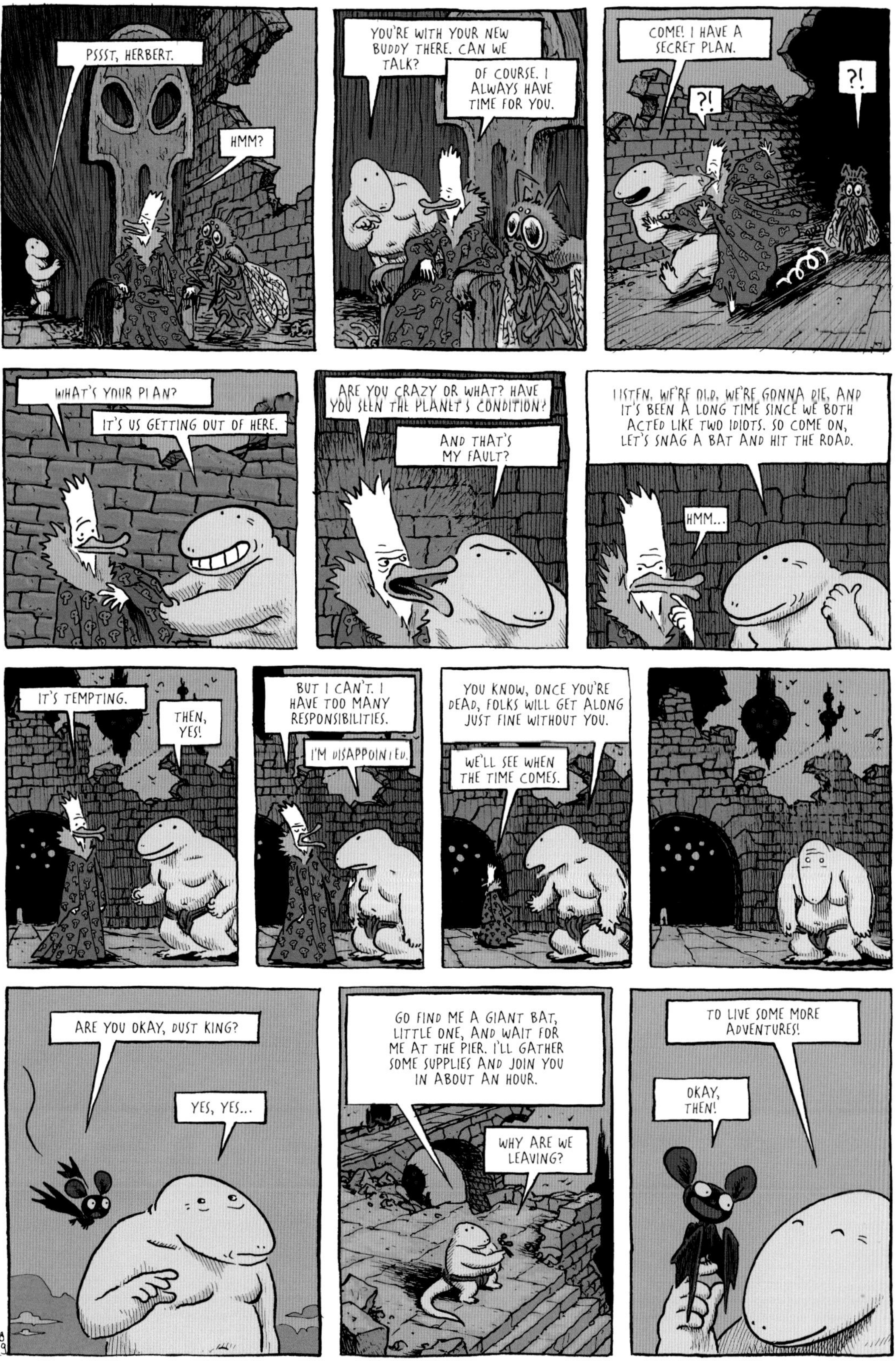
PSSST, HERBERT.
HMM?
YOU'RE WITH YOUR NEW BUDDY THERE. CAN WE TALK?
OF COURSE. I ALWAYS HAVE TIME FOR YOU.
COME! I HAVE A SECRET PLAN.
?!
?!
WHAT'S YOUR PLAN?
IT'S US GETTING OUT OF HERE.
ARE YOU CRAZY OR WHAT? HAVE YOU SEEN THE PLANET'S CONDITION?
AND THAT'S MY FAULT?
LISTEN, WE'RE OLD, WE'RE GONNA DIE, AND IT'S BEEN A LONG TIME SINCE WE BOTH ACTED LIKE TWO IDIOTS. SO COME ON, LET'S SNAG A BAT AND HIT THE ROAD.
HMM...
IT'S TEMPTING.
THEN, YES!
BUT I CAN'T. I HAVE TOO MANY RESPONSIBILITIES.
I'M DISAPPOINTED.
YOU KNOW, ONCE YOU'RE DEAD, FOLKS WILL GET ALONG JUST FINE WITHOUT YOU.
WE'LL SEE WHEN THE TIME COMES.
ARE YOU OKAY, DUST KING?
YES, YES...
GO FIND ME A GIANT BAT, LITTLE ONE, AND WAIT FOR ME AT THE PIER. I'LL GATHER SOME SUPPLIES AND JOIN YOU IN ABOUT AN HOUR.
WHY ARE WE LEAVING?
TO LIVE SOME MORE ADVENTURES!
OKAY, THEN!

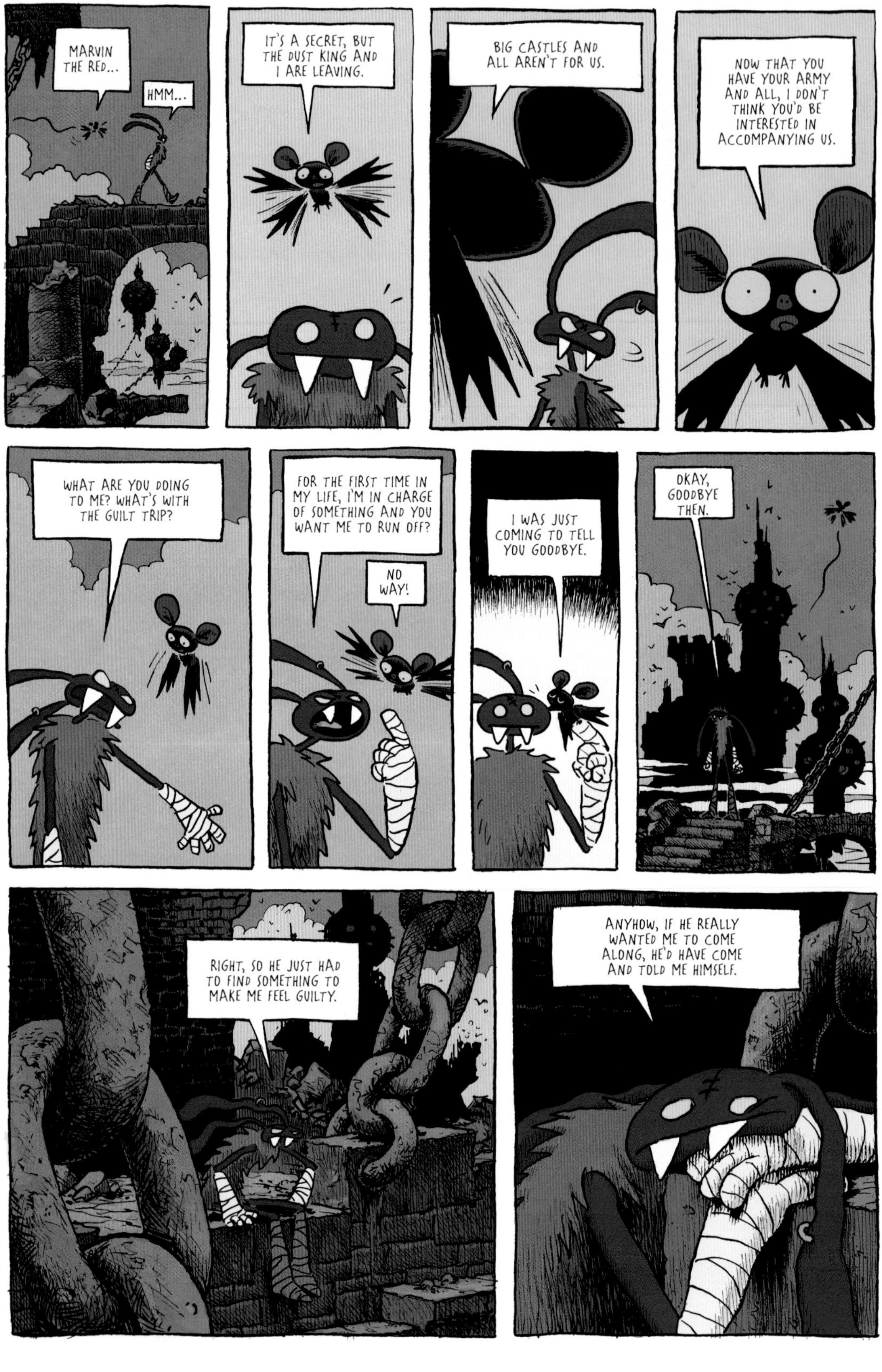
MARVIN THE RED...
HMM...
IT'S A SECRET, BUT THE DUST KING AND I ARE LEAVING.
BIG CASTLES AND ALL AREN'T FOR US.
NOW THAT YOU HAVE YOUR ARMY AND ALL, I DON'T THINK YOU'D BE INTERESTED IN ACCOMPANYING US.
WHAT ARE YOU DOING TO ME? WHAT'S WITH THE GUILT TRIP?
FOR THE FIRST TIME IN MY LIFE, I'M IN CHARGE OF SOMETHING AND YOU WANT ME TO RUN OFF?
NO WAY!
I WAS JUST COMING TO TELL YOU GOODBYE.
OKAY, GOODBYE THEN.
RIGHT, SO HE JUST HAD TO FIND SOMETHING TO MAKE ME FEEL GUILTY.
ANYHOW, IF HE REALLY WANTED ME TO COME ALONG, HE'D HAVE COME AND TOLD ME HIMSELF.

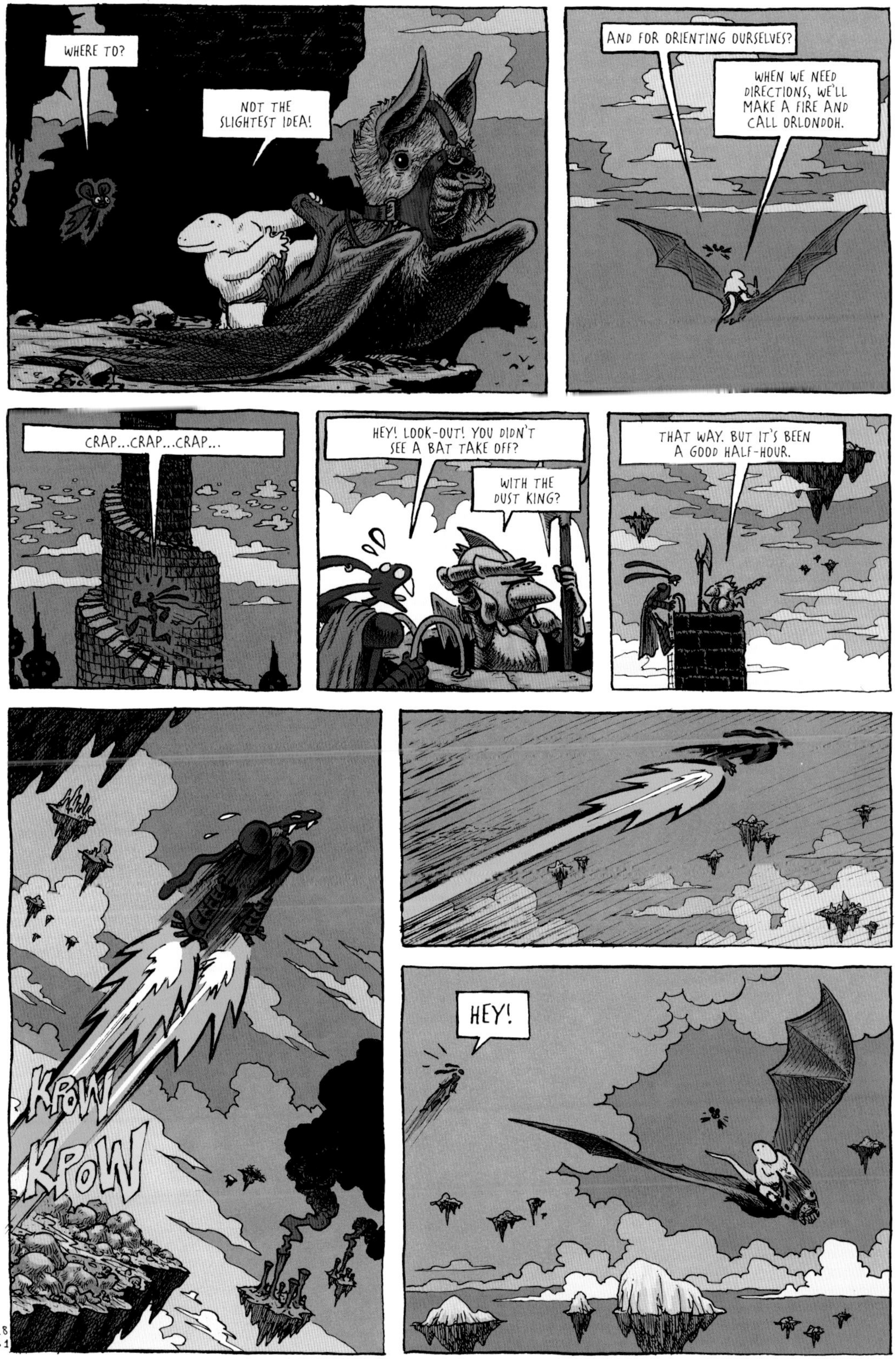
WHERE TO?
NOT THE SLIGHTEST IDEA!
AND FOR ORIENTING OURSELVES?
WHEN WE NEED DIRECTIONS, WE'LL MAKE A FIRE AND CALL ORLONDOH.
CRAP...CRAP...CRAP...
HEY! LOOK-OUT! YOU DIDN'T SEE A BAT TAKE OFF?
WITH THE DUST KING?
THAT WAY. BUT IT'S BEEN A GOOD HALF-HOUR.
KROW
KPOW
HEY!

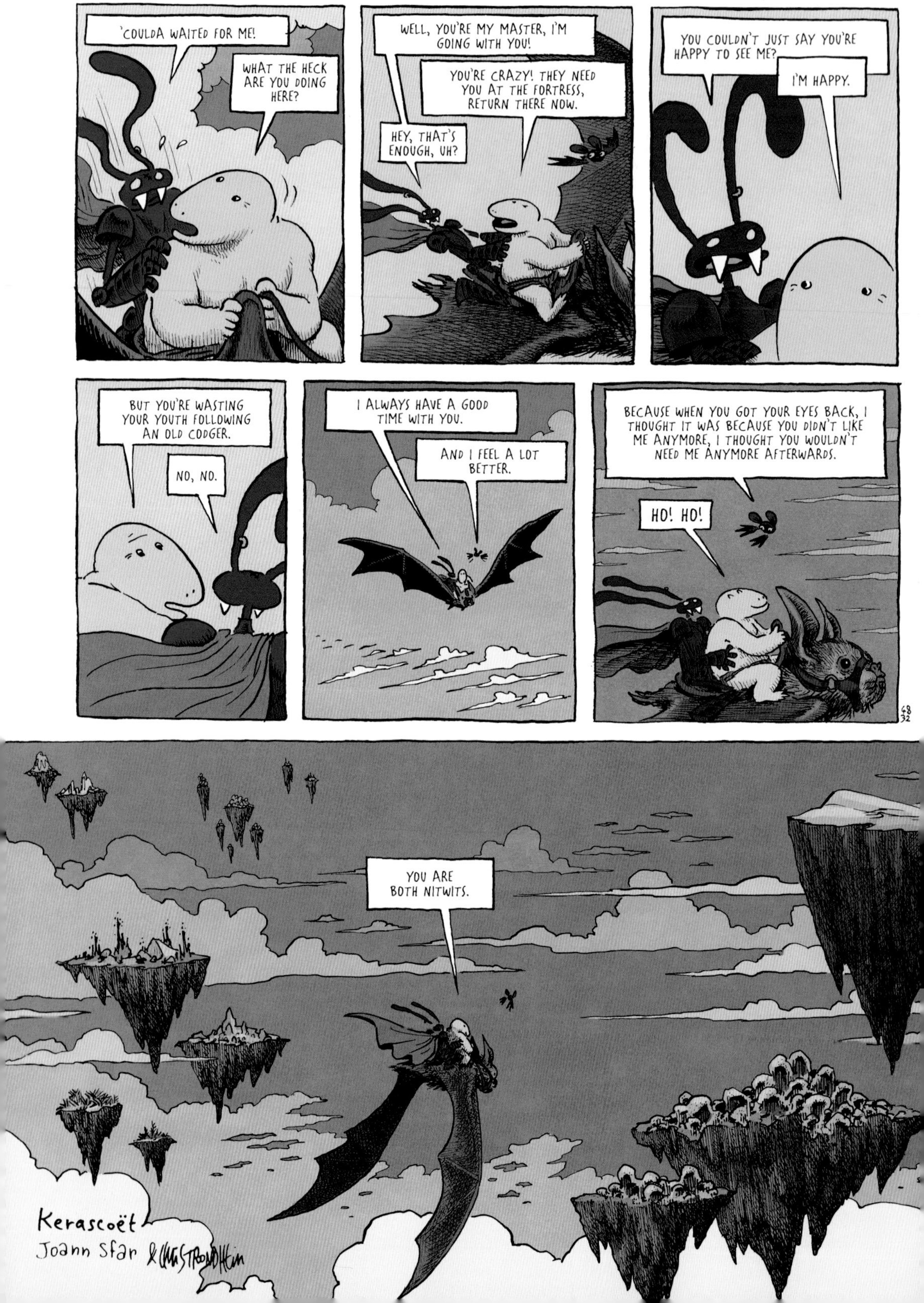
'COULDA WAITED FOR ME!
WHAT THE HECK ARE YOU DOING HERE?
WELL, YOU'RE MY MASTER, I'M GOING WITH YOU!
YOU'RE CRAZY! THEY NEED YOU AT THE FORTRESS, RETURN THERE NOW.
HEY, THAT'S ENOUGH, UH?
YOU COULDN'T JUST SAY YOU'RE HAPPY TO SEE ME?
I'M HAPPY.
BUT YOU'RE WASTING YOUR YOUTH FOLLOWING AN OLD CODGER.
NO, NO.
I ALWAYS HAVE A GOOD TIME WITH YOU.
AND I FEEL A LOT BETTER.
BECAUSE WHEN YOU GOT YOUR EYES BACK, I THOUGHT IT WAS BECAUSE YOU DIDN'T LIKE ME ANYMORE, I THOUGHT YOU WOULDN'T NEED ME ANYMORE AFTERWARDS.
HO! HO!
48
32
YOU ARE BOTH NITWITS.
Kerascoët
Joann Sfar

REVOLUTIONS

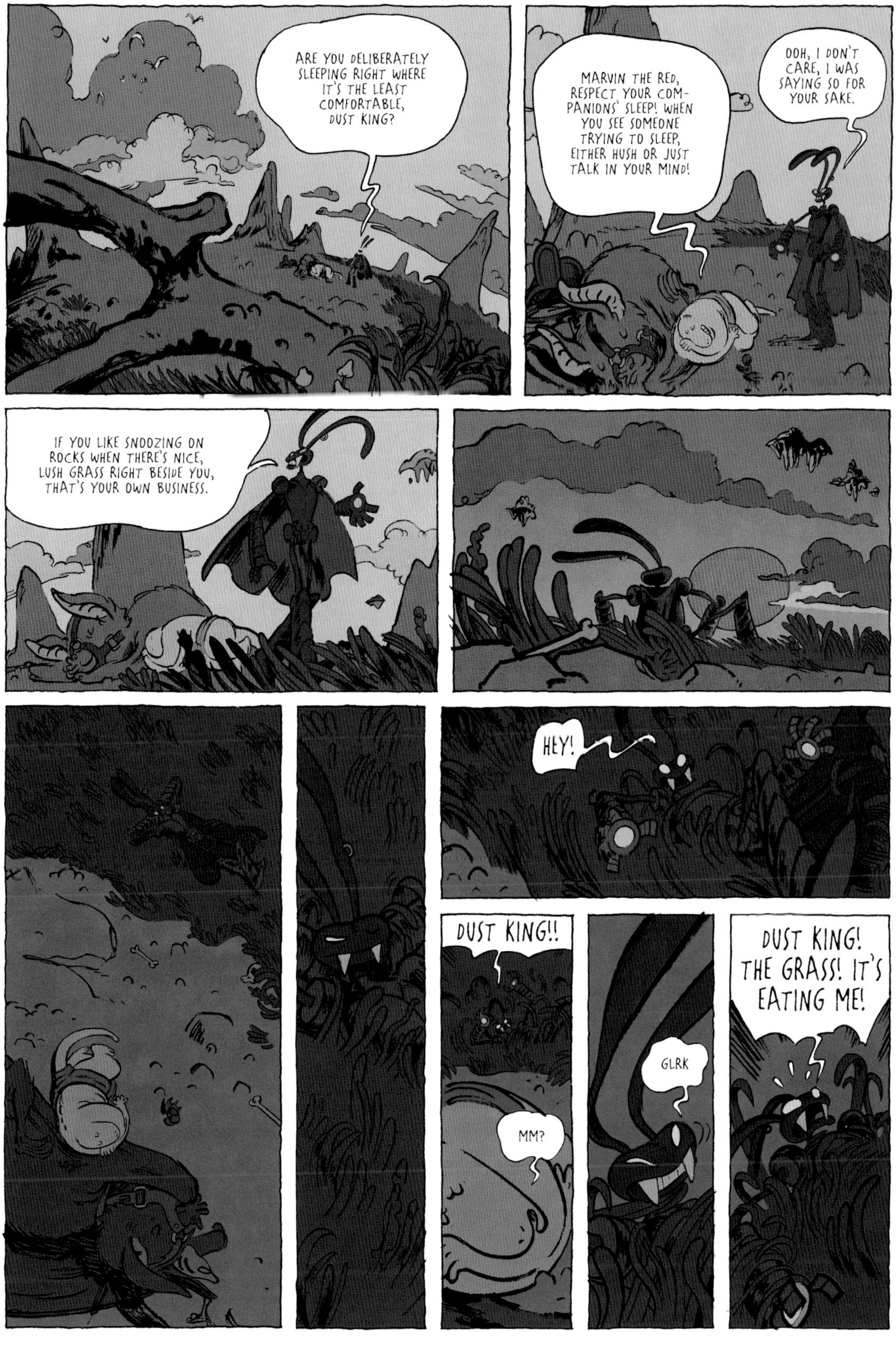

ARE YOU DELIBERATELY SLEEPING RIGHT WHERE IT'S THE LEAST COMFORTABLE, DUST KING?
MARVIN THE RED, RESPECT YOUR COMPANIONS' SLEEP! WHEN YOU SEE SOMEONE TRYING TO SLEEP, EITHER HUSH OR JUST TALK IN YOUR MIND!
OOH, I DON'T CARE, I WAS SAYING SO FOR YOUR SAKE.
IF YOU LIKE SNOOZING ON ROCKS WHEN THERE'S NICE, LUSH GRASS RIGHT BESIDE YOU, THAT'S YOUR OWN BUSINESS.
HEY!
DUST KING!!
MM?
GLRK
DUST KING! THE GRASS! IT'S EATING ME!

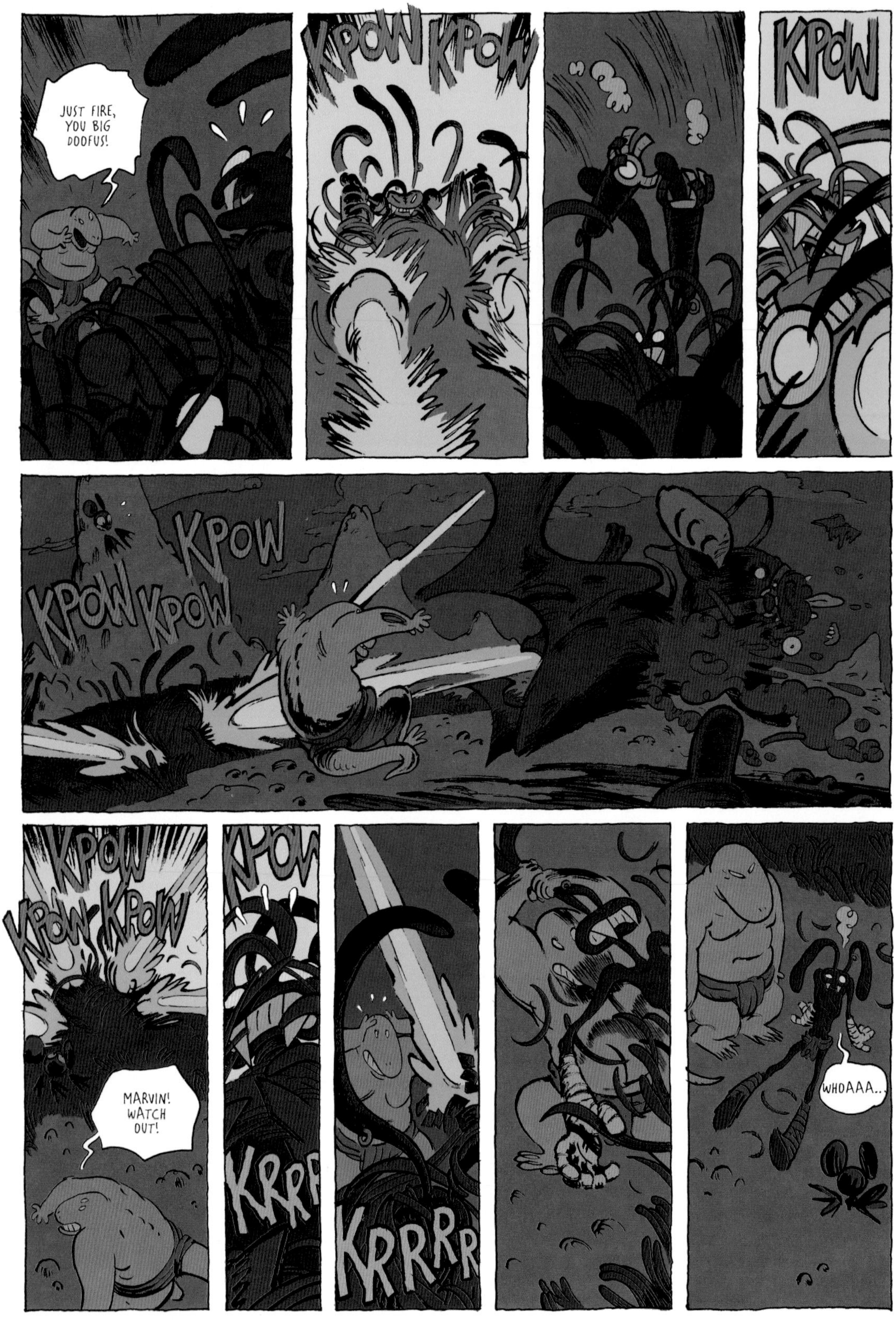
JUST FIRE, YOU BIG DOOFUS!
KPOW KPOW
KPOW
KPOW
KPOW KPOW
KPOW
KPOW KPOW
MARVIN! WATCH OUT!
KPOW
KRRR
KRRRR
WHOAAA...

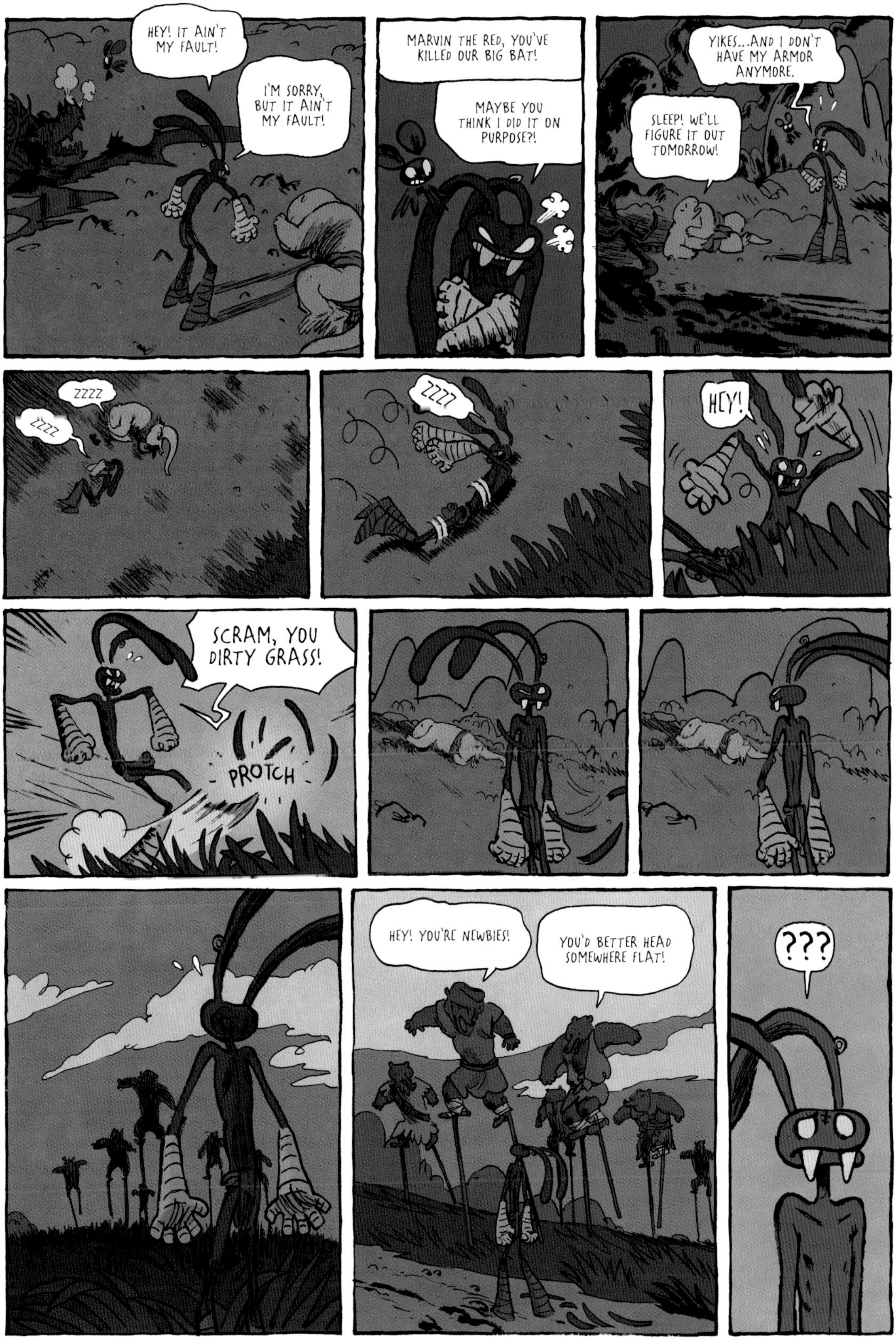
HEY! IT AIN'T MY FAULT!
I'M SORRY, BUT IT AIN'T MY FAULT!
MARVIN THE RED, YOU'VE KILLED OUR BIG BAT!
MAYBE YOU THINK I DID IT ON PURPOSE?!
YIKES...AND I DON'T HAVE MY ARMOR ANYMORE.
SLEEP! WE'LL FIGURE IT OUT TOMORROW!
ZZZZ
ZZZZ
ZZZZ
HEY!
SCRAM, YOU DIRTY GRASS!
PROTCH
HEY! YOU'RE NEWBIES!
YOU'D BETTER HEAD SOMEWHERE FLAT!
???

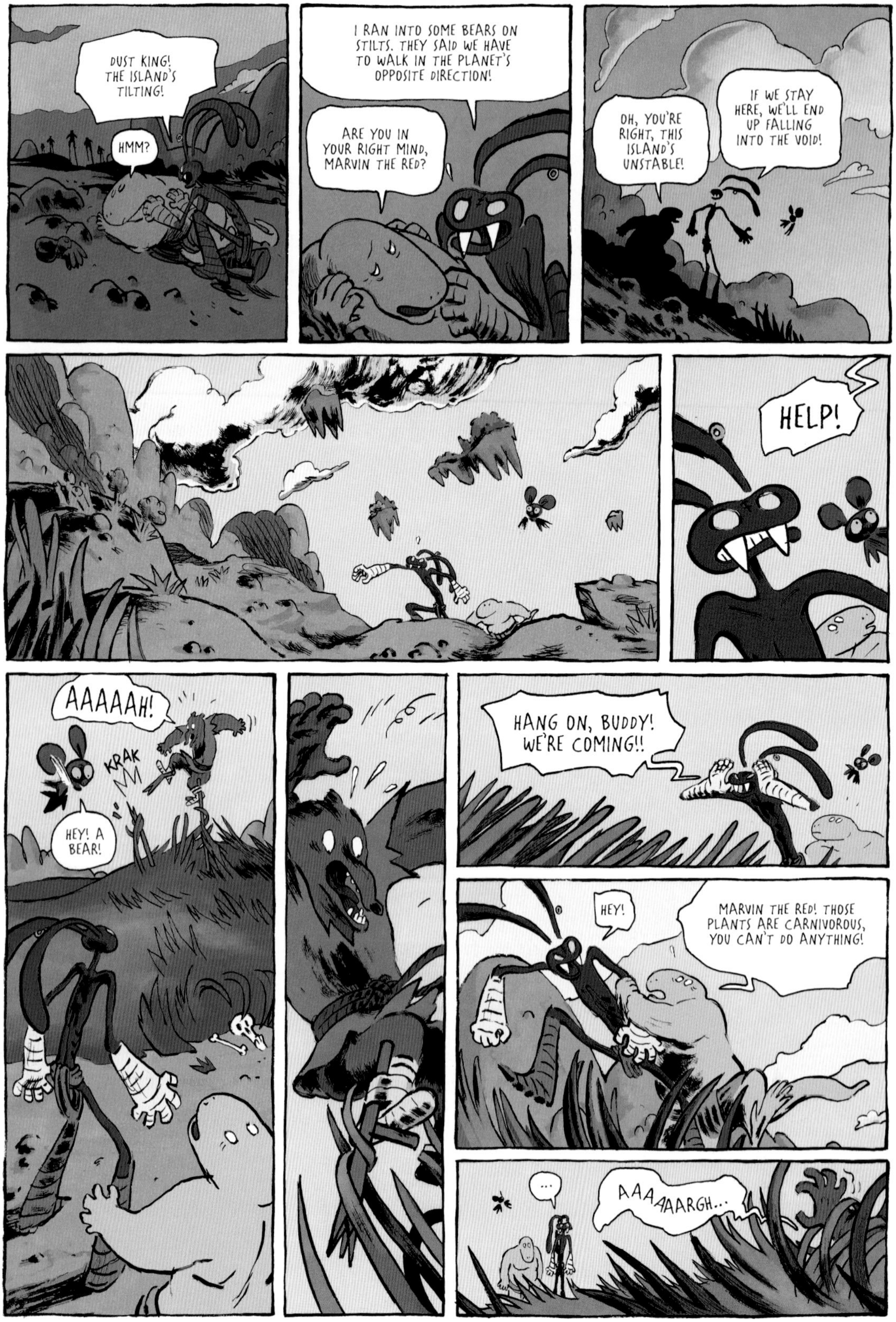
DUST KING! THE ISLAND'S TILTING!
HMM?
I RAN INTO SOME BEARS ON STILTS. THEY SAID WE HAVE TO WALK IN THE PLANET'S OPPOSITE DIRECTION!
ARE YOU IN YOUR RIGHT MIND, MARVIN THE RED?
OH, YOU'RE RIGHT, THIS ISLAND'S UNSTABLE!
IF WE STAY HERE, WE'LL END UP FALLING INTO THE VOID!
HELP!
AAAAAH!
KRAK
HEY! A BEAR!
HANG ON, BUDDY! WE'RE COMING!!
HEY!
MARVIN THE RED! THOSE PLANTS ARE CARNIVOROUS, YOU CAN'T DO ANYTHING!
...
AAAAAARGH...

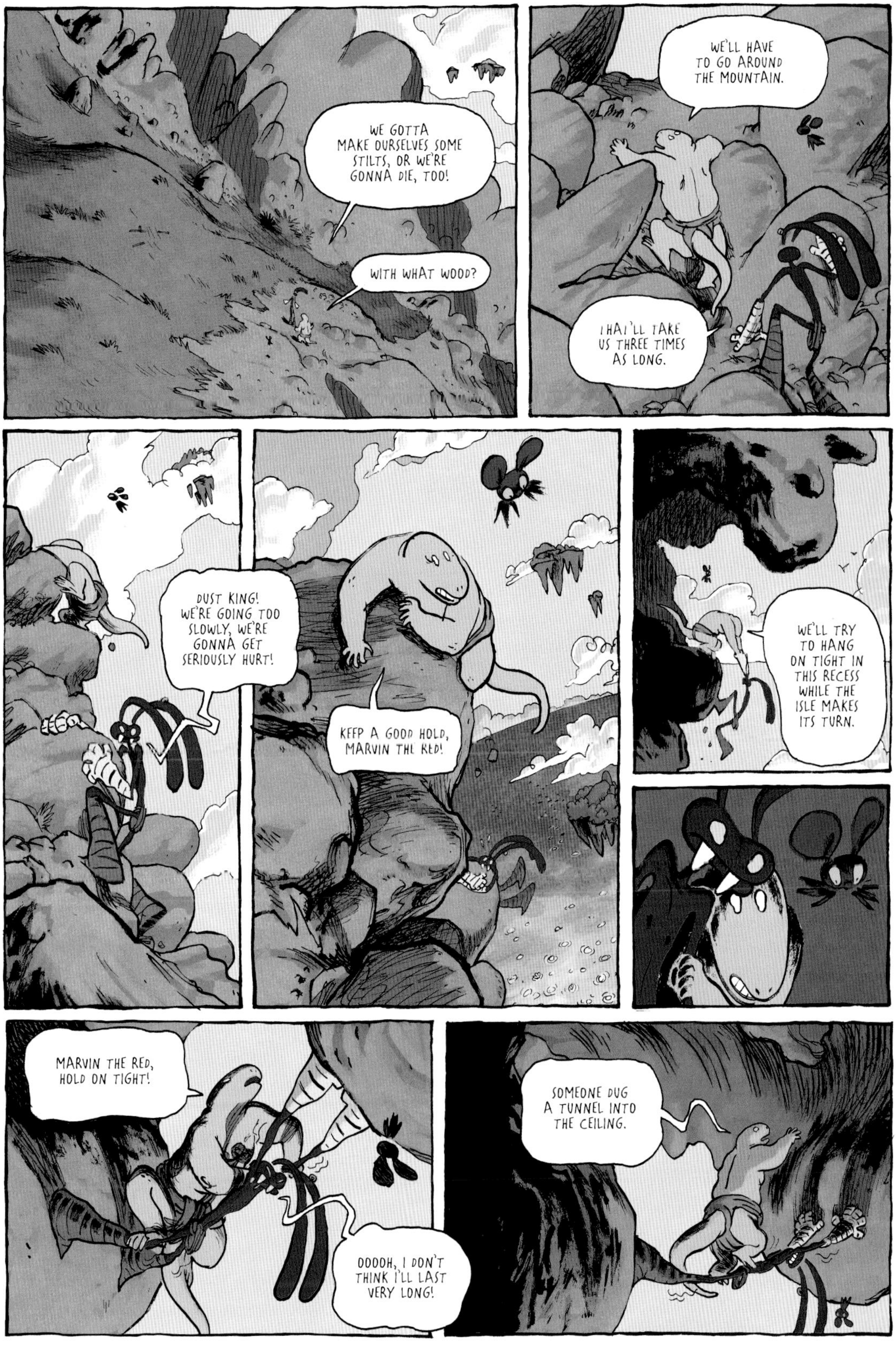
WE GOTTA MAKE OURSELVES SOME STILTS, OR WE'RE GONNA DIE, TOO!
WITH WHAT WOOD?
WE'LL HAVE TO GO AROUND THE MOUNTAIN.
THAT'LL TAKE US THREE TIMES AS LONG.
DUST KING! WE'RE GOING TOO SLOWLY, WE'RE GONNA GET SERIOUSLY HURT!
KEEP A GOOD HOLD, MARVIN THE RED!
WE'LL TRY TO HANG ON TIGHT IN THIS RECESS WHILE THE ISLE MAKES ITS TURN.
MARVIN THE RED, HOLD ON TIGHT!
OOOOH, I DON'T THINK I'LL LAST VERY LONG!
SOMEONE DUG A TUNNEL INTO THE CEILING.

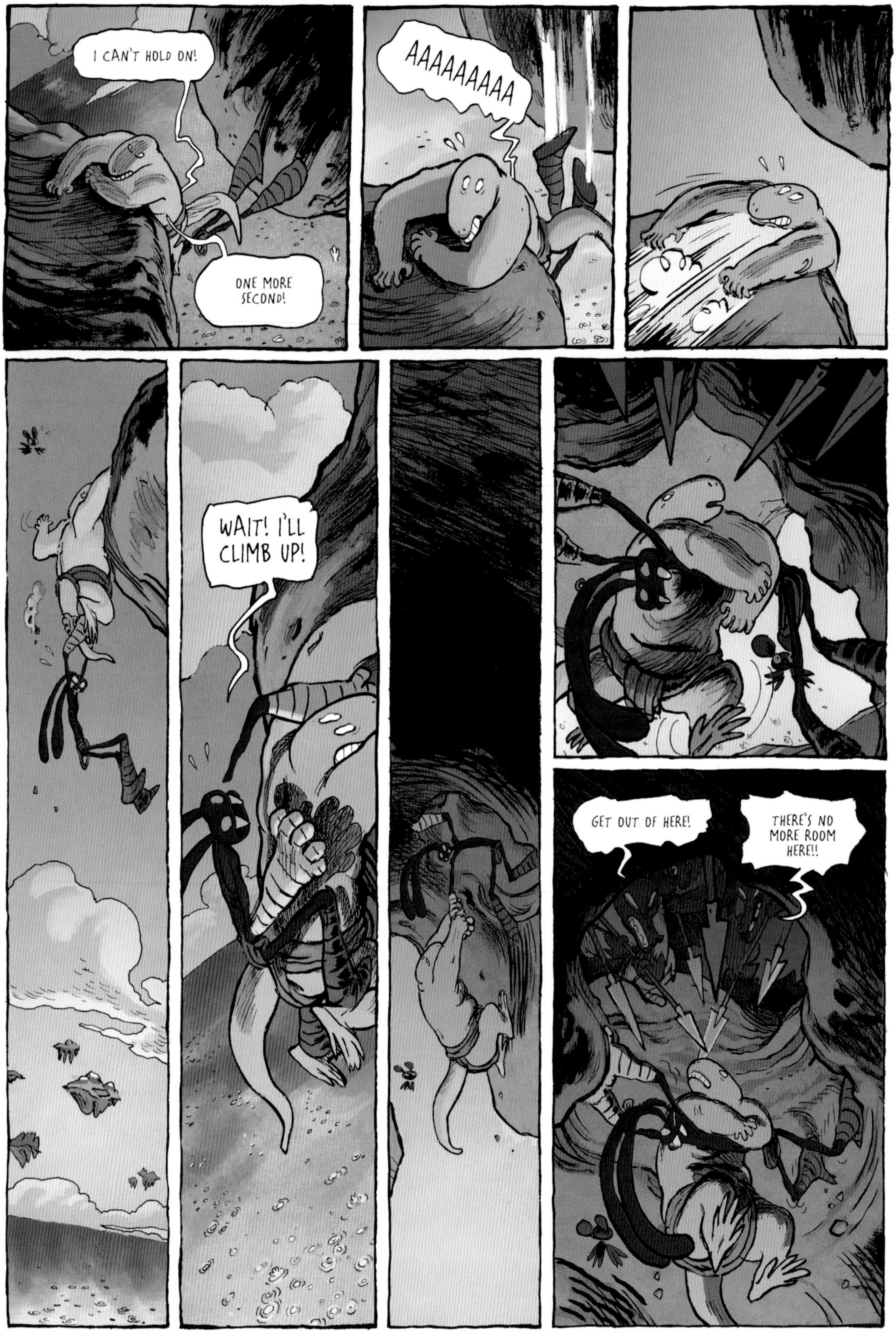
I CAN'T HOLD ON!
ONE MORE SECOND!
AAAAAAAAA
WAIT! I'LL CLIMB UP!
GET OUT OF HERE!
THERE'S NO MORE ROOM HERE!!

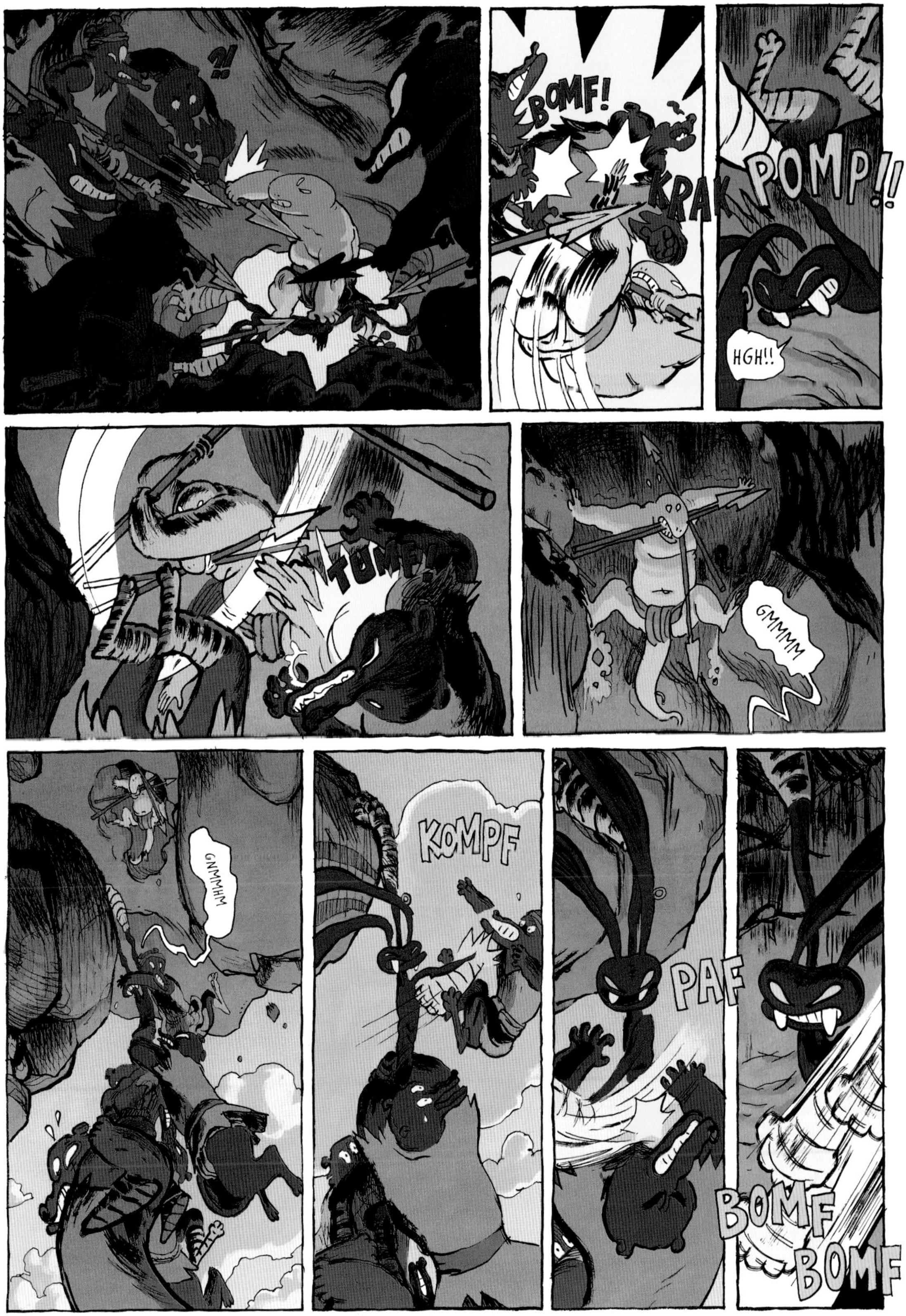
BOMF!
KRAK
POMP!!
HGH!!
TUMF
GMMMM
GNMMHM
KOMPF
PAF
BOMF
BOMF

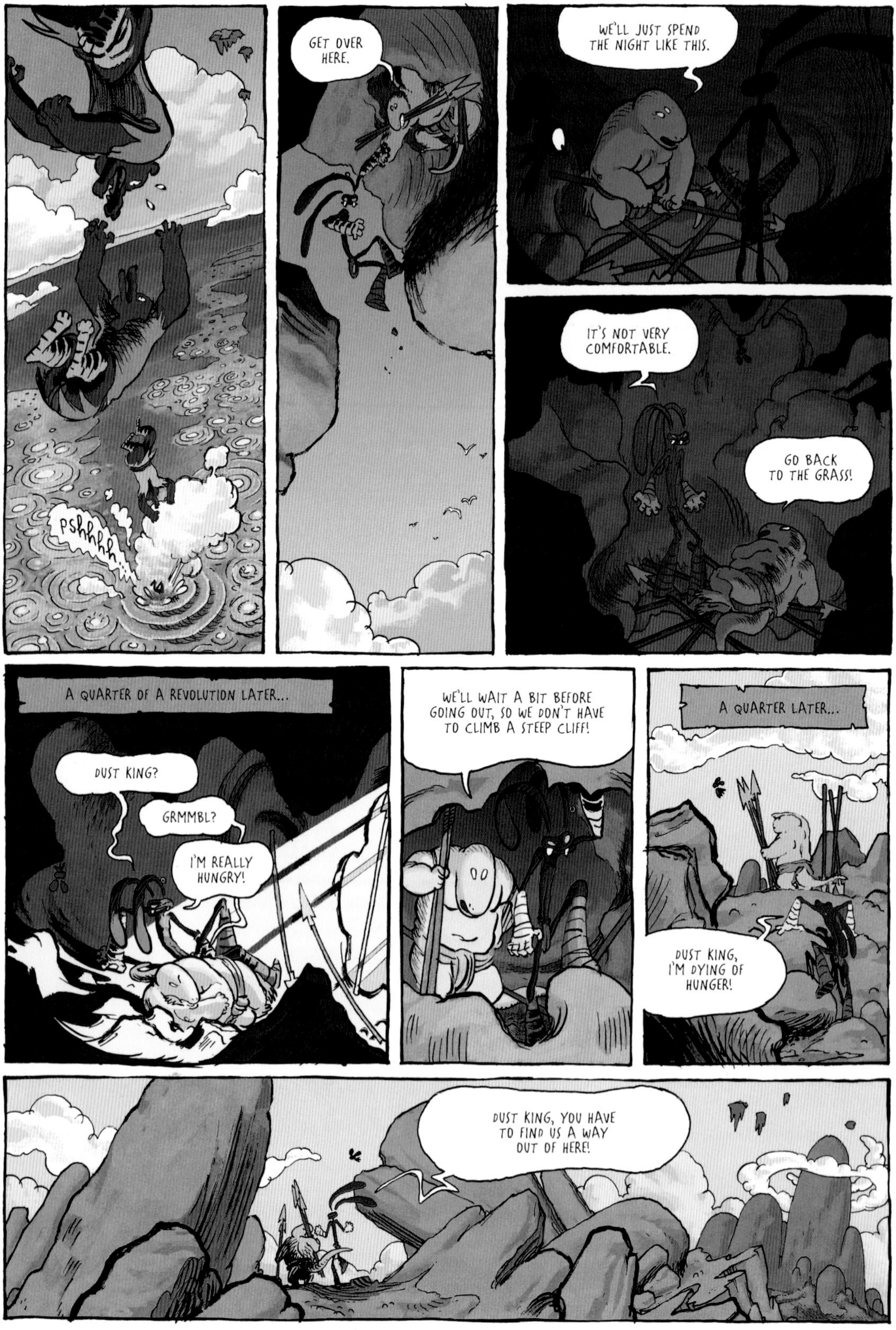
PSHHHHH...
GET OVER HERE.
WE'LL JUST SPEND THE NIGHT LIKE THIS.
IT'S NOT VERY COMFORTABLE.
GO BACK TO THE GRASS!
A QUARTER OF A REVOLUTION LATER...
DUST KING?
GRMMBL?
I'M REALLY HUNGRY!
WE'LL WAIT A BIT BEFORE GOING OUT, SO WE DON'T HAVE TO CLIMB A STEEP CLIFF!
A QUARTER LATER...
DUST KING, I'M DYING OF HUNGER!
DUST KING, YOU HAVE TO FIND US A WAY OUT OF HERE!

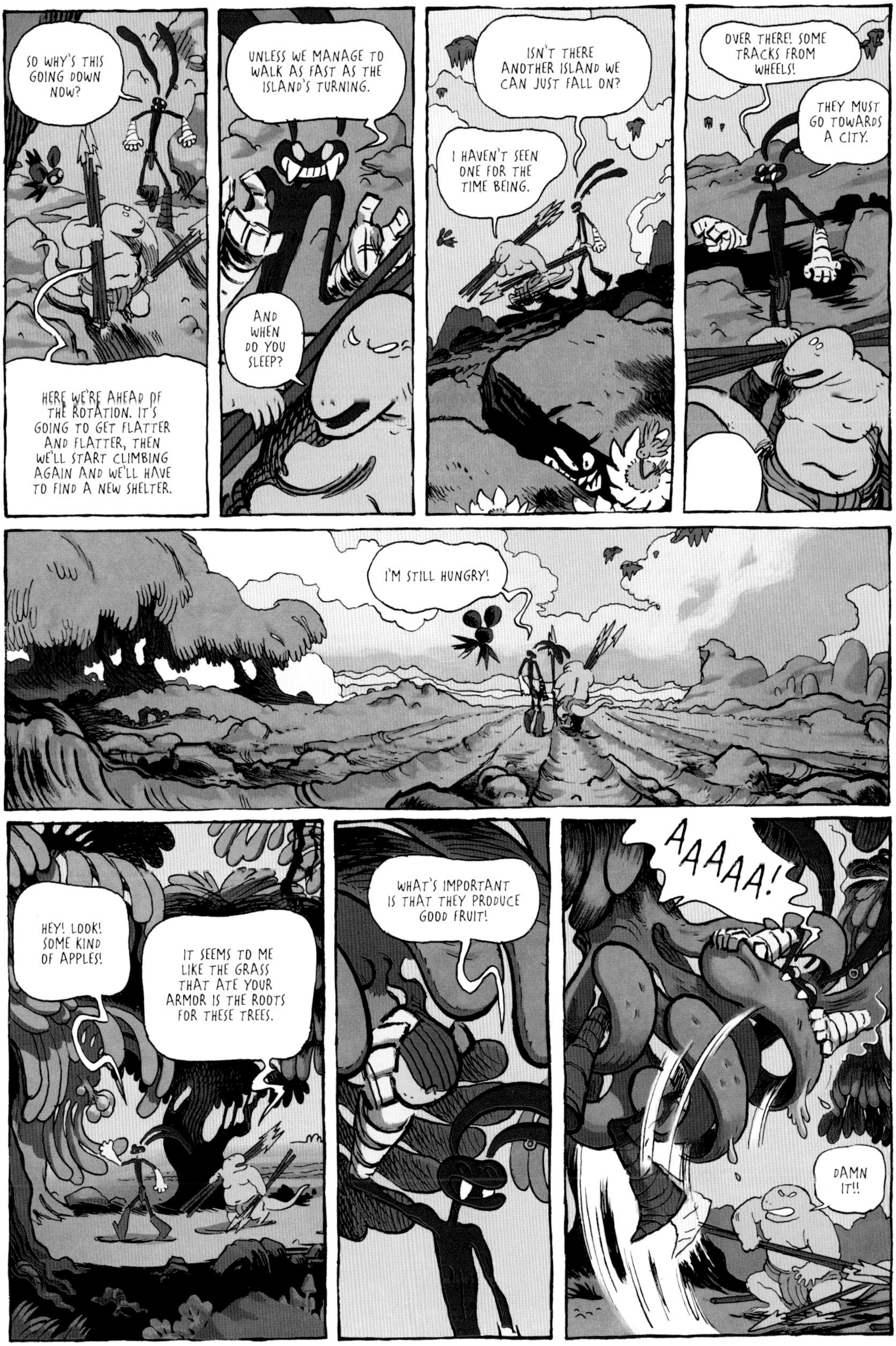
SO WHY'S THIS GOING DOWN NOW?
HERE WE'RE AHEAD OF THE ROTATION. IT'S GOING TO GET FLATTER AND FLATTER, THEN WE'LL START CLIMBING AGAIN AND WE'LL HAVE TO FIND A NEW SHELTER.
UNLESS WE MANAGE TO WALK AS FAST AS THE ISLAND'S TURNING.
AND WHEN DO YOU SLEEP?
ISN'T THERE ANOTHER ISLAND WE CAN JUST FALL ON?
I HAVEN'T SEEN ONE FOR THE TIME BEING.
OVER THERE! SOME TRACKS FROM WHEELS!
THEY MUST GO TOWARDS A CITY.
I'M STILL HUNGRY!
HEY! LOOK! SOME KIND OF APPLES!
IT SEEMS TO ME LIKE THE GRASS THAT ATE YOUR ARMOR IS THE ROOTS FOR THESE TREES.
WHAT'S IMPORTANT IS THAT THEY PRODUCE GOOD FRUIT!
AAAAA!
DAMN IT!!

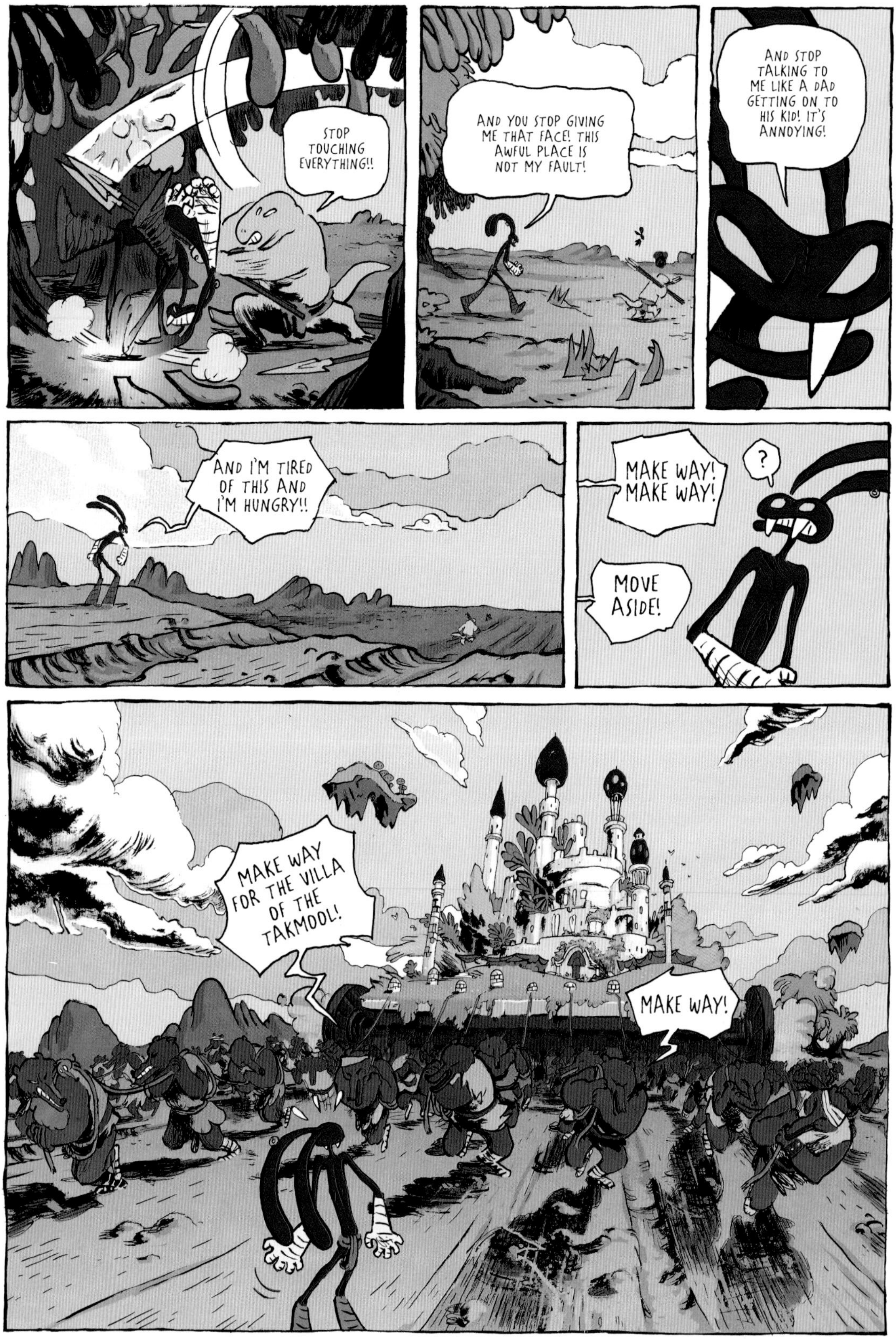
STOP TOUCHING EVERYTHING!!
AND YOU STOP GIVING ME THAT FACE! THIS AWFUL PLACE IS NOT MY FAULT!
AND STOP TALKING TO ME LIKE A DAD GETTING ON TO HIS KID! IT'S ANNOYING!
AND I'M TIRED OF THIS AND I'M HUNGRY!!
MAKE WAY! MAKE WAY!
?
MOVE ASIDE!
MAKE WAY FOR THE VILLA OF THE TAKMOOL!
MAKE WAY!

IS THERE ANYTHING TO EAT IN THERE?

FOR THOSE WHO PULL.

AND YOU CAN'T EAT FIRST THEN WORK AFTERWARDS?

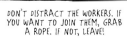

DON'T DISTRACT THE WORKERS. IF YOU WANT TO JOIN THEM, GRAB A ROPE. IF NOT, LEAVE!

HOW LONG DO YOU GOTTA WORK TO GET SOMETHING TO EAT?

YOU PULL FOR EIGHT HOURS AND, FOR EIGHT HOURS AFTERWARDS, YOU'RE ENTITLED TO REST IN THE GARDENS OF THE TAKMOOL.

AND THE EIGHT HOURS AFTER?

YOU PULL AGAIN. IT'S WHAT WE CALL THE THREE BY EIGHT.

MARVIN THE RED?!

WHAT ARE YOU DOING?

I'M WORKING! CAN'T YOU SEE?

ORLONDOH!

ORLONDOH, COME IN!

YES, MARVIN!

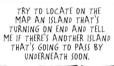
TRY TO LOCATE ON THE MAP AN ISLAND THAT'S TURNING ON END AND TELL ME IF THERE'S ANOTHER ISLAND THAT'S GOING TO PASS BY UNDERNEATH SOON.

UHH, I'LL SEE ABOUT IT AND CONTACT YOU LATER.

WE'RE IN THE MIDDLE OF AN OLF ATTACK HERE!

HEY!

EXCUSE ME...HOW DO YOU GET ANY REST?

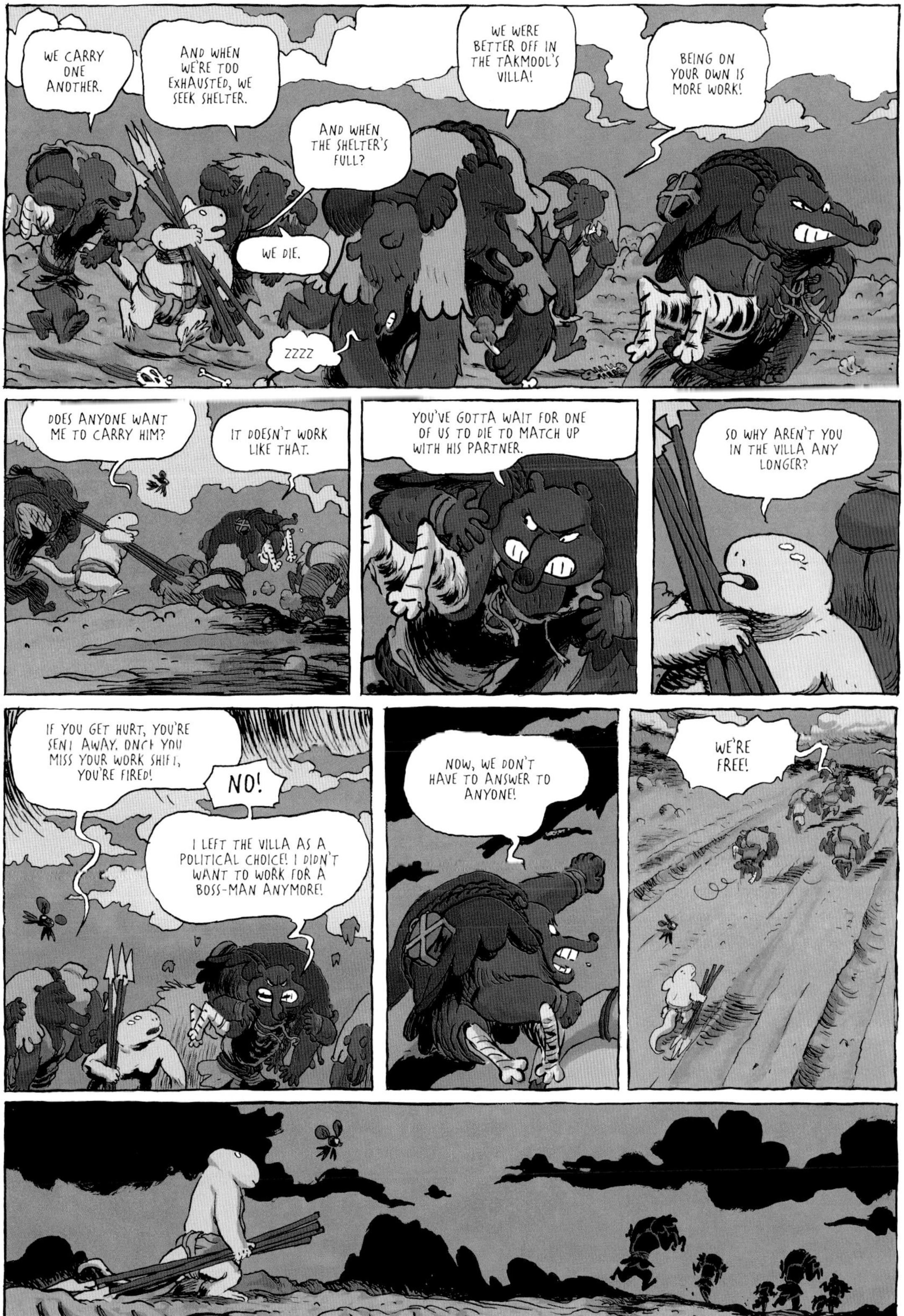
WE CARRY ONE ANOTHER.
AND WHEN WE'RE TOO EXHAUSTED, WE SEEK SHELTER.
AND WHEN THE SHELTER'S FULL?
WE DIE.
ZZZZ
WE WERE BETTER OFF IN THE TAKMOOL'S VILLA!
BEING ON YOUR OWN IS MORE WORK!
DOES ANYONE WANT ME TO CARRY HIM?
IT DOESN'T WORK LIKE THAT.
YOU'VE GOTTA WAIT FOR ONE OF US TO DIE TO MATCH UP WITH HIS PARTNER.
SO WHY AREN'T YOU IN THE VILLA ANY LONGER?
IF YOU GET HURT, YOU'RE SENT AWAY. ONCE YOU MISS YOUR WORK SHIFT, YOU'RE FIRED!
NO!
I LEFT THE VILLA AS A POLITICAL CHOICE! I DIDN'T WANT TO WORK FOR A BOSS-MAN ANYMORE!
NOW, WE DON'T HAVE TO ANSWER TO ANYONE!
WE'RE FREE!

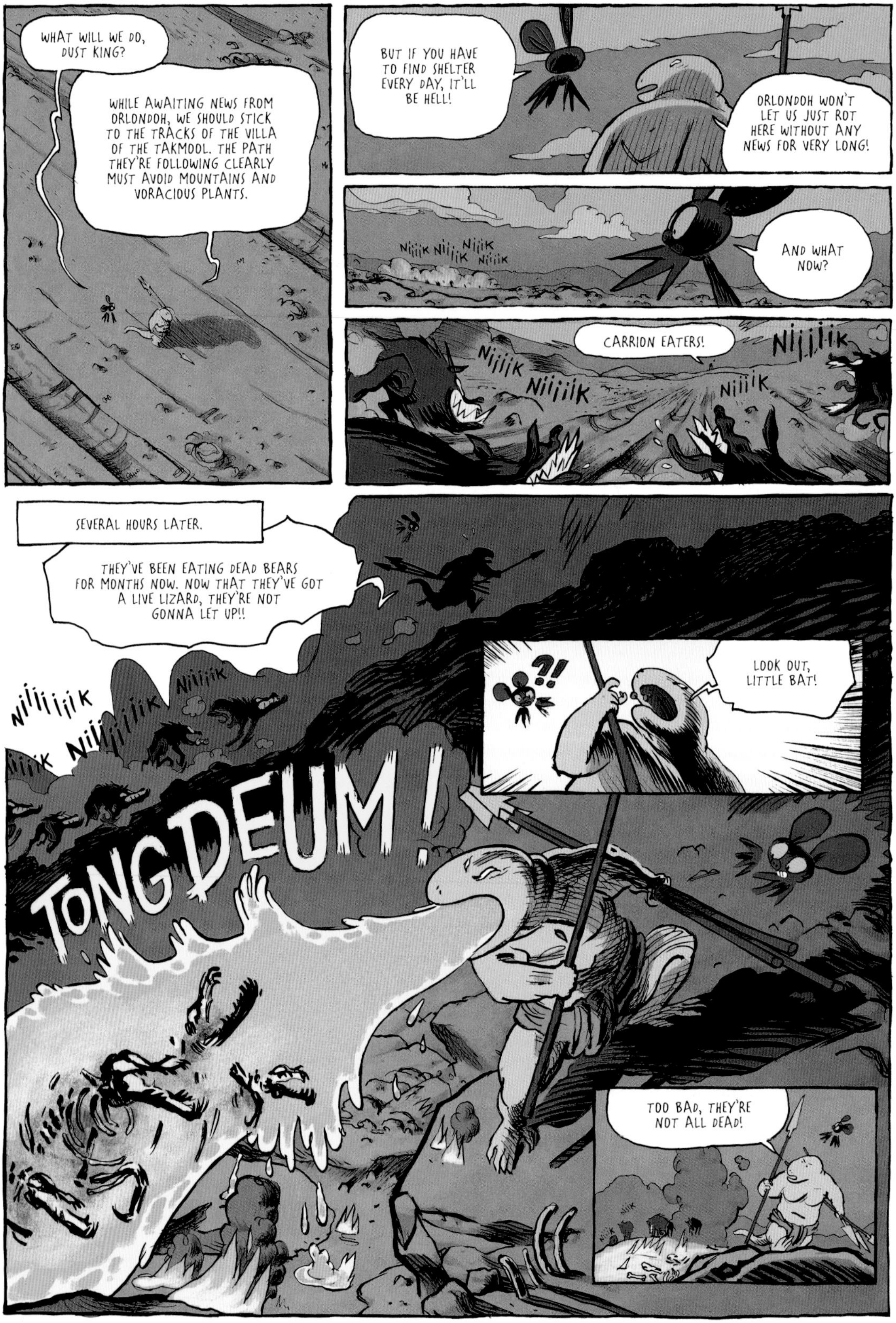
WHAT WILL WE DO, DUST KING?
WHILE AWAITING NEWS FROM ORLONDOH, WE SHOULD STICK TO THE TRACKS OF THE VILLA OF THE TAKMOOL. THE PATH THEY'RE FOLLOWING CLEARLY MUST AVOID MOUNTAINS AND VORACIOUS PLANTS.
BUT IF YOU HAVE TO FIND SHELTER EVERY DAY, IT'LL BE HELL!
ORLONDOH WON'T LET US JUST ROT HERE WITHOUT ANY NEWS FOR VERY LONG!
NIIIK NIIIK NIIIK NIIIK
AND WHAT NOW?
CARRION EATERS!
NIIIIK NIIIIK NIIIK NIIIIK
SEVERAL HOURS LATER.
THEY'VE BEEN EATING DEAD BEARS FOR MONTHS NOW. NOW THAT THEY'VE GOT A LIVE LIZARD, THEY'RE NOT GONNA LET UP!!
NIIIIIIK NIIIIIIK NIIIIK
?!!
LOOK OUT, LITTLE BAT!
TONGDEUM!
TOO BAD, THEY'RE NOT ALL DEAD!

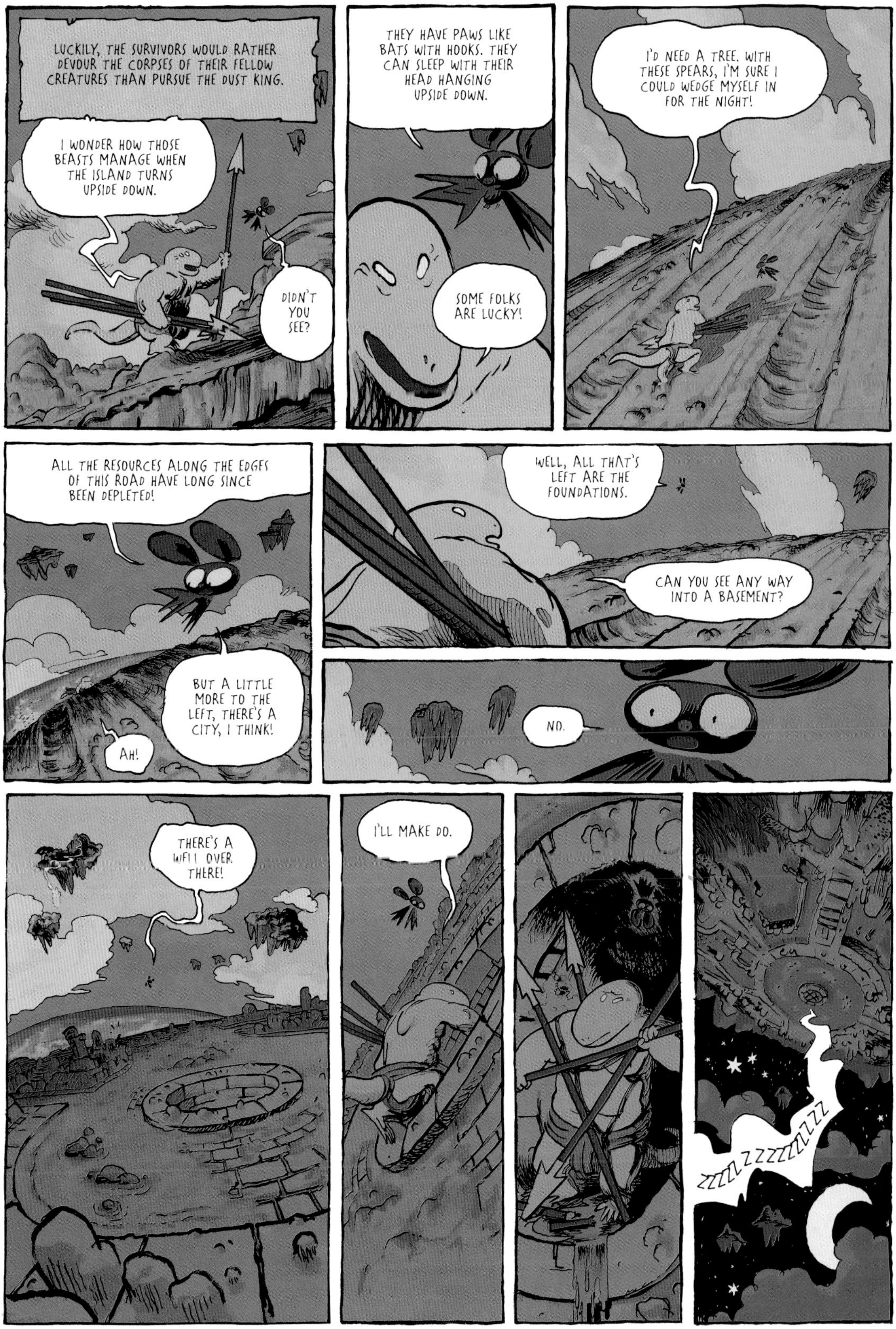
LUCKILY, THE SURVIVORS WOULD RATHER DEVOUR THE CORPSES OF THEIR FELLOW CREATURES THAN PURSUE THE DUST KING.
I WONDER HOW THOSE BEASTS MANAGE WHEN THE ISLAND TURNS UPSIDE DOWN.
DIDN'T YOU SEE?
THEY HAVE PAWS LIKE BATS WITH HOOKS. THEY CAN SLEEP WITH THEIR HEAD HANGING UPSIDE DOWN.
SOME FOLKS ARE LUCKY!
I'D NEED A TREE. WITH THESE SPEARS, I'M SURE I COULD WEDGE MYSELF IN FOR THE NIGHT!
ALL THE RESOURCES ALONG THE EDGES OF THIS ROAD HAVE LONG SINCE BEEN DEPLETED!
BUT A LITTLE MORE TO THE LEFT, THERE'S A CITY, I THINK!
AH!
WELL, ALL THAT'S LEFT ARE THE FOUNDATIONS.
CAN YOU SEE ANY WAY INTO A BASEMENT?
NO.
THERE'S A WELL OVER THERE!
I'LL MAKE DO.
ZZZZL ZZZZZZZZZZZ

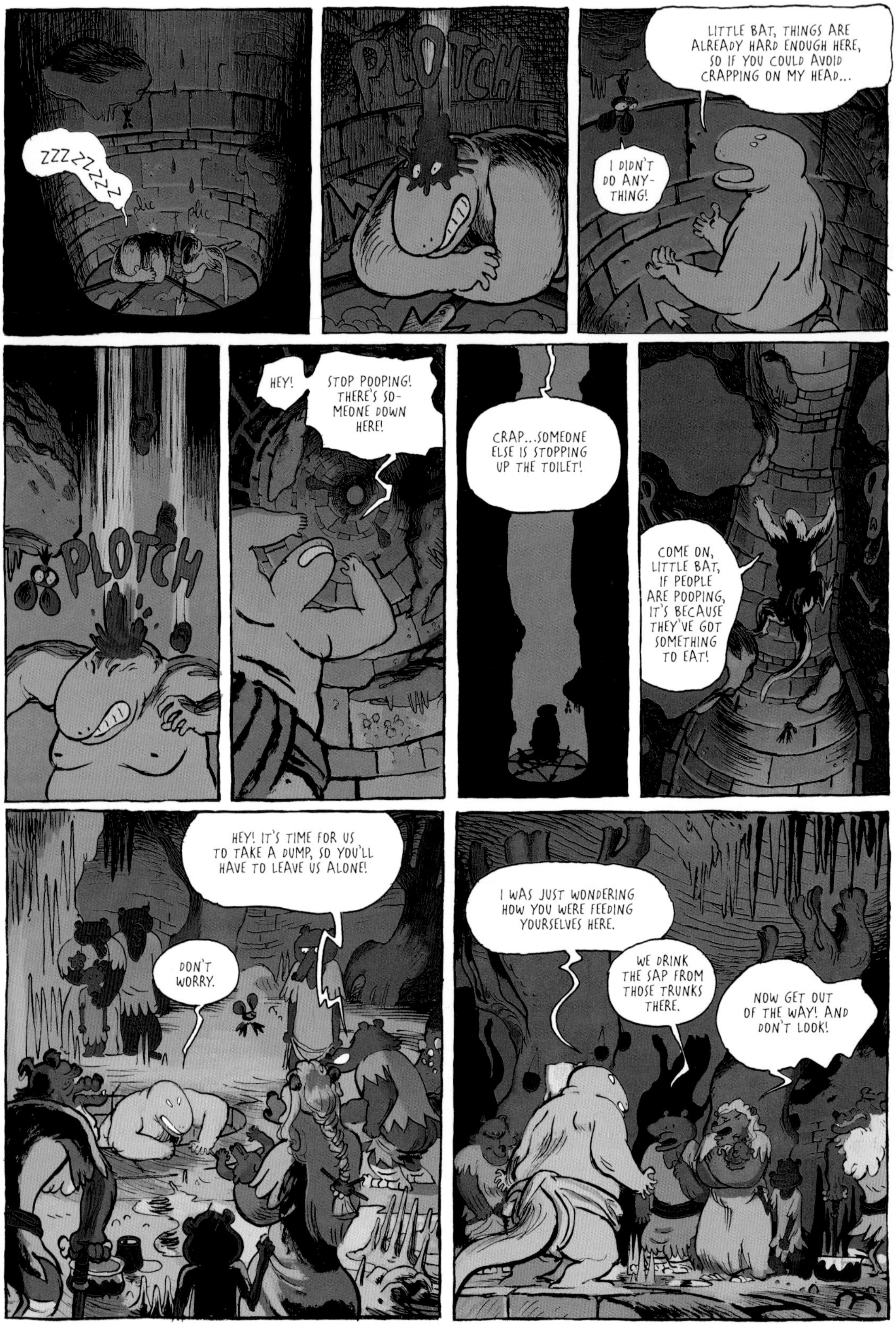
ZZZZZZZZ
plic
plic
PLOTCH
LITTLE BAT, THINGS ARE ALREADY HARD ENOUGH HERE, SO IF YOU COULD AVOID CRAPPING ON MY HEAD...
I DIDN'T DO ANY-THING!
PLOTCH
HEY!
STOP POOPING! THERE'S SO-MEONE DOWN HERE!
CRAP...SOMEONE ELSE IS STOPPING UP THE TOILET!
COME ON, LITTLE BAT, IF PEOPLE ARE POOPING, IT'S BECAUSE THEY'VE GOT SOMETHING TO EAT!
HEY! IT'S TIME FOR US TO TAKE A DUMP, SO YOU'LL HAVE TO LEAVE US ALONE!
DON'T WORRY.
I WAS JUST WONDERING HOW YOU WERE FEEDING YOURSELVES HERE.
WE DRINK THE SAP FROM THOSE TRUNKS THERE.
NOW GET OUT OF THE WAY! AND DON'T LOOK!

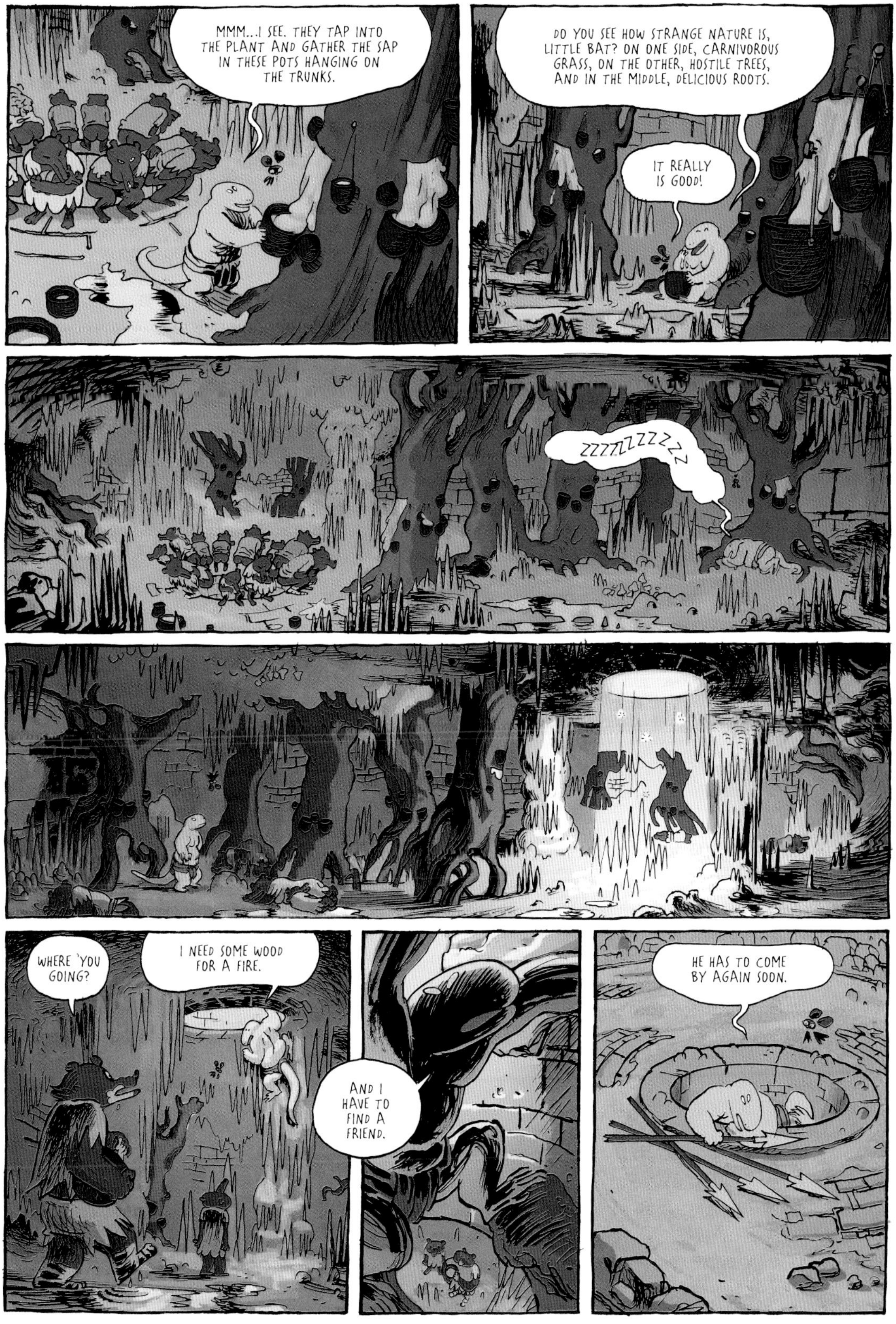
MMM...I SEE. THEY TAP INTO THE PLANT AND GATHER THE SAP IN THESE POTS HANGING ON THE TRUNKS.
DO YOU SEE HOW STRANGE NATURE IS, LITTLE BAT? ON ONE SIDE, CARNIVOROUS GRASS, ON THE OTHER, HOSTILE TREES, AND IN THE MIDDLE, DELICIOUS ROOTS.
IT REALLY IS GOOD!
ZZZZZZZZZZZ
WHERE 'YOU GOING?
I NEED SOME WOOD FOR A FIRE.
AND I HAVE TO FIND A FRIEND.
HE HAS TO COME BY AGAIN SOON.

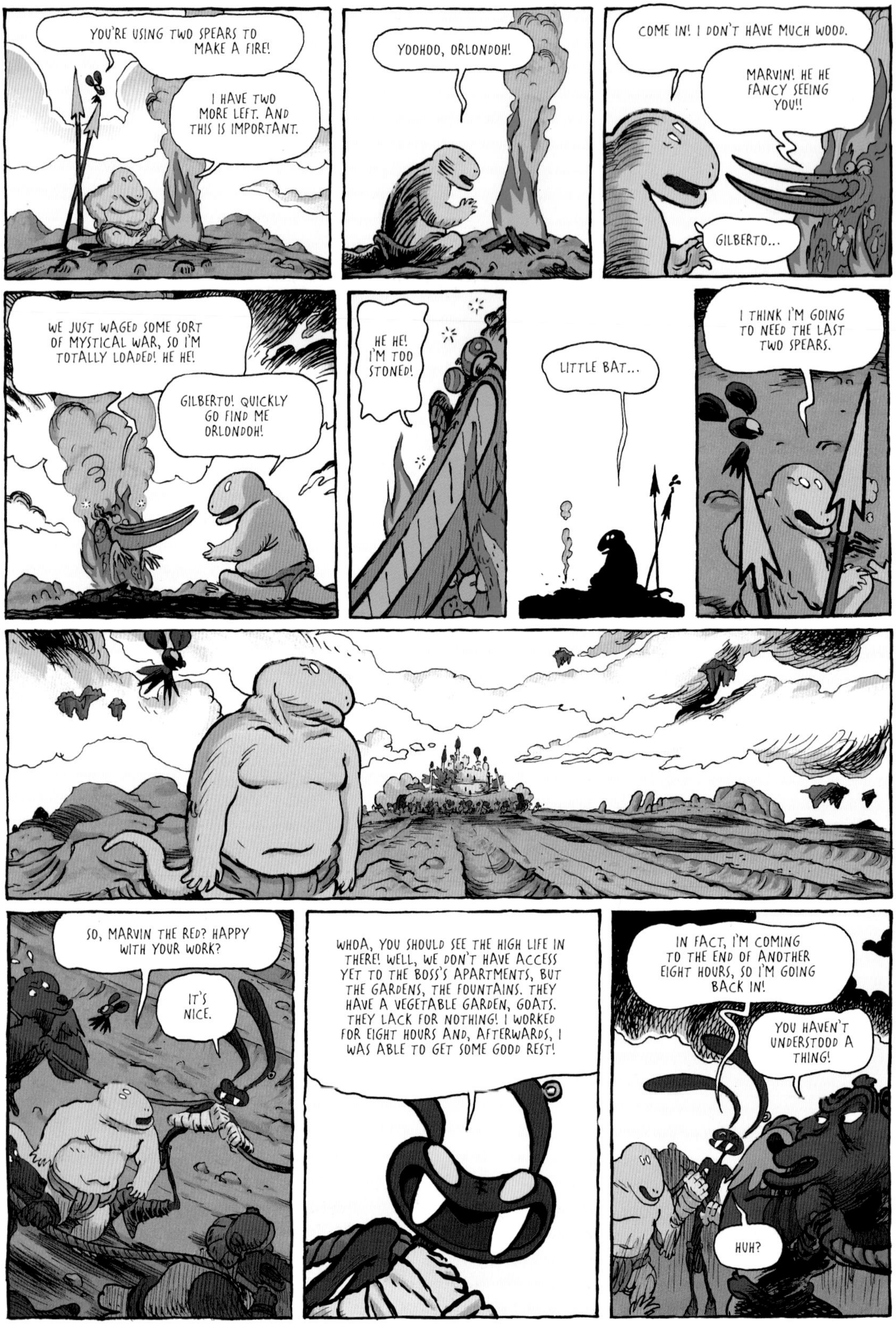
YOU'RE USING TWO SPEARS TO MAKE A FIRE!
I HAVE TWO MORE LEFT. AND THIS IS IMPORTANT.
YOOHOO, ORLONDOH!
COME IN! I DON'T HAVE MUCH WOOD.
MARVIN! HE HE FANCY SEEING YOU!!
GILBERTO...
WE JUST WAGED SOME SORT OF MYSTICAL WAR, SO I'M TOTALLY LOADED! HE HE!
GILBERTO! QUICKLY GO FIND ME ORLONDOH!
HE HE! I'M TOO STONED!
LITTLE BAT...
I THINK I'M GOING TO NEED THE LAST TWO SPEARS.
SO, MARVIN THE RED? HAPPY WITH YOUR WORK?
IT'S NICE.
WHOA, YOU SHOULD SEE THE HIGH LIFE IN THERE! WELL, WE DON'T HAVE ACCESS YET TO THE BOSS'S APARTMENTS, BUT THE GARDENS, THE FOUNTAINS. THEY HAVE A VEGETABLE GARDEN, GOATS. THEY LACK FOR NOTHING! I WORKED FOR EIGHT HOURS AND, AFTERWARDS, I WAS ABLE TO GET SOME GOOD REST!
IN FACT, I'M COMING TO THE END OF ANOTHER EIGHT HOURS, SO I'M GOING BACK IN!
YOU HAVEN'T UNDERSTOOD A THING!
HUH?

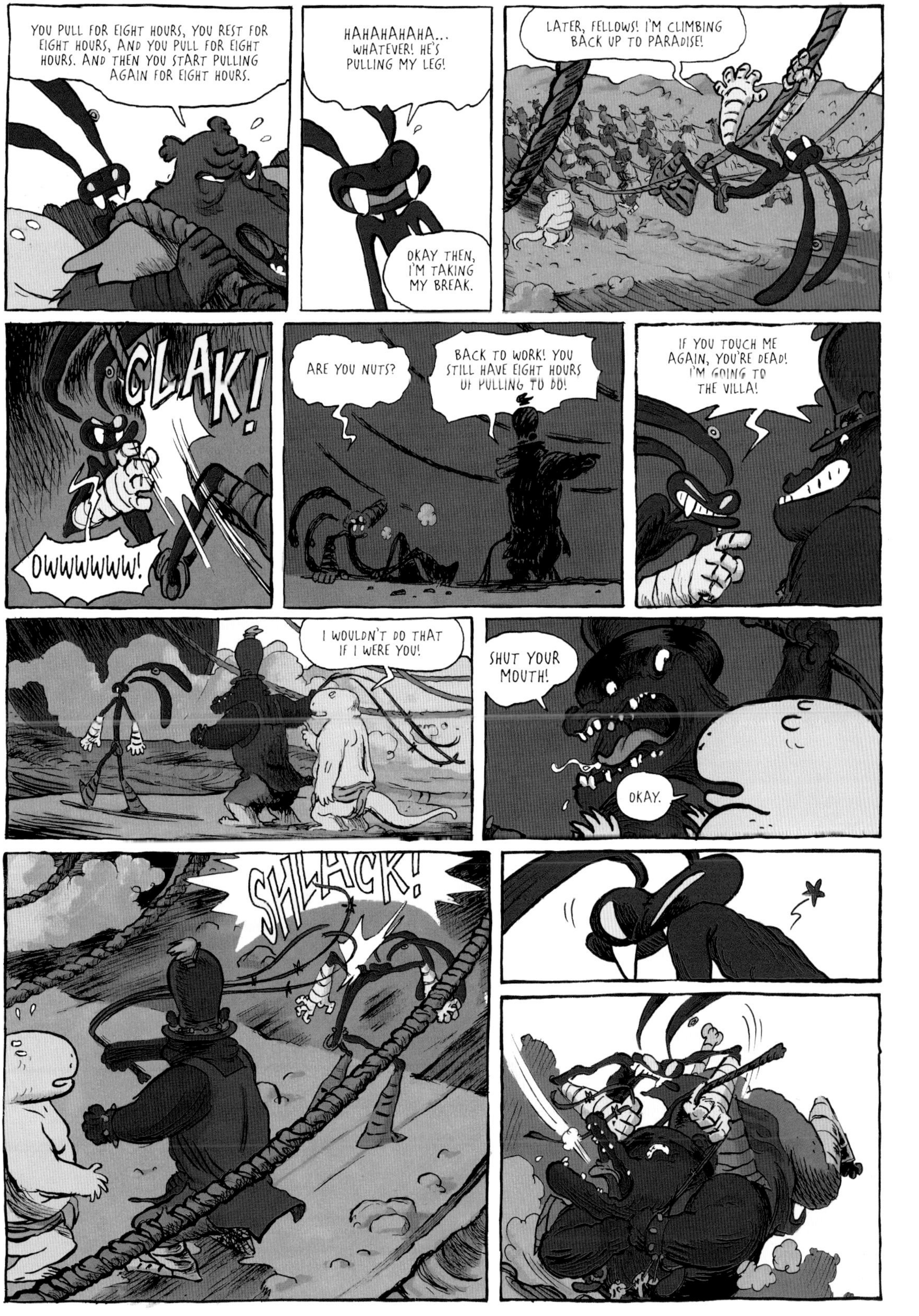

YOU PULL FOR EIGHT HOURS, YOU REST FOR EIGHT HOURS, AND YOU PULL FOR EIGHT HOURS. AND THEN YOU START PULLING AGAIN FOR EIGHT HOURS.
HAHAHAHAHA... WHATEVER! HE'S PULLING MY LEG!
OKAY THEN, I'M TAKING MY BREAK.
LATER, FELLOWS! I'M CLIMBING BACK UP TO PARADISE!
CLAK!
OWWWWWW!
ARE YOU NUTS?
BACK TO WORK! YOU STILL HAVE EIGHT HOURS OF PULLING TO DO!
IF YOU TOUCH ME AGAIN, YOU'RE DEAD! I'M GOING TO THE VILLA!
I WOULDN'T DO THAT IF I WERE YOU!
SHUT YOUR MOUTH!
OKAY.
SHLACK!

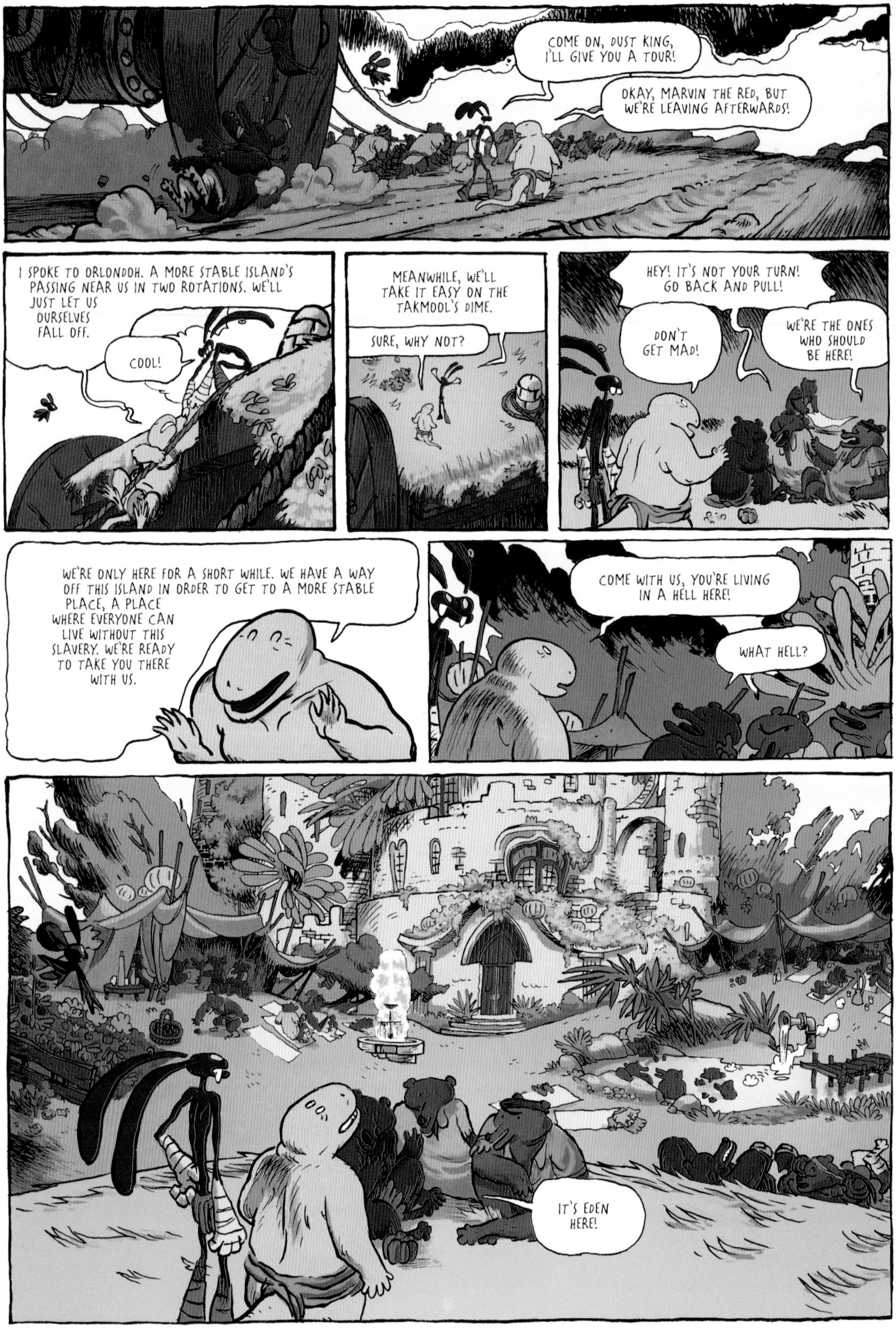
COME ON, DUST KING, I'LL GIVE YOU A TOUR!
OKAY, MARVIN THE RED, BUT WE'RE LEAVING AFTERWARDS!
I SPOKE TO ORLONDOH. A MORE STABLE ISLAND'S PASSING NEAR US IN TWO ROTATIONS. WE'LL JUST LET US OURSELVES FALL OFF.
COOL!
MEANWHILE, WE'LL TAKE IT EASY ON THE TAKMOOL'S DIME.
SURE, WHY NOT?
HEY! IT'S NOT YOUR TURN! GO BACK AND PULL!
DON'T GET MAD!
WE'RE THE ONES WHO SHOULD BE HERE!
WE'RE ONLY HERE FOR A SHORT WHILE. WE HAVE A WAY OFF THIS ISLAND IN ORDER TO GET TO A MORE STABLE PLACE, A PLACE WHERE EVERYONE CAN LIVE WITHOUT THIS SLAVERY. WE'RE READY TO TAKE YOU THERE WITH US.
COME WITH US, YOU'RE LIVING IN A HELL HERE!
WHAT HELL?
IT'S EDEN HERE!

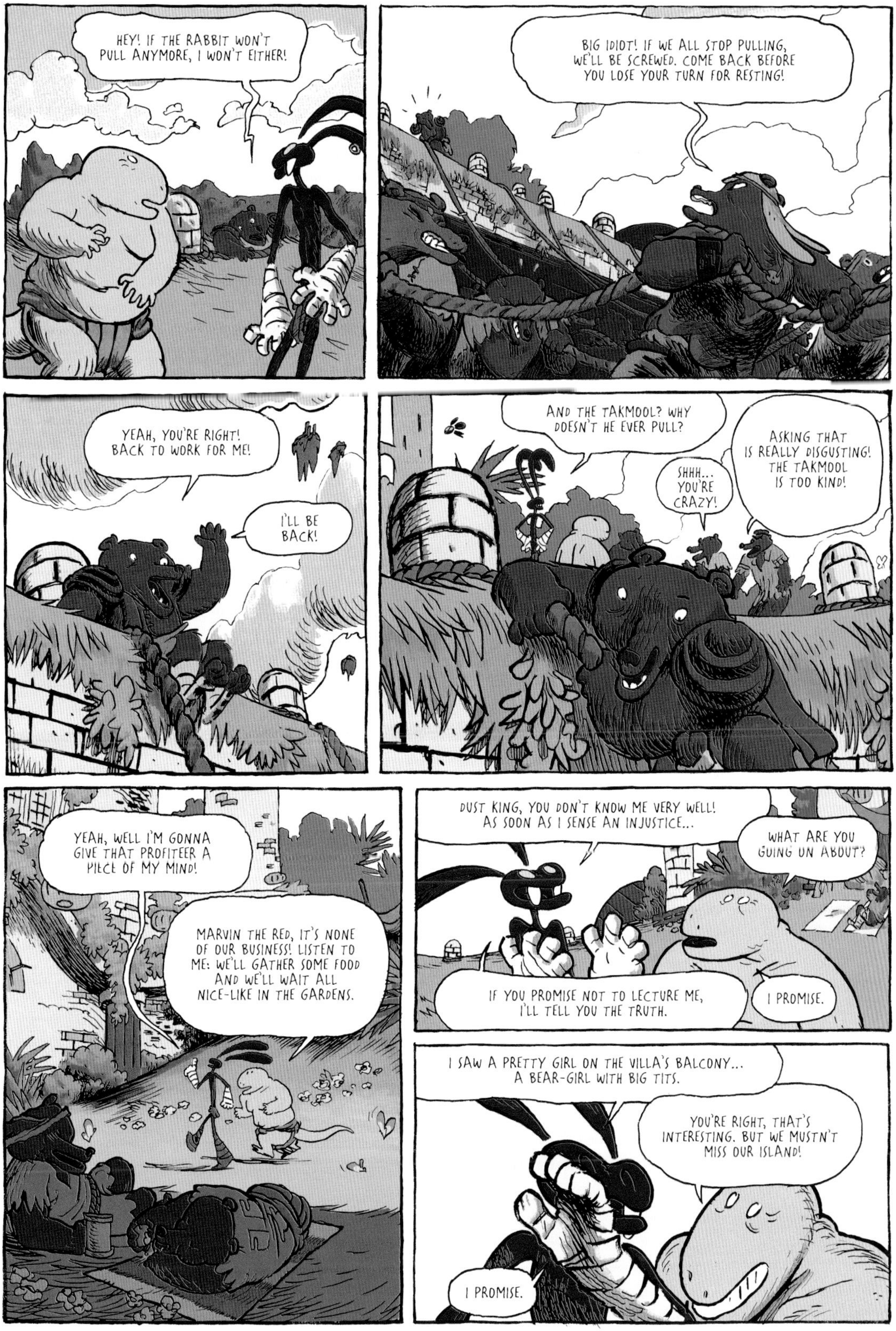
HEY! IF THE RABBIT WON'T PULL ANYMORE, I WON'T EITHER!
BIG IDIOT! IF WE ALL STOP PULLING, WE'LL BE SCREWED. COME BACK BEFORE YOU LOSE YOUR TURN FOR RESTING!
YEAH, YOU'RE RIGHT! BACK TO WORK FOR ME!
I'LL BE BACK!
AND THE TAKMOOL? WHY DOESN'T HE EVER PULL?
SHHH... YOU'RE CRAZY!
ASKING THAT IS REALLY DISGUSTING! THE TAKMOOL IS TOO KIND!
YEAH, WELL I'M GONNA GIVE THAT PROFITEER A PIECE OF MY MIND!
MARVIN THE RED, IT'S NONE OF OUR BUSINESS! LISTEN TO ME: WE'LL GATHER SOME FOOD AND WE'LL WAIT ALL NICE-LIKE IN THE GARDENS.
DUST KING, YOU DON'T KNOW ME VERY WELL! AS SOON AS I SENSE AN INJUSTICE...
WHAT ARE YOU GOING ON ABOUT?
IF YOU PROMISE NOT TO LECTURE ME, I'LL TELL YOU THE TRUTH.
I PROMISE.
I SAW A PRETTY GIRL ON THE VILLA'S BALCONY... A BEAR-GIRL WITH BIG TITS.
YOU'RE RIGHT, THAT'S INTERESTING. BUT WE MUSTN'T MISS OUR ISLAND!
I PROMISE.

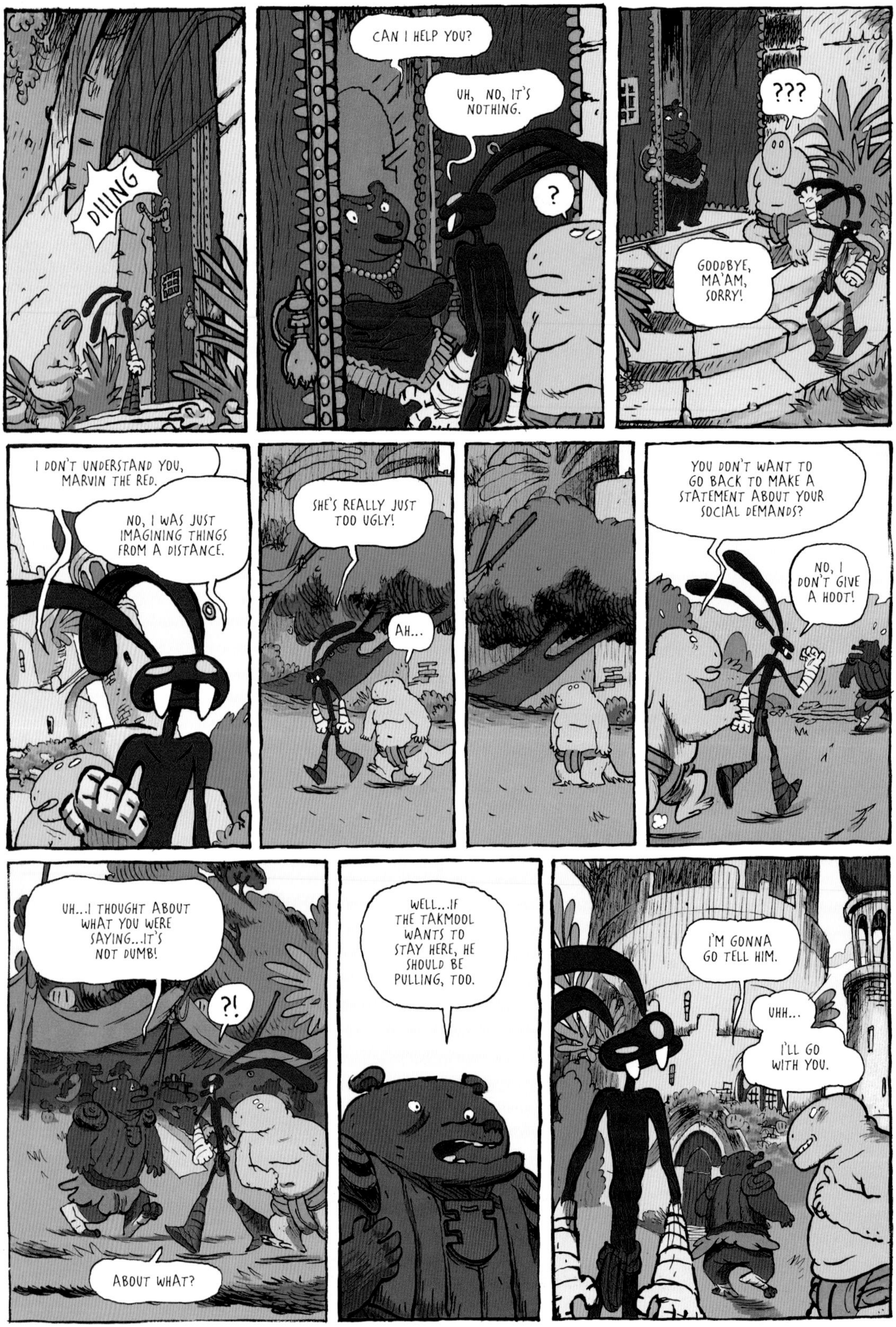
DIIIING
CAN I HELP YOU?
UH, NO, IT'S NOTHING.
?
???
GOODBYE, MA'AM, SORRY!
I DON'T UNDERSTAND YOU, MARVIN THE RED.
NO, I WAS JUST IMAGINING THINGS FROM A DISTANCE.
SHE'S REALLY JUST TOO UGLY!
AH...
YOU DON'T WANT TO GO BACK TO MAKE A STATEMENT ABOUT YOUR SOCIAL DEMANDS?
NO, I DON'T GIVE A HOOT!
UH...I THOUGHT ABOUT WHAT YOU WERE SAYING...IT'S NOT DUMB!
?!
ABOUT WHAT?
WELL...IF THE TAKMOOL WANTS TO STAY HERE, HE SHOULD BE PULLING, TOO.
I'M GONNA GO TELL HIM.
UHH...
I'LL GO WITH YOU.

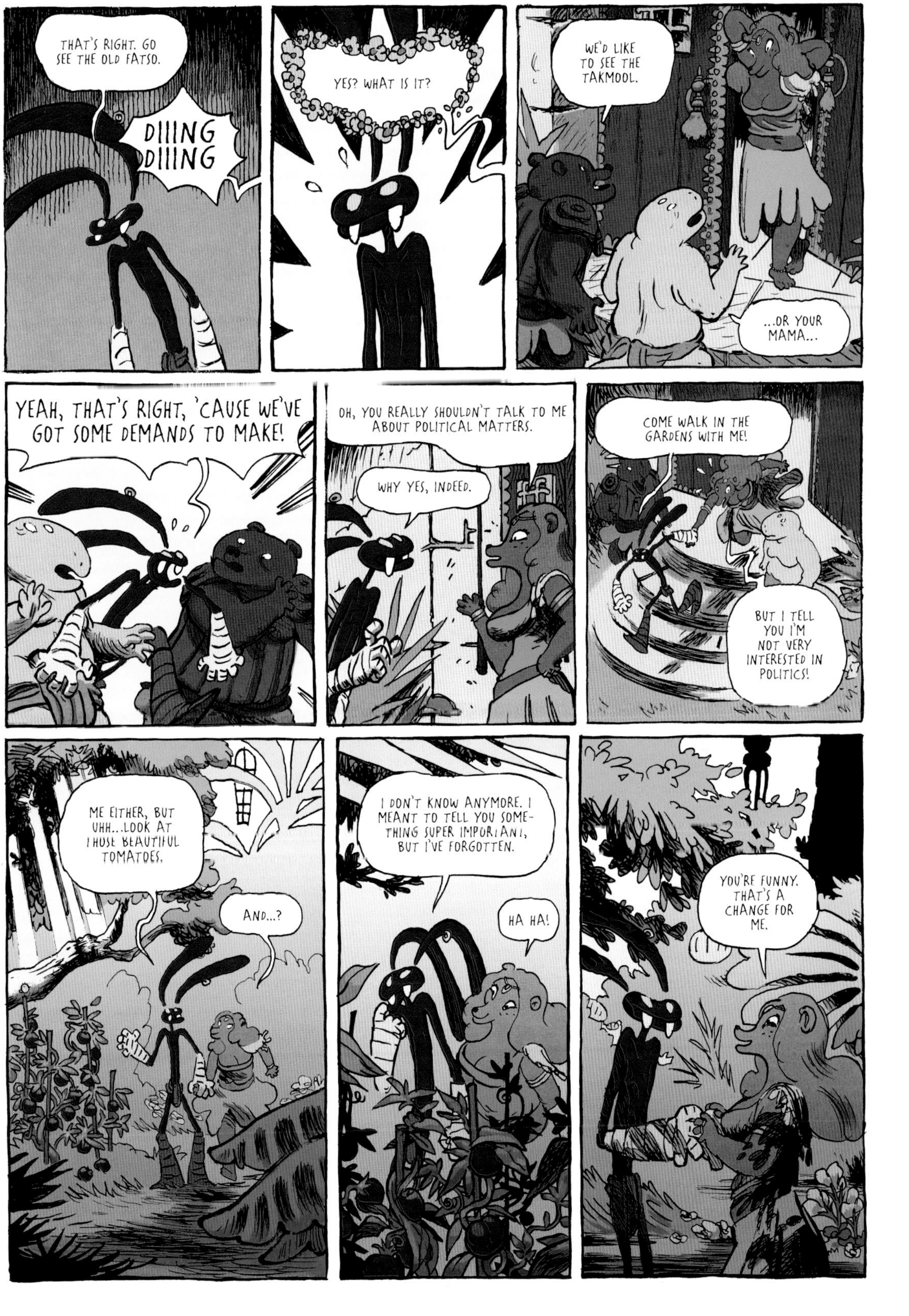
THAT'S RIGHT. GO SEE THE OLD FATSO.
DIIING DIIING
YES? WHAT IS IT?
WE'D LIKE TO SEE THE TAKMOOL.
...OR YOUR MAMA...
YEAH, THAT'S RIGHT, 'CAUSE WE'VE GOT SOME DEMANDS TO MAKE!
OH, YOU REALLY SHOULDN'T TALK TO ME ABOUT POLITICAL MATTERS.
WHY YES, INDEED.
COME WALK IN THE GARDENS WITH ME!
BUT I TELL YOU I'M NOT VERY INTERESTED IN POLITICS!
ME EITHER, BUT UHH...LOOK AT THOSE BEAUTIFUL TOMATOES.
AND...?
I DON'T KNOW ANYMORE. I MEANT TO TELL YOU SOMETHING SUPER IMPORTANT, BUT I'VE FORGOTTEN.
HA HA!
YOU'RE FUNNY. THAT'S A CHANGE FOR ME.

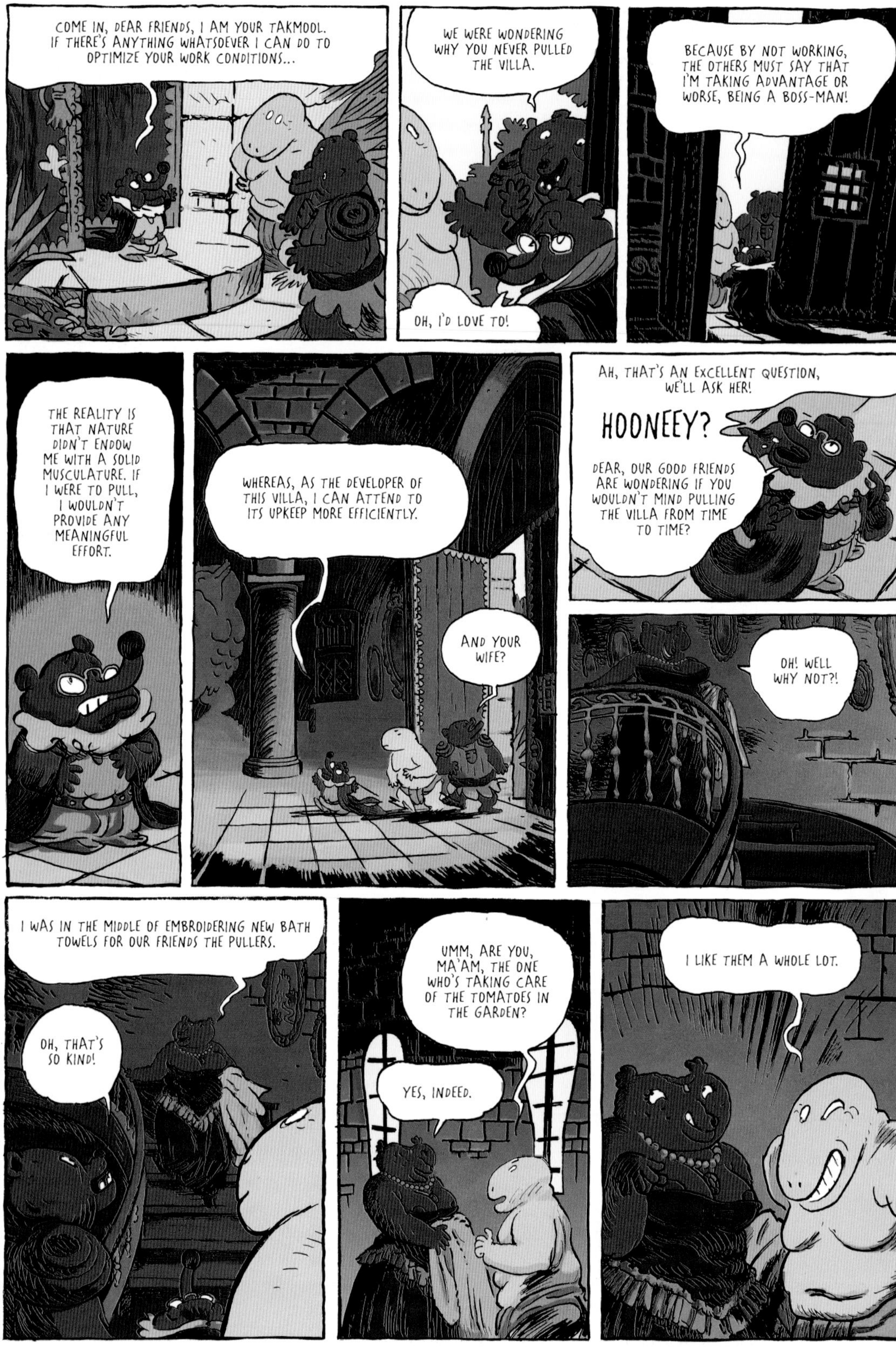
COME IN, DEAR FRIENDS, I AM YOUR TAKMOOL. IF THERE'S ANYTHING WHATSOEVER I CAN DO TO OPTIMIZE YOUR WORK CONDITIONS...
WE WERE WONDERING WHY YOU NEVER PULLED THE VILLA.
OH, I'D LOVE TO!
BECAUSE BY NOT WORKING, THE OTHERS MUST SAY THAT I'M TAKING ADVANTAGE OR WORSE, BEING A BOSS-MAN!
THE REALITY IS THAT NATURE DIDN'T ENDOW ME WITH A SOLID MUSCULATURE. IF I WERE TO PULL, I WOULDN'T PROVIDE ANY MEANINGFUL EFFORT.
WHEREAS, AS THE DEVELOPER OF THIS VILLA, I CAN ATTEND TO ITS UPKEEP MORE EFFICIENTLY.
AND YOUR WIFE?
AH, THAT'S AN EXCELLENT QUESTION, WE'LL ASK HER!
HOONEEY?
DEAR, OUR GOOD FRIENDS ARE WONDERING IF YOU WOULDN'T MIND PULLING THE VILLA FROM TIME TO TIME?
OH! WELL WHY NOT?!
I WAS IN THE MIDDLE OF EMBROIDERING NEW BATH TOWELS FOR OUR FRIENDS THE PULLERS.
OH, THAT'S SO KIND!
UMM, ARE YOU, MA'AM, THE ONE WHO'S TAKING CARE OF THE TOMATOES IN THE GARDEN?
YES, INDEED.
I LIKE THEM A WHOLE LOT.

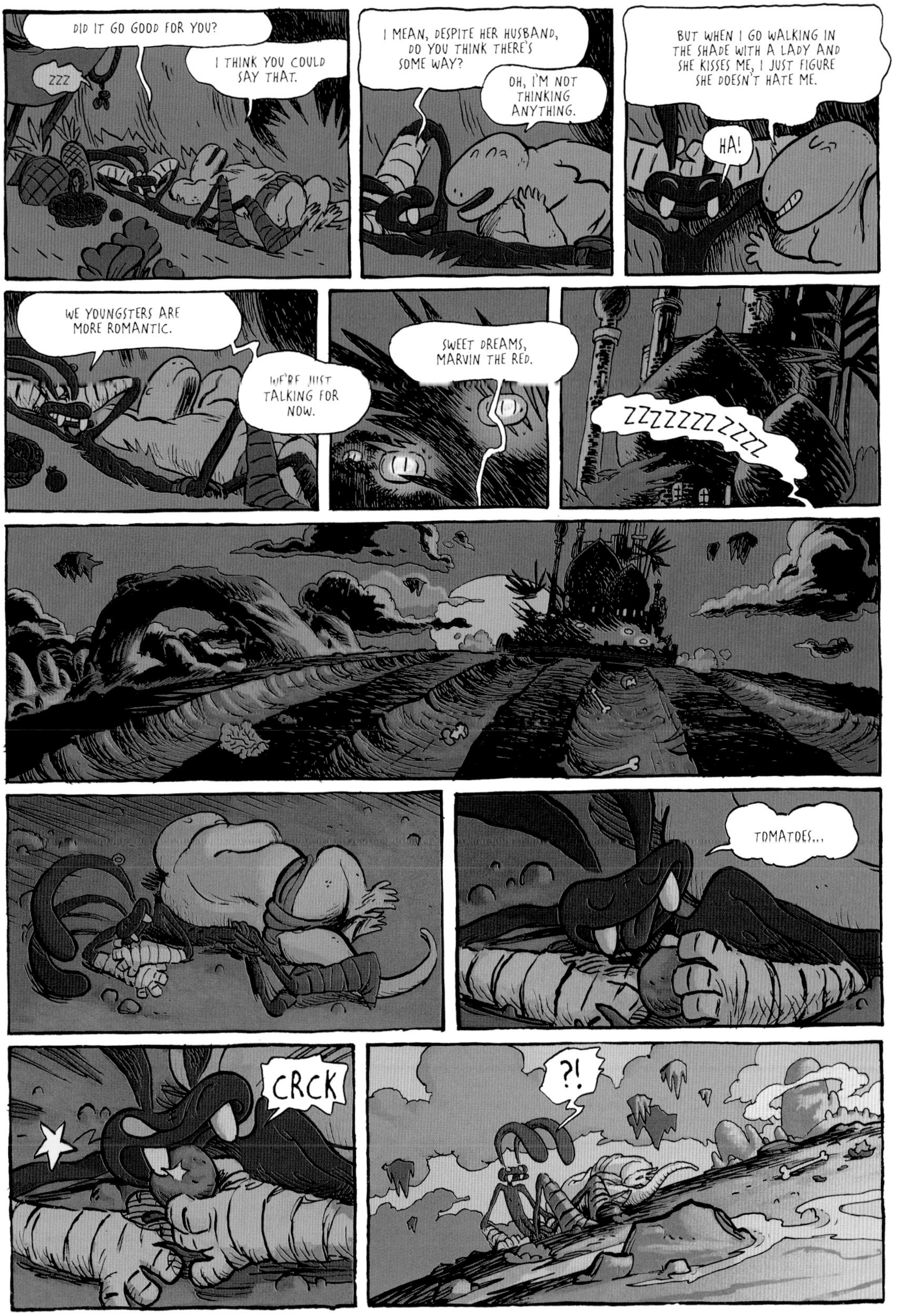
DID IT GO GOOD FOR YOU?
ZZZ
I THINK YOU COULD SAY THAT.
I MEAN, DESPITE HER HUSBAND, DO YOU THINK THERE'S SOME WAY?
OH, I'M NOT THINKING ANYTHING.
BUT WHEN I GO WALKING IN THE SHADE WITH A LADY AND SHE KISSES ME, I JUST FIGURE SHE DOESN'T HATE ME.
HA!
WE YOUNGSTERS ARE MORE ROMANTIC.
WE'RE JUST TALKING FOR NOW.
SWEET DREAMS, MARVIN THE RED.
ZZZZZZZZZZZ
TOMATOES...
CRCK
?!

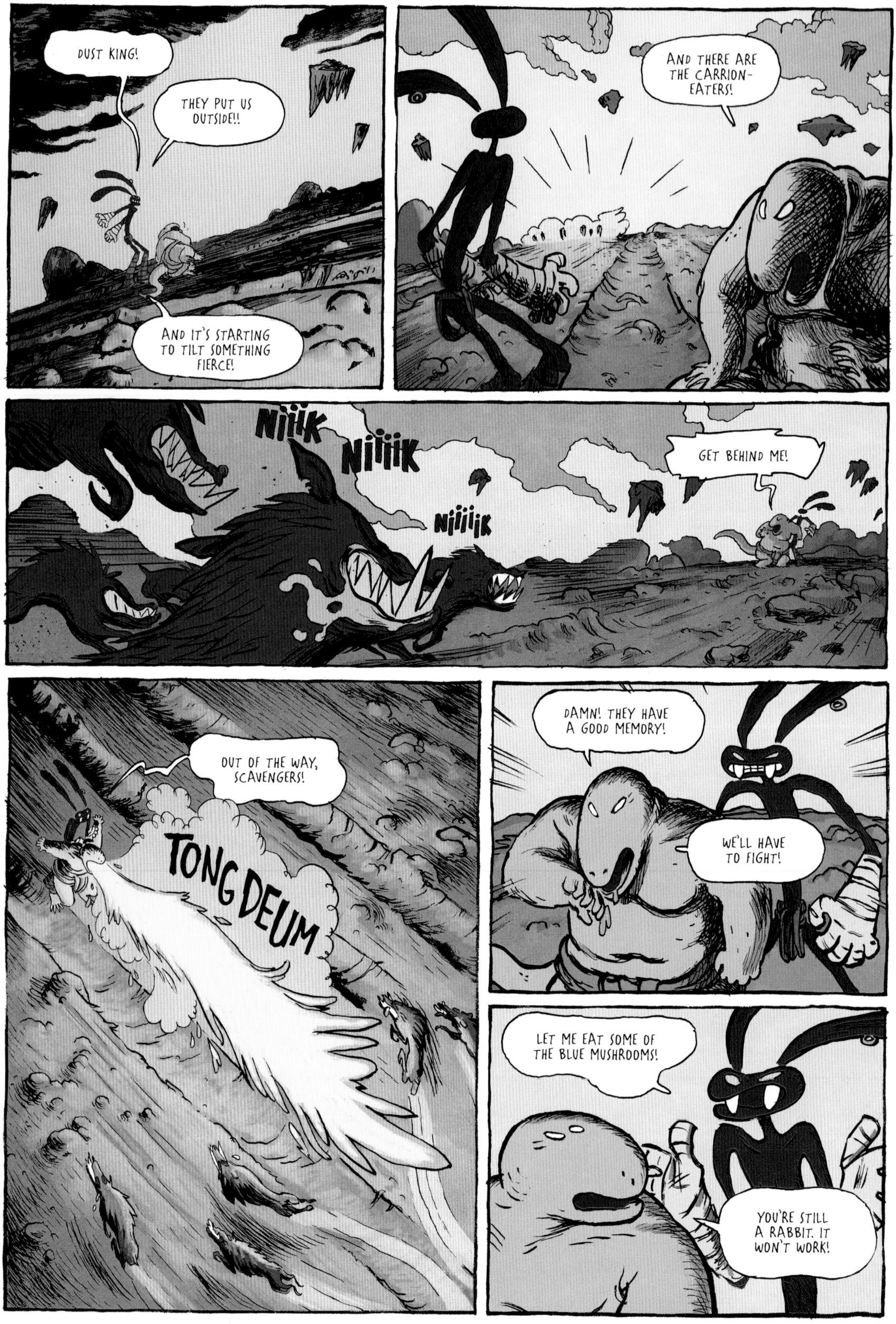
DUST KING!
THEY PUT US OUTSIDE!!
AND IT'S STARTING TO TILT SOMETHING FIERCE!
AND THERE ARE THE CARRION-EATERS!
NIIIK
NIIIIK
NIIIIK
GET BEHIND ME!
OUT OF THE WAY, SCAVENGERS!
TONG DEUM
DAMN! THEY HAVE A GOOD MEMORY!
WE'LL HAVE TO FIGHT!
LET ME EAT SOME OF THE BLUE MUSHROOMS!
YOU'RE STILL A RABBIT. IT WON'T WORK!

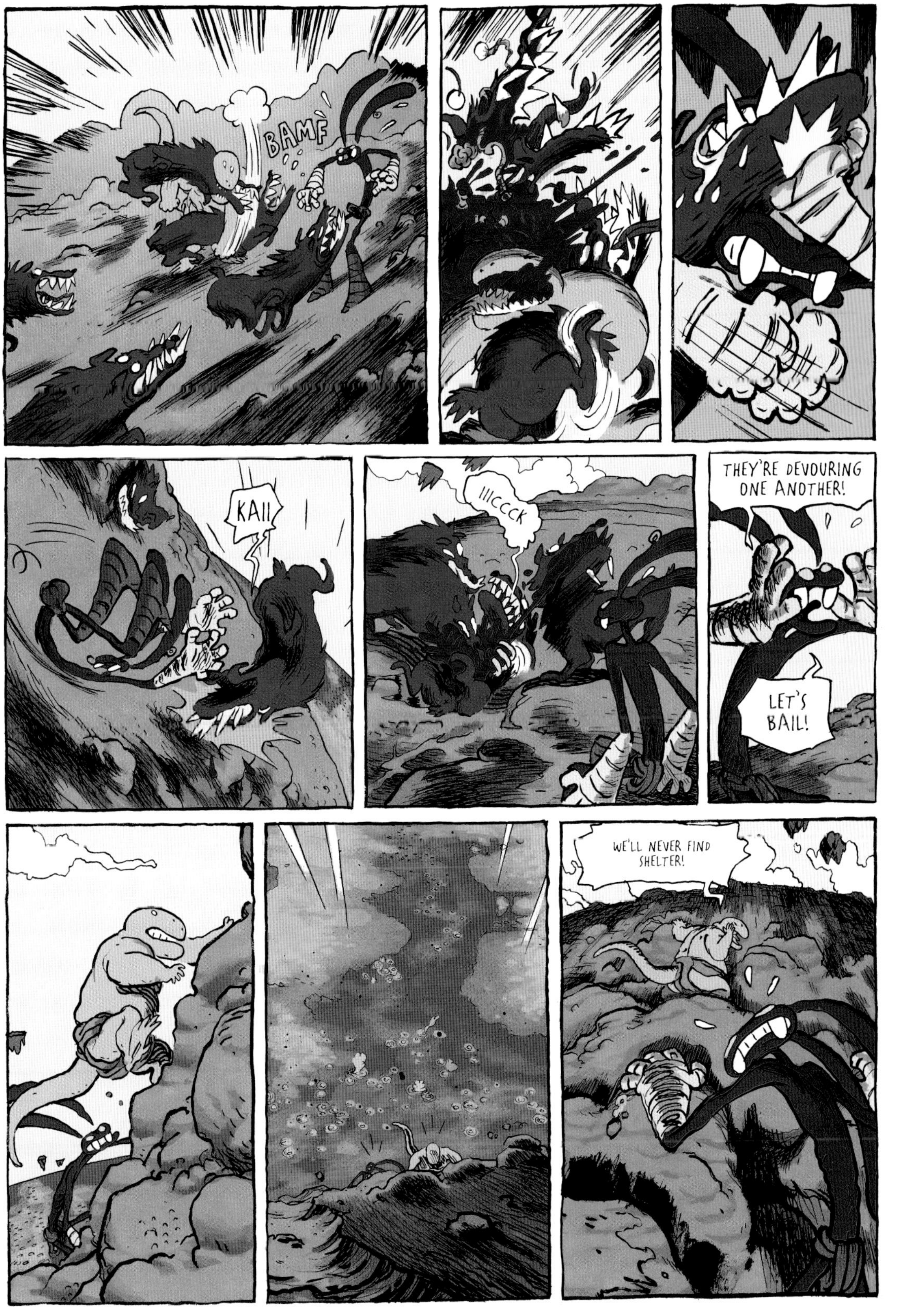
BAMF
KAII
IIICCCK
THEY'RE DEVOURING ONE ANOTHER!
LET'S BAIL!
WE'LL NEVER FIND SHELTER!

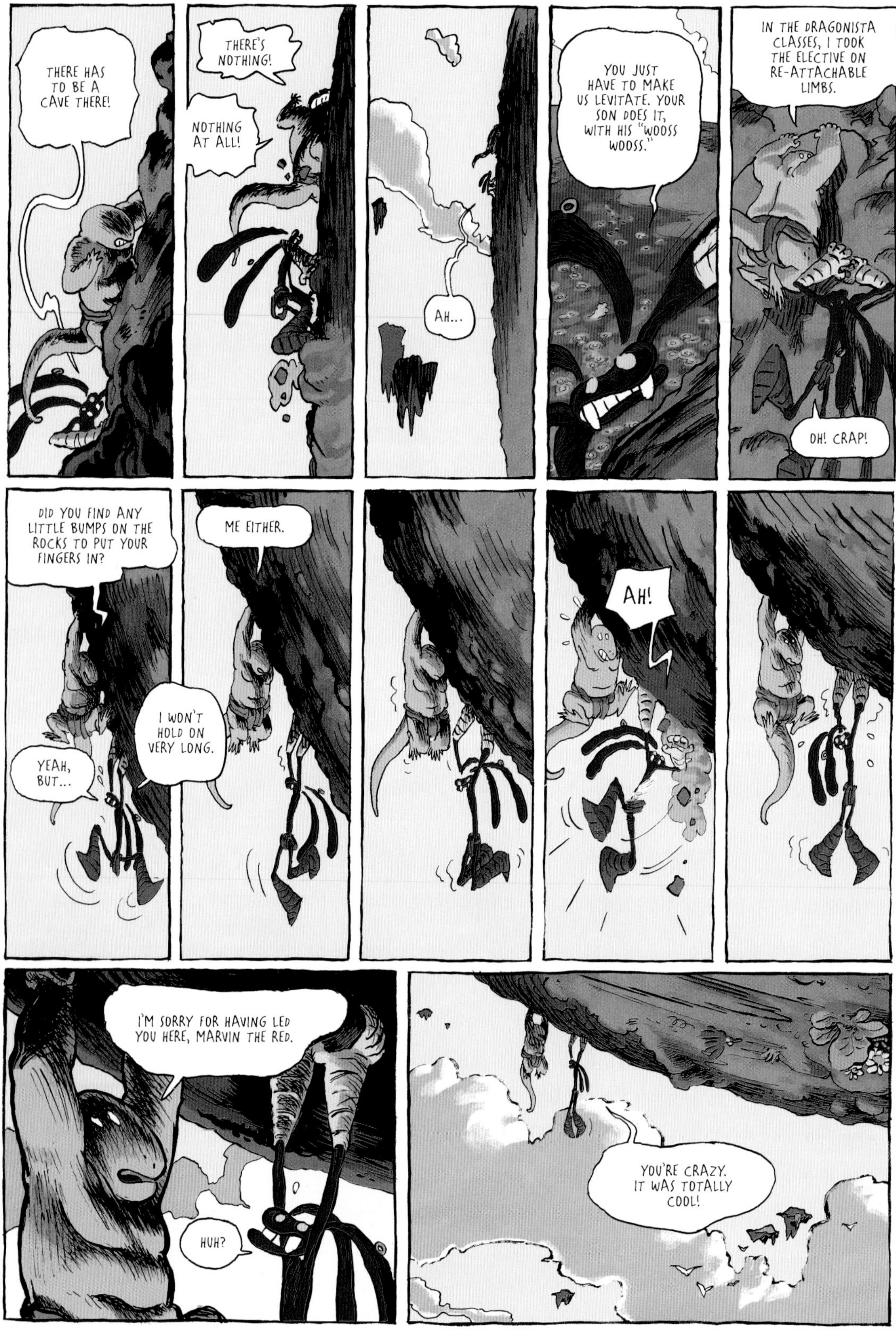

THERE HAS TO BE A CAVE THERE!
THERE'S NOTHING!
NOTHING AT ALL!
AH...
YOU JUST HAVE TO MAKE US LEVITATE. YOUR SON DOES IT, WITH HIS "WOOSS WOOSS."
IN THE DRAGONISTA CLASSES, I TOOK THE ELECTIVE ON RE-ATTACHABLE LIMBS.
OH! CRAP!
DID YOU FIND ANY LITTLE BUMPS ON THE ROCKS TO PUT YOUR FINGERS IN?
YEAH, BUT...
I WON'T HOLD ON VERY LONG.
ME EITHER.
AH!
I'M SORRY FOR HAVING LED YOU HERE, MARVIN THE RED.
HUH?
YOU'RE CRAZY. IT WAS TOTALLY COOL!

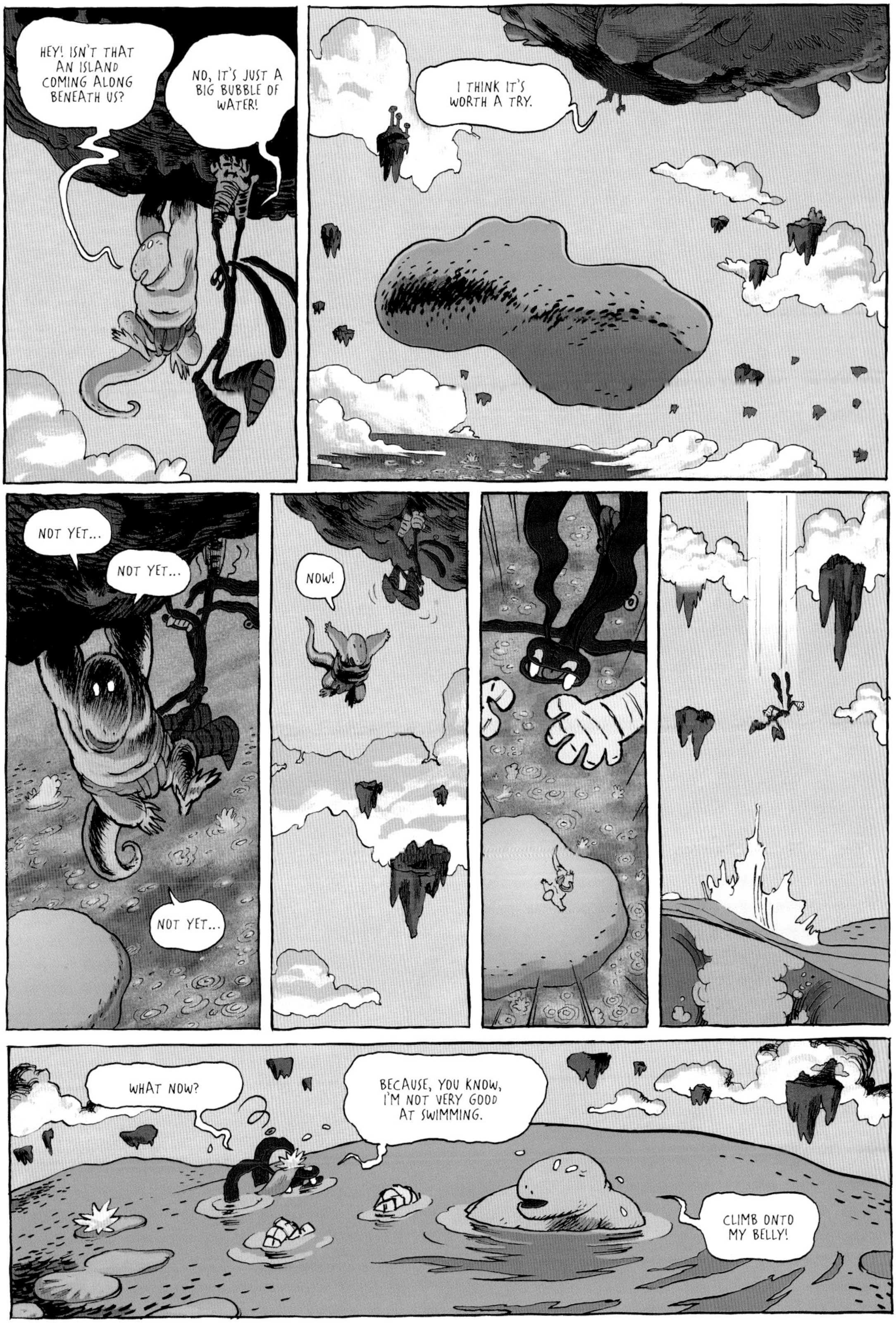
HEY! ISN'T THAT AN ISLAND COMING ALONG BENEATH US?
NO, IT'S JUST A BIG BUBBLE OF WATER!
I THINK IT'S WORTH A TRY.
NOT YET...
NOT YET...
NOT YET...
NOW!
WHAT NOW?
BECAUSE, YOU KNOW, I'M NOT VERY GOOD AT SWIMMING.
CLIMB ONTO MY BELLY!

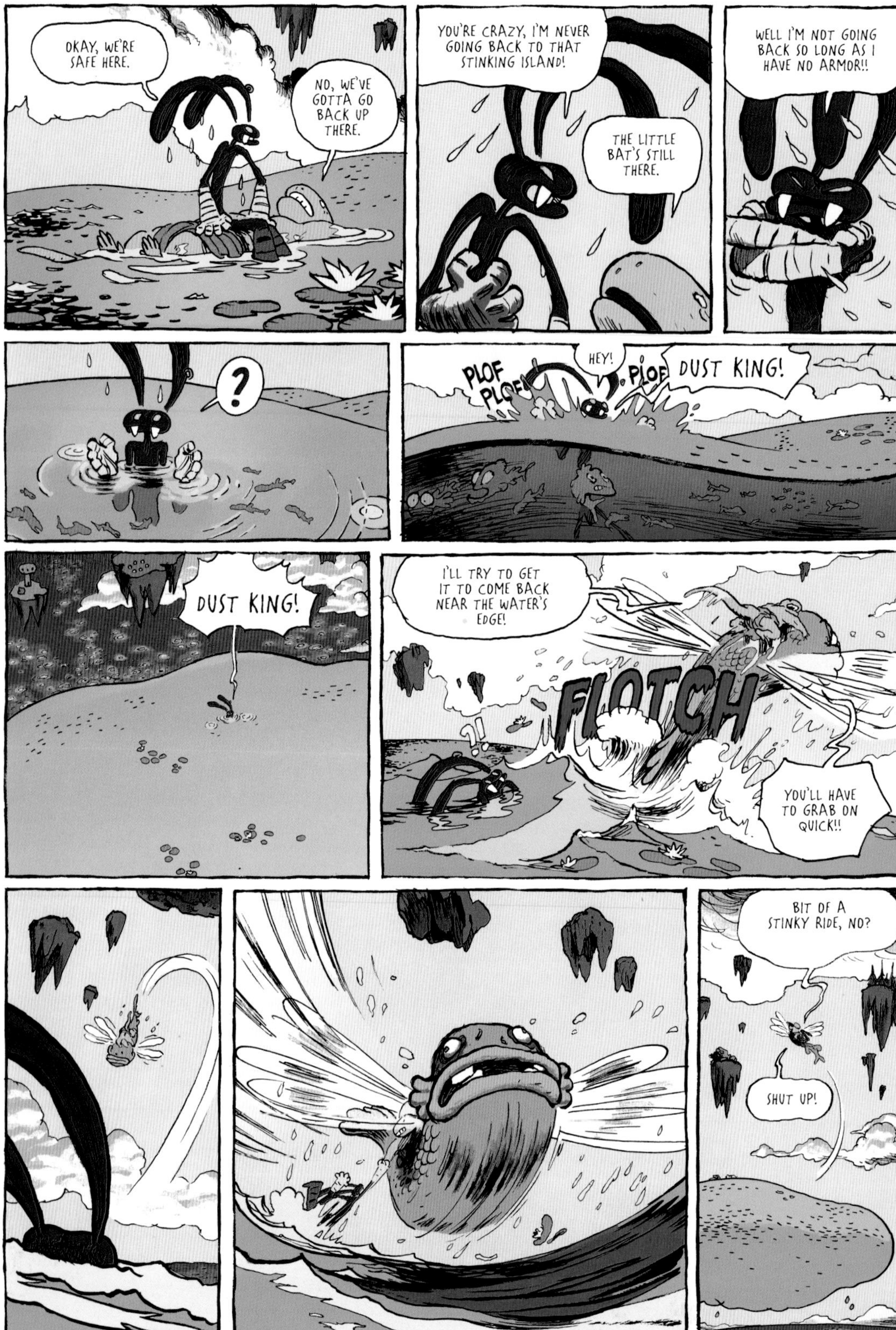
OKAY, WE'RE SAFE HERE.
NO, WE'VE GOTTA GO BACK UP THERE.
YOU'RE CRAZY, I'M NEVER GOING BACK TO THAT STINKING ISLAND!
THE LITTLE BAT'S STILL THERE.
WELL I'M NOT GOING BACK SO LONG AS I HAVE NO ARMOR!!
?
PLOF PLOF
HEY!
PLOF
DUST KING!
DUST KING!
I'LL TRY TO GET IT TO COME BACK NEAR THE WATER'S EDGE!
FLOTCH
YOU'LL HAVE TO GRAB ON QUICK!!
BIT OF A STINKY RIDE, NO?
SHUT UP!

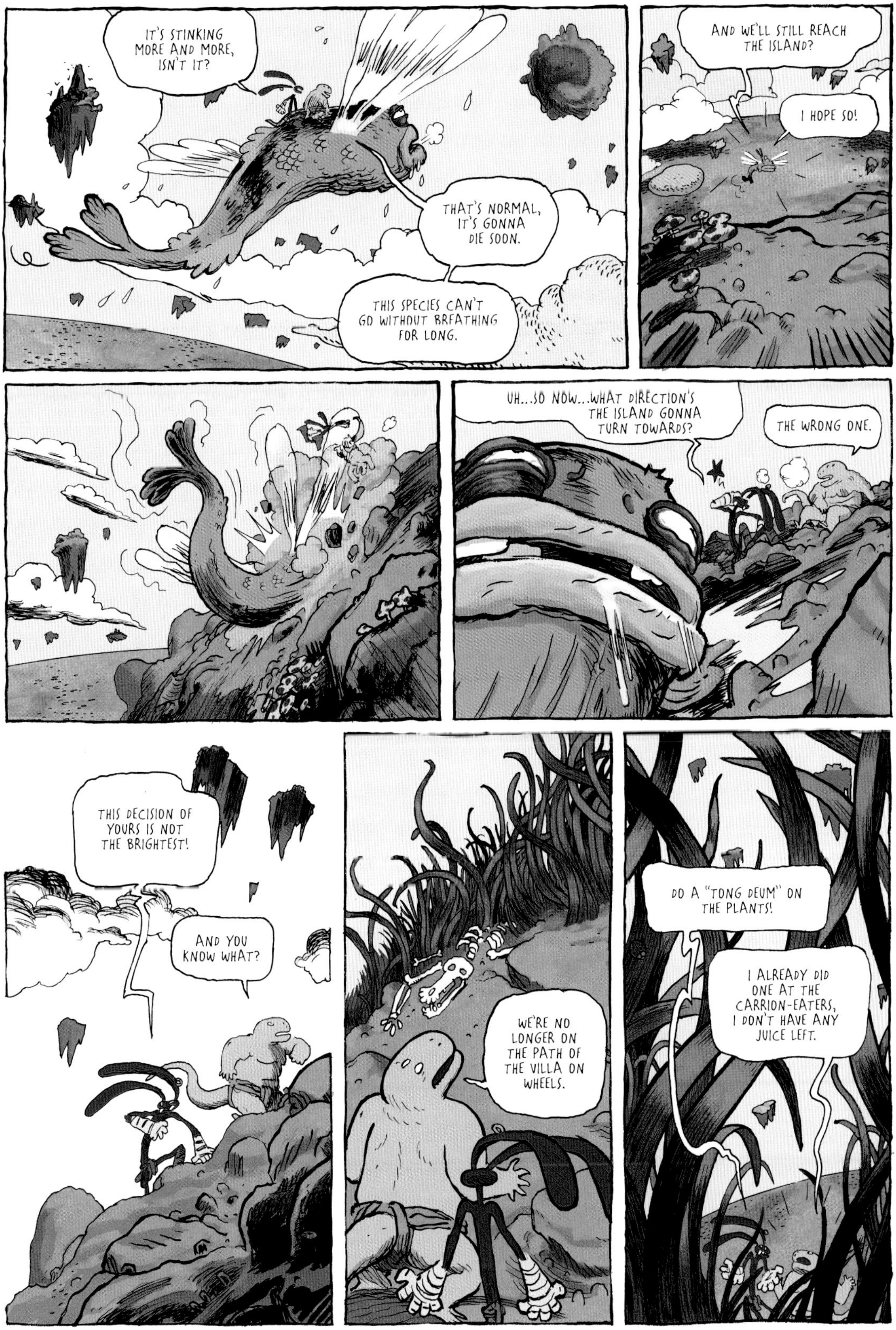
IT'S STINKING MORE AND MORE, ISN'T IT?
THAT'S NORMAL, IT'S GONNA DIE SOON.
THIS SPECIES CAN'T GO WITHOUT BREATHING FOR LONG.
AND WE'LL STILL REACH THE ISLAND?
I HOPE SO!
UH...SO NOW...WHAT DIRECTION'S THE ISLAND GONNA TURN TOWARDS?
THE WRONG ONE.
THIS DECISION OF YOURS IS NOT THE BRIGHTEST!
AND YOU KNOW WHAT?
WE'RE NO LONGER ON THE PATH OF THE VILLA ON WHEELS.
DO A "TONG DEUM" ON THE PLANTS!
I ALREADY DID ONE AT THE CARRION-EATERS, I DON'T HAVE ANY JUICE LEFT.

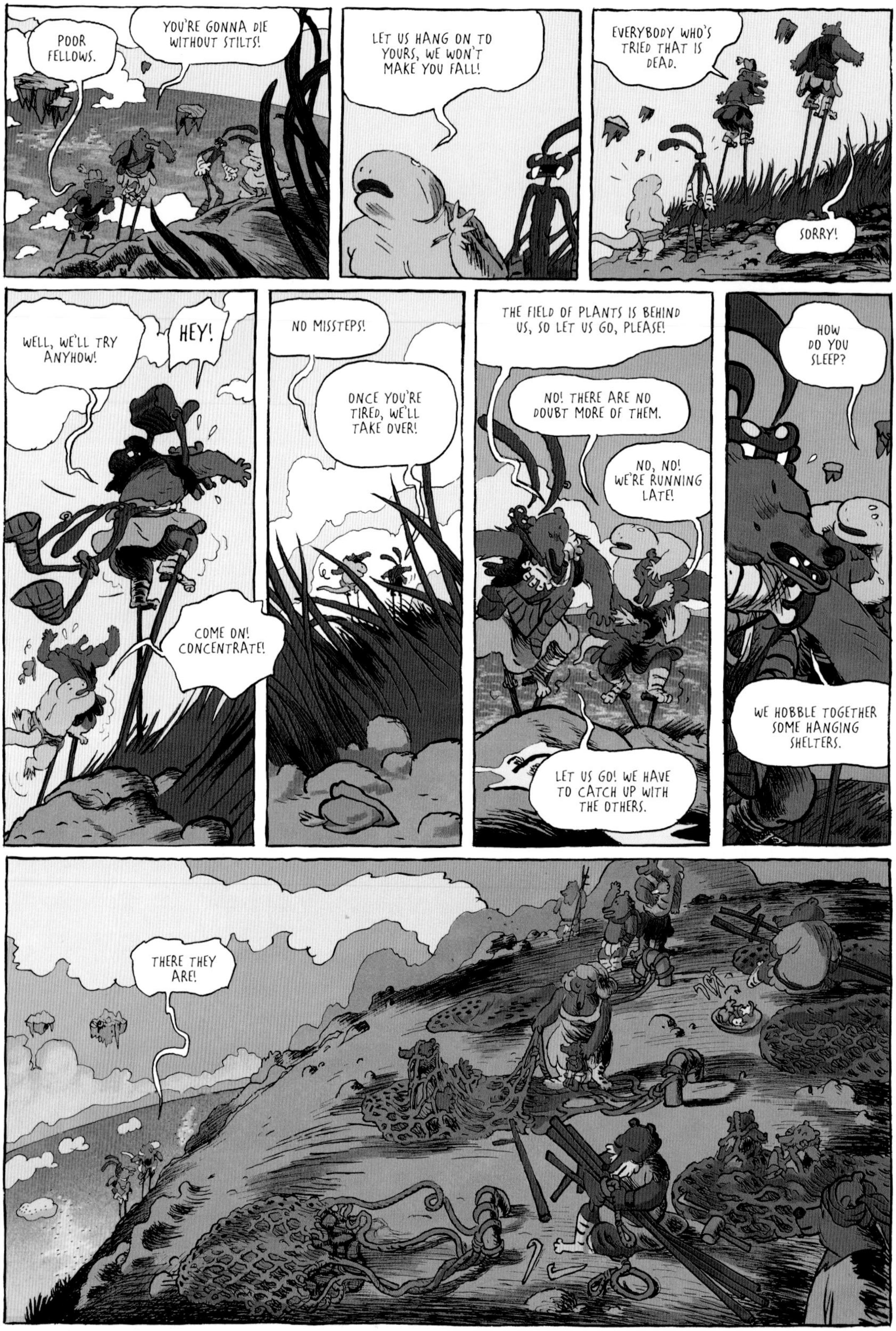
POOR FELLOWS.
YOU'RE GONNA DIE WITHOUT STILTS!
LET US HANG ON TO YOURS, WE WON'T MAKE YOU FALL!
EVERYBODY WHO'S TRIED THAT IS DEAD.
SORRY!
WELL, WE'LL TRY ANYHOW!
HEY!
COME ON! CONCENTRATE!
NO MISSTEPS!
ONCE YOU'RE TIRED, WE'LL TAKE OVER!
THE FIELD OF PLANTS IS BEHIND US, SO LET US GO, PLEASE!
NO! THERE ARE NO DOUBT MORE OF THEM.
NO, NO! WE'RE RUNNING LATE!
LET US GO! WE HAVE TO CATCH UP WITH THE OTHERS.
HOW DO YOU SLEEP?
WE HOBBLE TOGETHER SOME HANGING SHELTERS.
THERE THEY ARE!

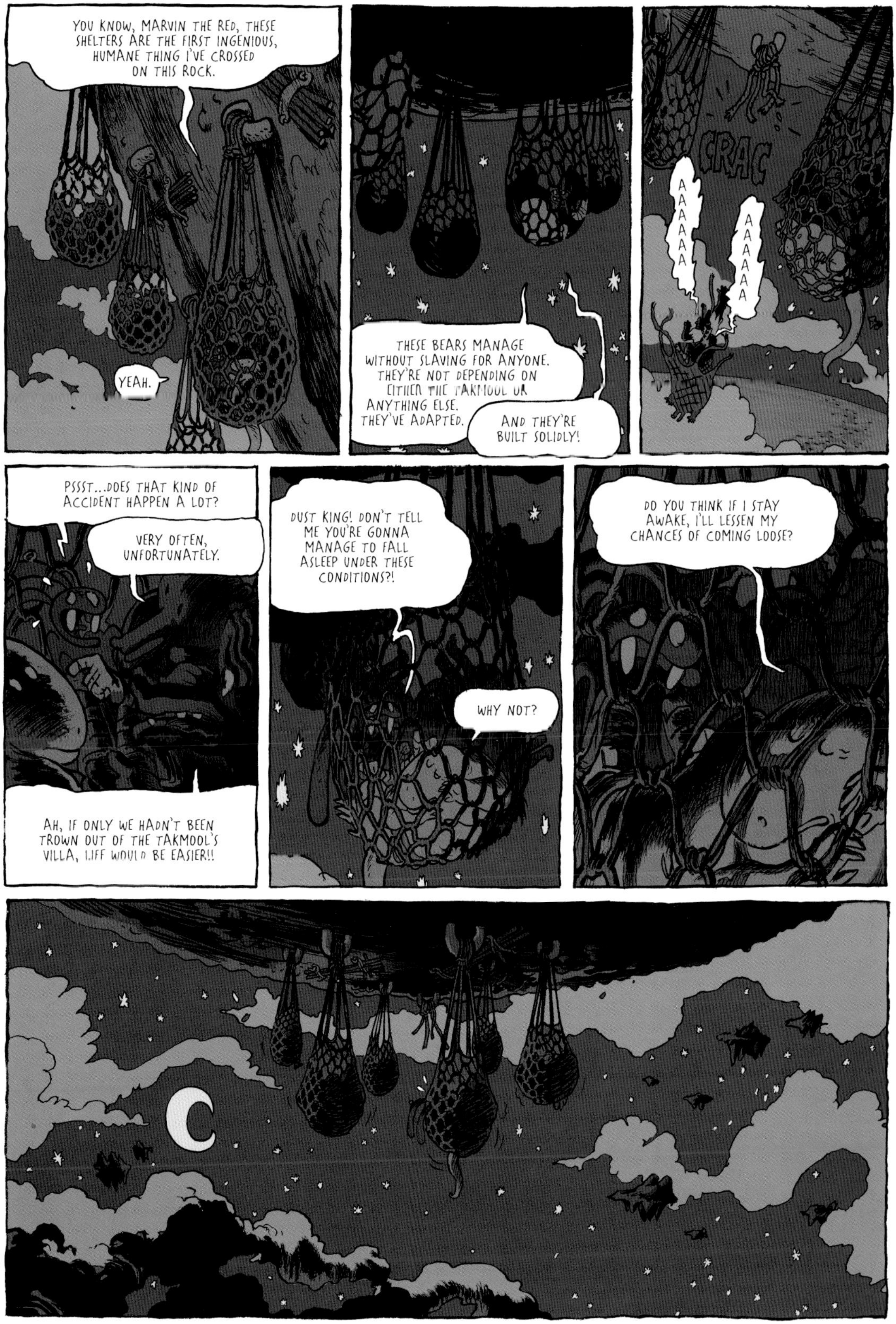
YOU KNOW, MARVIN THE RED, THESE SHELTERS ARE THE FIRST INGENIOUS, HUMANE THING I'VE CROSSED ON THIS ROCK.
YEAH.
THESE BEARS MANAGE WITHOUT SLAVING FOR ANYONE. THEY'RE NOT DEPENDING ON EITHER THE TAKMOOL OR ANYTHING ELSE. THEY'VE ADAPTED.
AND THEY'RE BUILT SOLIDLY!
CRAC
AAAAAA
AAAAAA
PSSST...DOES THAT KIND OF ACCIDENT HAPPEN A LOT?
VERY OFTEN, UNFORTUNATELY.
AH, IF ONLY WE HADN'T BEEN TROWN OUT OF THE TAKMOOL'S VILLA, LIFE WOULD BE EASIER!!
DUST KING! DON'T TELL ME YOU'RE GONNA MANAGE TO FALL ASLEEP UNDER THESE CONDITIONS?!
WHY NOT?
DO YOU THINK IF I STAY AWAKE, I'LL LESSEN MY CHANCES OF COMING LOOSE?

PAPA! PAPA! THE LITTLE BAT TELLS ME ITS FRIENDS ARE BACK!

AH...

I WAS SURE THEY'D COME BACK!

YOU KNOW, THAT'S AN EXCELLENT BIT OF NEWS YOU'VE TOLD ME, FARFALLE. LET'S GO WELCOME THEM RIGHT AWAY!

DIING DIING

MY DEAR FRIENDS! WHAT A JOY!

AH! YOU CERTAINLY WORRIED US!

WE SEARCHED EVERYWHERE FOR YOU!

VONGOLA! COME SEE WHO'S BACK!

OOH! I'M SO HAPPY!!

STAY FOR DINNER. MY WIFE HAS MADE SOME PASTA.

HEY, YOU KNOW, THERE'S NO POINT IN TAKING US FOR FOOLS!

WHAT DO YOU MEAN BY THAT?

MY YOUNG COMRADE IS EXPRESSING WITHOUT DETOUR THAT WE KNOW FULL WELL YOU'RE THE ONE WHO THREW US OUT!

KNOW THAT IT'S SOLELY OUT OF CONSIDERATION FOR YOUR WIFE AND DAUGHTER PRESENT HERE THAT WE HAVEN'T KILLED YOU YET.

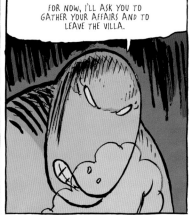

FOR NOW, I'LL ASK YOU TO GATHER YOUR AFFAIRS AND TO LEAVE THE VILLA.

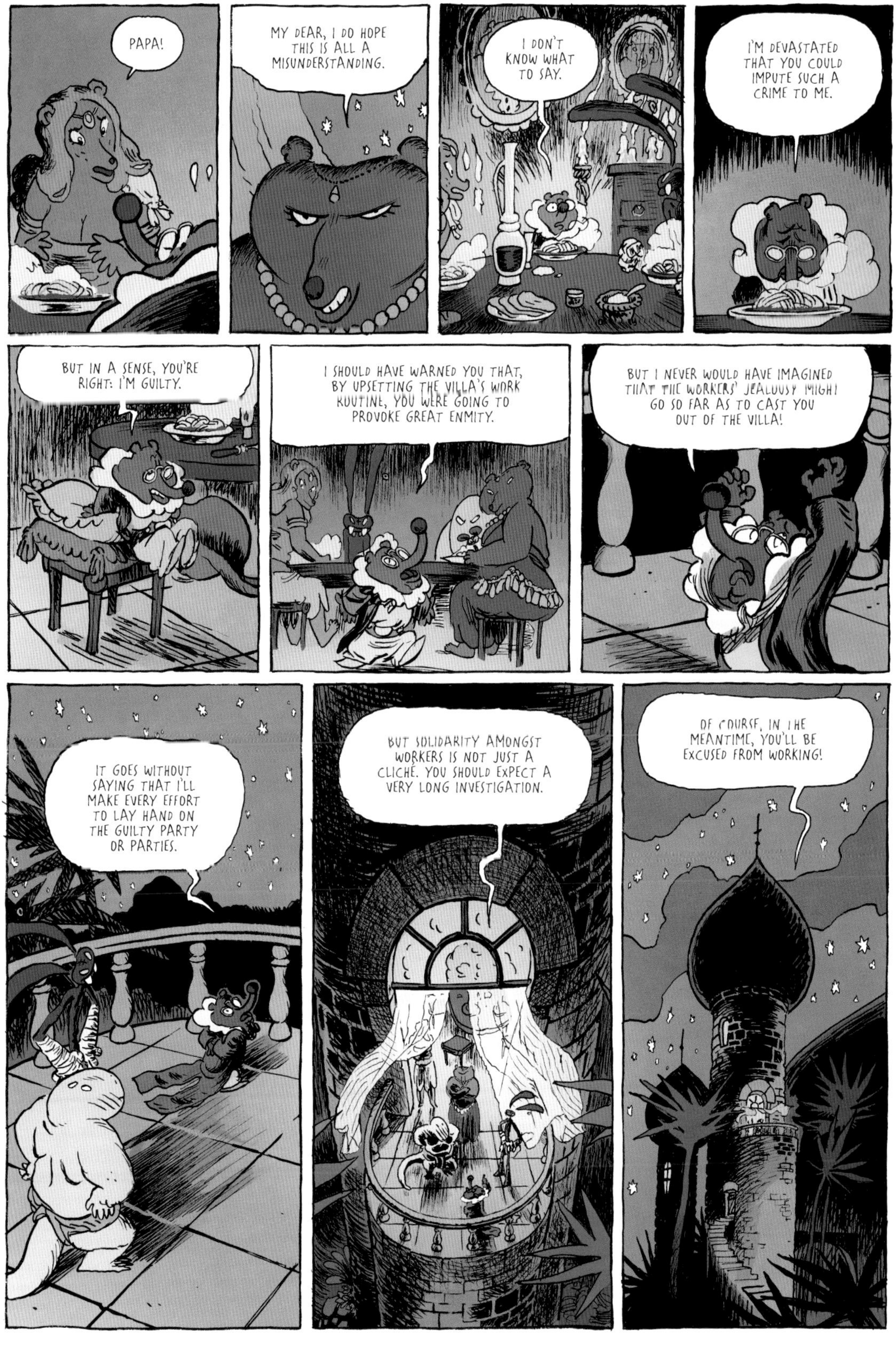
PAPA!
MY DEAR, I DO HOPE THIS IS ALL A MISUNDERSTANDING.
I DON'T KNOW WHAT TO SAY.
I'M DEVASTATED THAT YOU COULD IMPUTE SUCH A CRIME TO ME.
BUT IN A SENSE, YOU'RE RIGHT: I'M GUILTY.
I SHOULD HAVE WARNED YOU THAT, BY UPSETTING THE VILLA'S WORK ROUTINE, YOU WERE GOING TO PROVOKE GREAT ENMITY.
BUT I NEVER WOULD HAVE IMAGINED THAT THE WORKERS' JEALOUSY MIGHT GO SO FAR AS TO CAST YOU OUT OF THE VILLA!
IT GOES WITHOUT SAYING THAT I'LL MAKE EVERY EFFORT TO LAY HAND ON THE GUILTY PARTY OR PARTIES.
BUT SOLIDARITY AMONGST WORKERS IS NOT JUST A CLICHÉ. YOU SHOULD EXPECT A VERY LONG INVESTIGATION.
OF COURSE, IN THE MEANTIME, YOU'LL BE EXCUSED FROM WORKING!

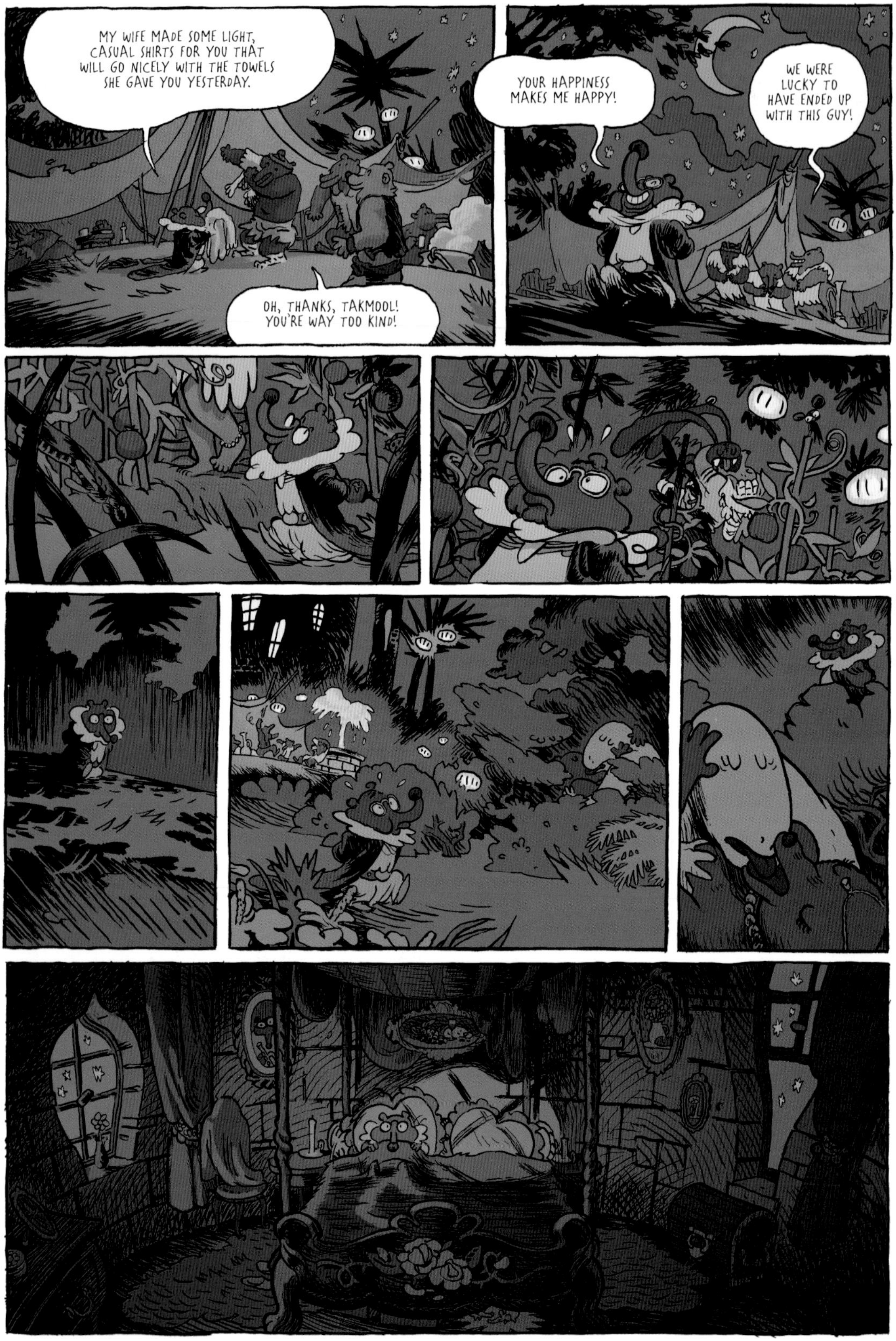
MY WIFE MADE SOME LIGHT, CASUAL SHIRTS FOR YOU THAT WILL GO NICELY WITH THE TOWELS SHE GAVE YOU YESTERDAY.
OH, THANKS, TAKMOOL! YOU'RE WAY TOO KIND!
YOUR HAPPINESS MAKES ME HAPPY!
WE WERE LUCKY TO HAVE ENDED UP WITH THIS GUY!

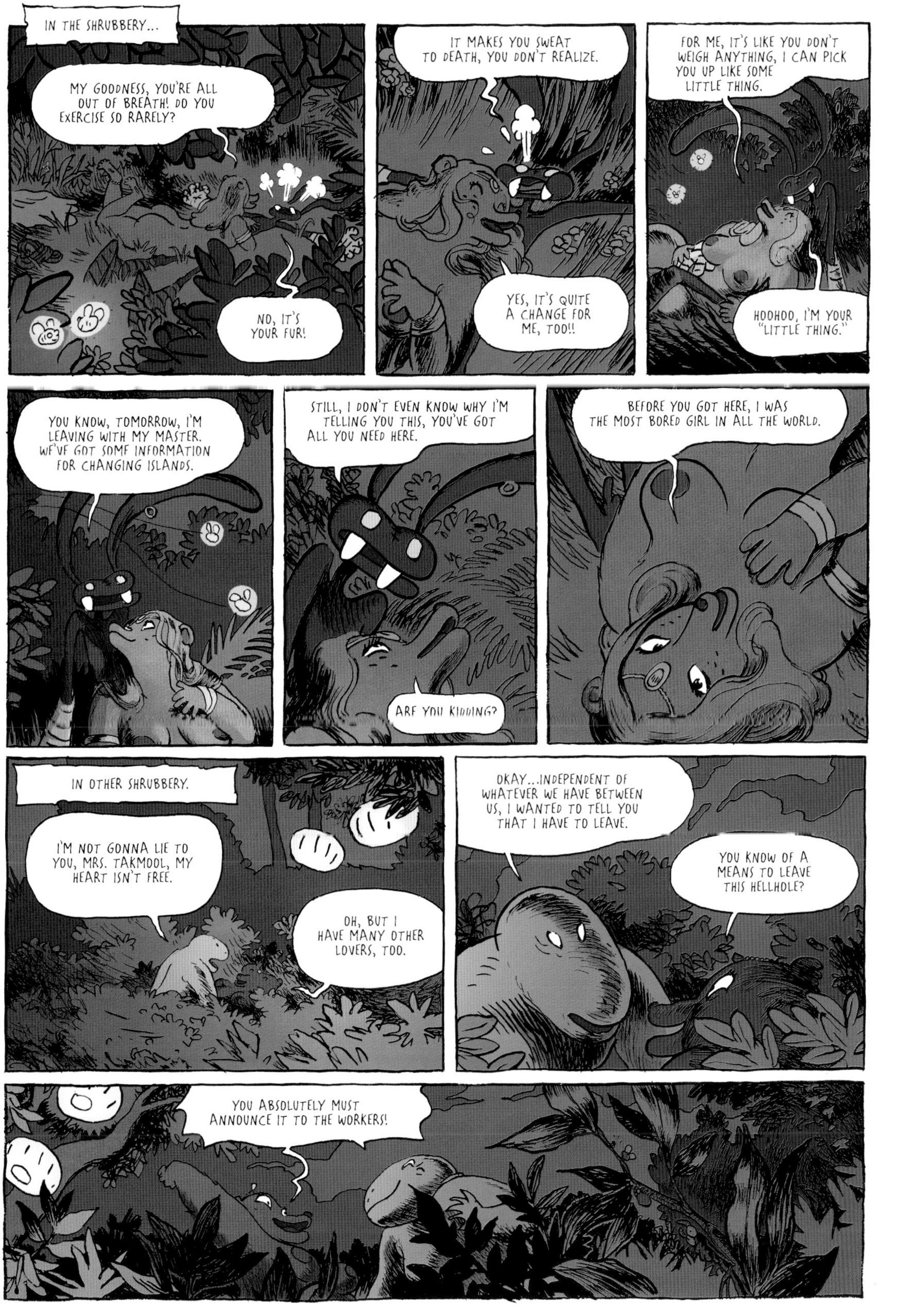
IN THE SHRUBBERY...
MY GOODNESS, YOU'RE ALL OUT OF BREATH! DO YOU EXERCISE SO RARELY?
NO, IT'S YOUR FUR!
IT MAKES YOU SWEAT TO DEATH, YOU DON'T REALIZE.
YES, IT'S QUITE A CHANGE FOR ME, TOO!!
FOR ME, IT'S LIKE YOU DON'T WEIGH ANYTHING, I CAN PICK YOU UP LIKE SOME LITTLE THING.
HOOHOO, I'M YOUR "LITTLE THING."
YOU KNOW, TOMORROW, I'M LEAVING WITH MY MASTER. WE'VE GOT SOME INFORMATION FOR CHANGING ISLANDS.
STILL, I DON'T EVEN KNOW WHY I'M TELLING YOU THIS, YOU'VE GOT ALL YOU NEED HERE.
ARE YOU KIDDING?
BEFORE YOU GOT HERE, I WAS THE MOST BORED GIRL IN ALL THE WORLD.
IN OTHER SHRUBBERY.
I'M NOT GONNA LIE TO YOU, MRS. TAKMOOL, MY HEART ISN'T FREE.
OH, BUT I HAVE MANY OTHER LOVERS, TOO.
OKAY...INDEPENDENT OF WHATEVER WE HAVE BETWEEN US, I WANTED TO TELL YOU THAT I HAVE TO LEAVE.
YOU KNOW OF A MEANS TO LEAVE THIS HELLHOLE?
YOU ABSOLUTELY MUST ANNOUNCE IT TO THE WORKERS!

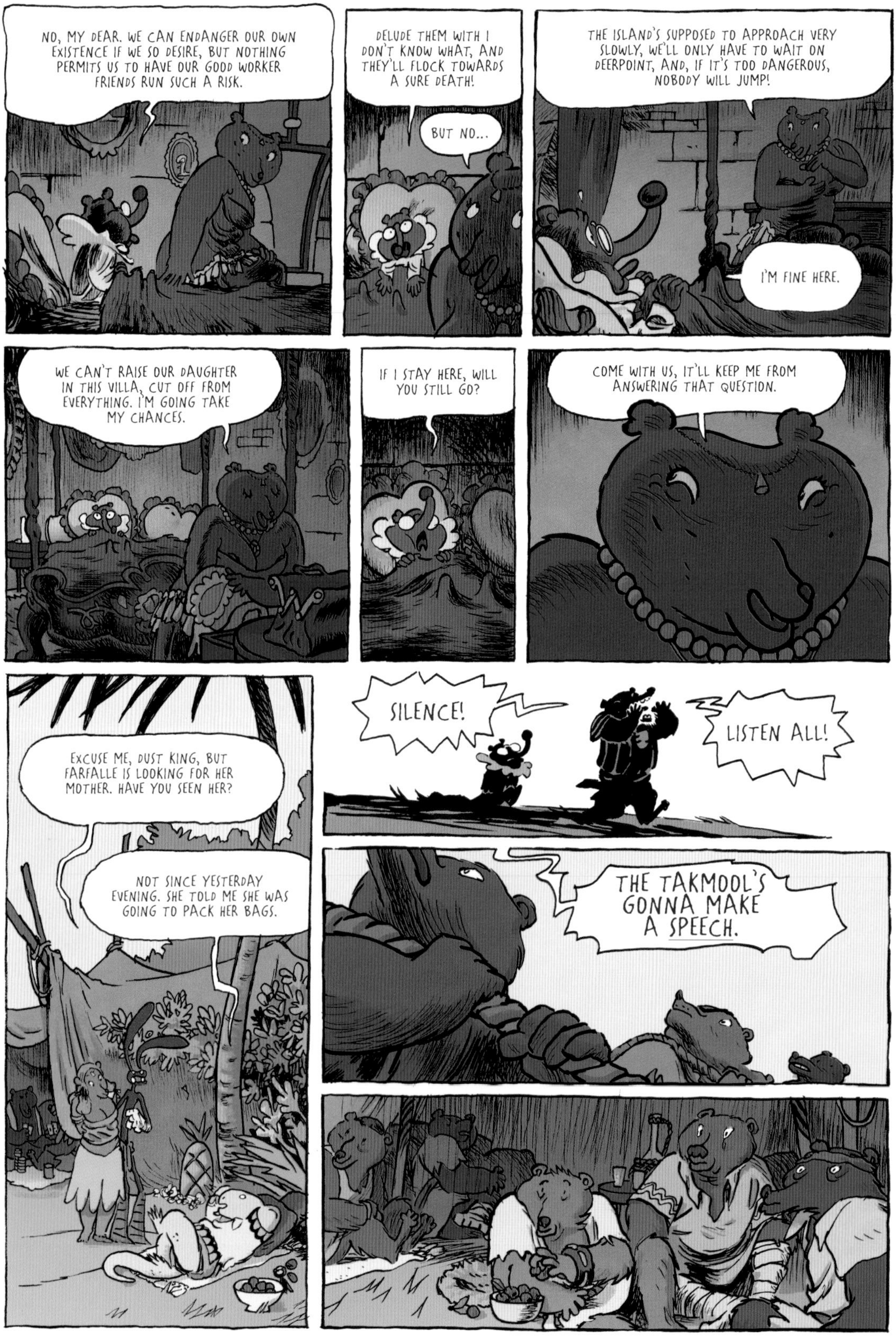
NO, MY DEAR. WE CAN ENDANGER OUR OWN EXISTENCE IF WE SO DESIRE, BUT NOTHING PERMITS US TO HAVE OUR GOOD WORKER FRIENDS RUN SUCH A RISK.
DELUDE THEM WITH I DON'T KNOW WHAT, AND THEY'LL FLOCK TOWARDS A SURE DEATH!
BUT NO...
THE ISLAND'S SUPPOSED TO APPROACH VERY SLOWLY, WE'LL ONLY HAVE TO WAIT ON DEERPOINT, AND, IF IT'S TOO DANGEROUS, NOBODY WILL JUMP!
I'M FINE HERE.
WE CAN'T RAISE OUR DAUGHTER IN THIS VILLA, CUT OFF FROM EVERYTHING. I'M GOING TAKE MY CHANCES.
IF I STAY HERE, WILL YOU STILL GO?
COME WITH US, IT'LL KEEP ME FROM ANSWERING THAT QUESTION.
EXCUSE ME, DUST KING, BUT FARFALLE IS LOOKING FOR HER MOTHER. HAVE YOU SEEN HER?
NOT SINCE YESTERDAY EVENING. SHE TOLD ME SHE WAS GOING TO PACK HER BAGS.
SILENCE!
LISTEN ALL!
THE TAKMOOL'S GONNA MAKE A SPEECH.

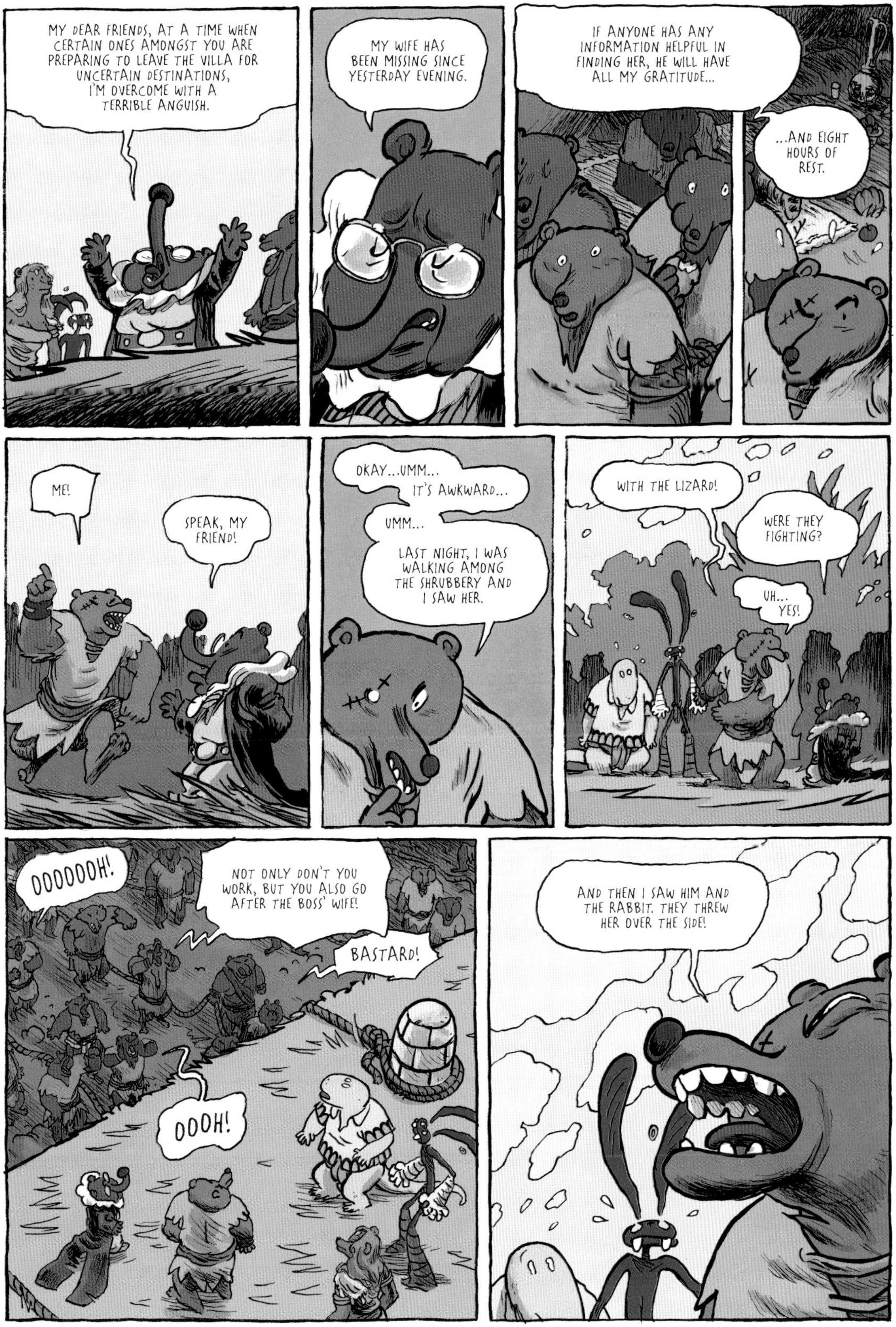
MY DEAR FRIENDS, AT A TIME WHEN CERTAIN ONES AMONGST YOU ARE PREPARING TO LEAVE THE VILLA FOR UNCERTAIN DESTINATIONS, I'M OVERCOME WITH A TERRIBLE ANGUISH.
MY WIFE HAS BEEN MISSING SINCE YESTERDAY EVENING.
IF ANYONE HAS ANY INFORMATION HELPFUL IN FINDING HER, HE WILL HAVE ALL MY GRATITUDE...
...AND EIGHT HOURS OF REST.
ME!
SPEAK, MY FRIEND!
OKAY...UMM...
IT'S AWKWARD...
UMM...
LAST NIGHT, I WAS WALKING AMONG THE SHRUBBERY AND I SAW HER.
WITH THE LIZARD!
WERE THEY FIGHTING?
UH... YES!
OOOOOOH!
NOT ONLY DON'T YOU WORK, BUT YOU ALSO GO AFTER THE BOSS' WIFE!
BASTARD!
OOOH!
AND THEN I SAW HIM AND THE RABBIT. THEY THREW HER OVER THE SIDE!

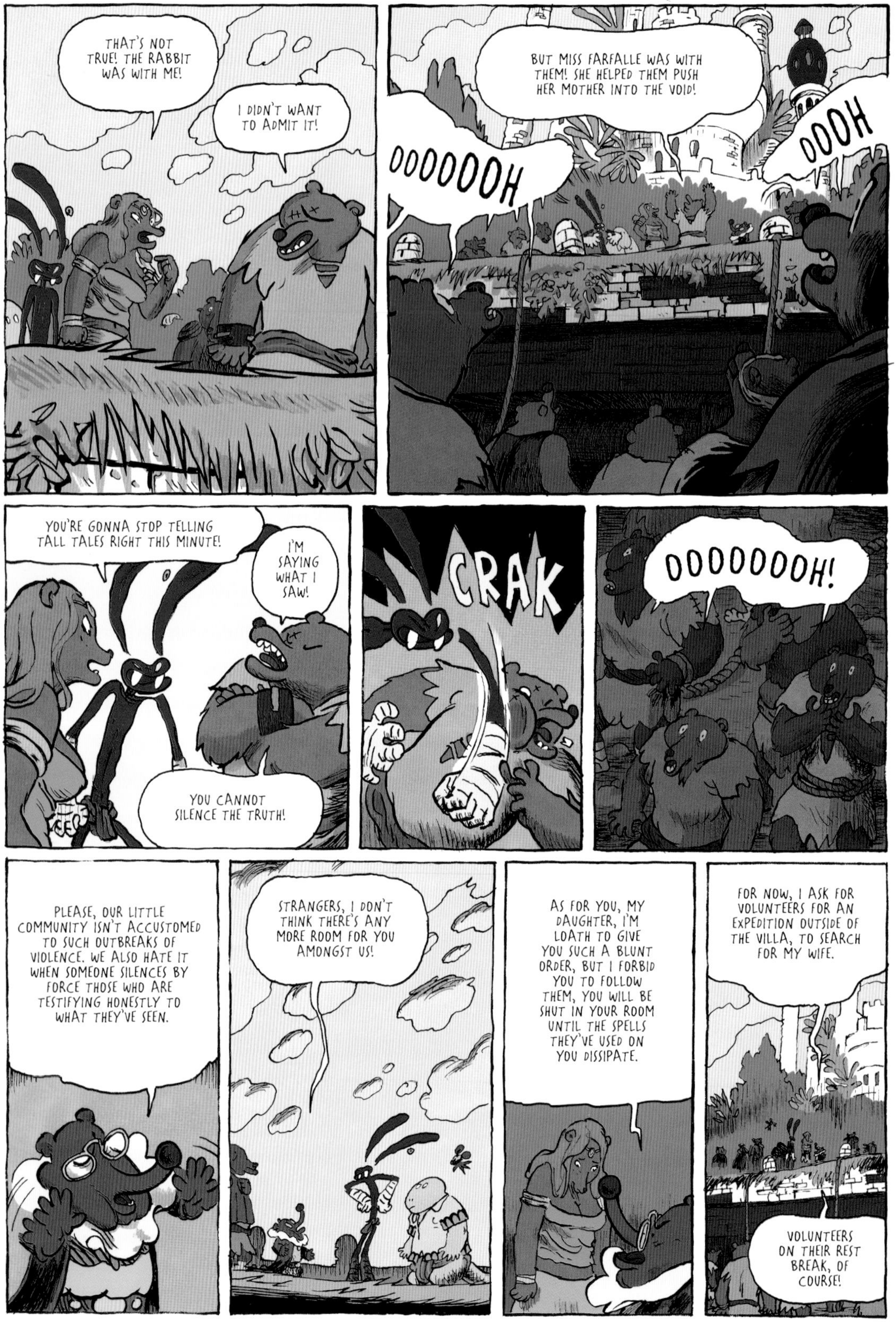
THAT'S NOT TRUE! THE RABBIT WAS WITH ME!
I DIDN'T WANT TO ADMIT IT!
BUT MISS FARFALLE WAS WITH THEM! SHE HELPED THEM PUSH HER MOTHER INTO THE VOID!
OOOOOOH
OOOH
YOU'RE GONNA STOP TELLING TALL TALES RIGHT THIS MINUTE!
I'M SAYING WHAT I SAW!
YOU CANNOT SILENCE THE TRUTH!
CRAK
OOOOOOOH!
PLEASE, OUR LITTLE COMMUNITY ISN'T ACCUSTOMED TO SUCH OUTBREAKS OF VIOLENCE. WE ALSO HATE IT WHEN SOMEONE SILENCES BY FORCE THOSE WHO ARE TESTIFYING HONESTLY TO WHAT THEY'VE SEEN.
STRANGERS, I DON'T THINK THERE'S ANY MORE ROOM FOR YOU AMONGST US!
AS FOR YOU, MY DAUGHTER, I'M LOATH TO GIVE YOU SUCH A BLUNT ORDER, BUT I FORBID YOU TO FOLLOW THEM, YOU WILL BE SHUT IN YOUR ROOM UNTIL THE SPELLS THEY'VE USED ON YOU DISSIPATE.
FOR NOW, I ASK FOR VOLUNTEERS FOR AN EXPEDITION OUTSIDE OF THE VILLA, TO SEARCH FOR MY WIFE.
VOLUNTEERS ON THEIR REST BREAK, OF COURSE!

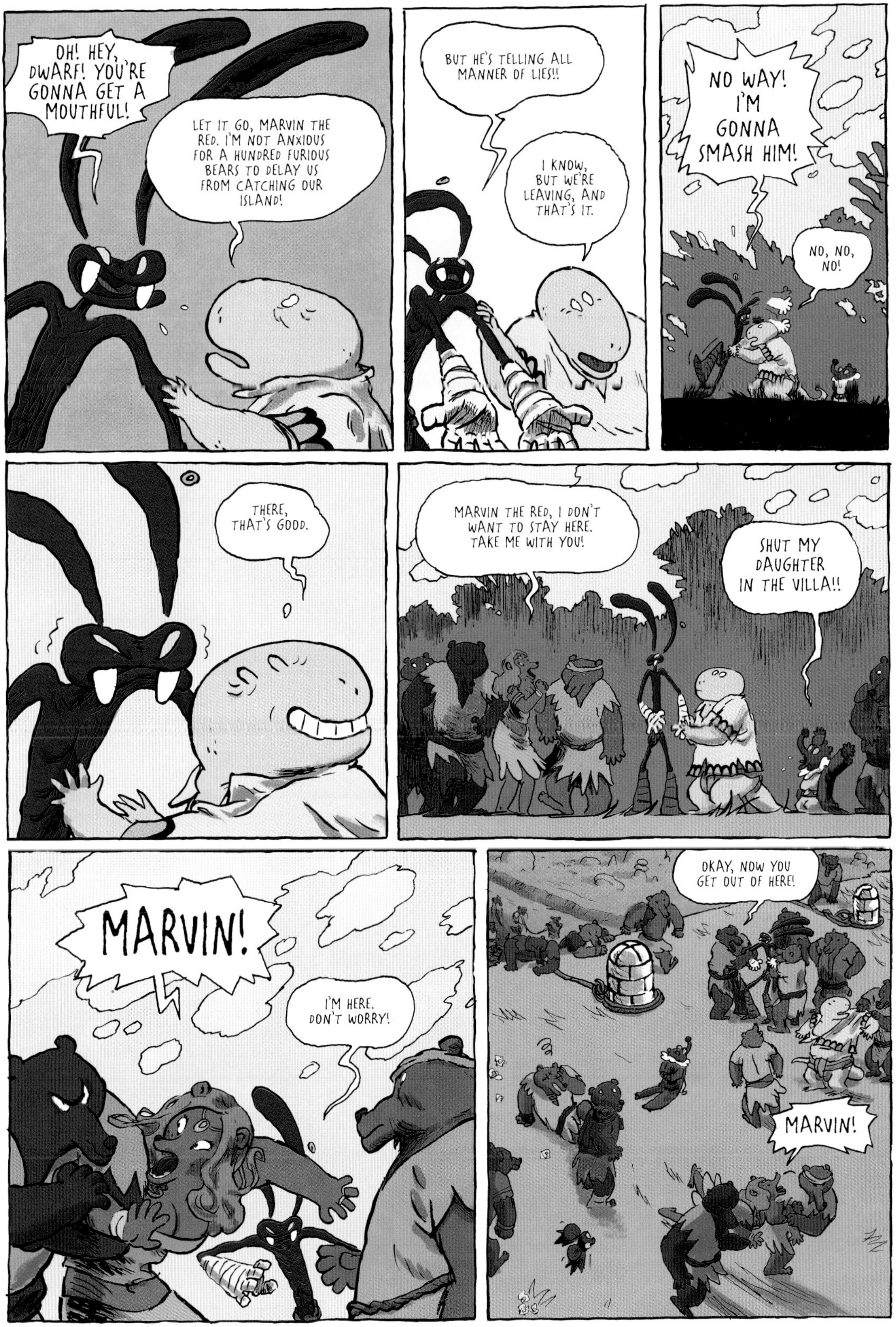
OH! HEY, DWARF! YOU'RE GONNA GET A MOUTHFUL!
LET IT GO, MARVIN THE RED. I'M NOT ANXIOUS FOR A HUNDRED FURIOUS BEARS TO DELAY US FROM CATCHING OUR ISLAND!
BUT HE'S TELLING ALL MANNER OF LIES!!
I KNOW, BUT WE'RE LEAVING, AND THAT'S IT.
NO WAY! I'M GONNA SMASH HIM!
NO, NO, NO!
THERE, THAT'S GOOD.
MARVIN THE RED, I DON'T WANT TO STAY HERE. TAKE ME WITH YOU!
SHUT MY DAUGHTER IN THE VILLA!!
MARVIN!
I'M HERE. DON'T WORRY!
OKAY, NOW YOU GET OUT OF HERE!
MARVIN!

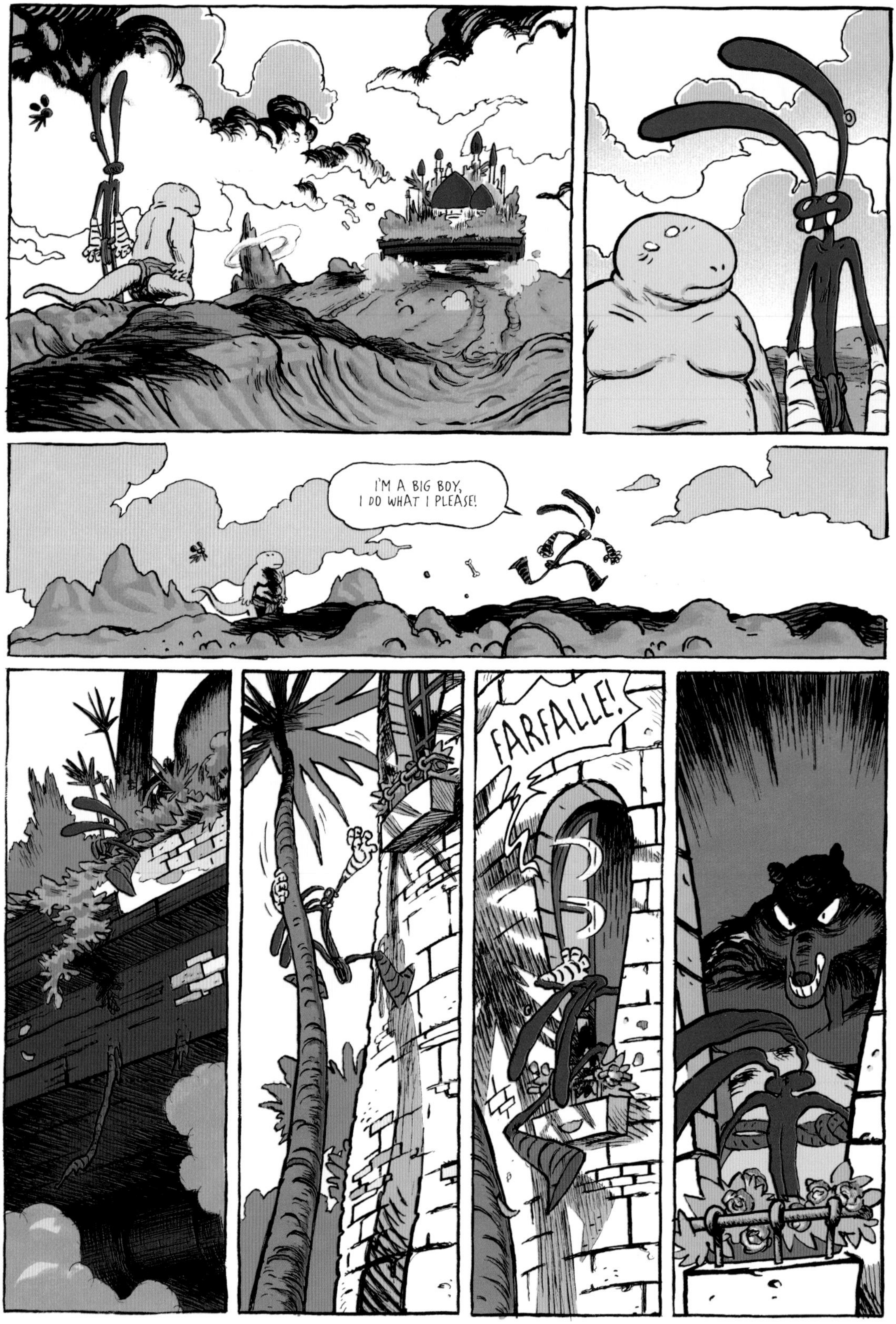
I'M A BIG BOY, I DO WHAT I PLEASE!
FARFALLE!

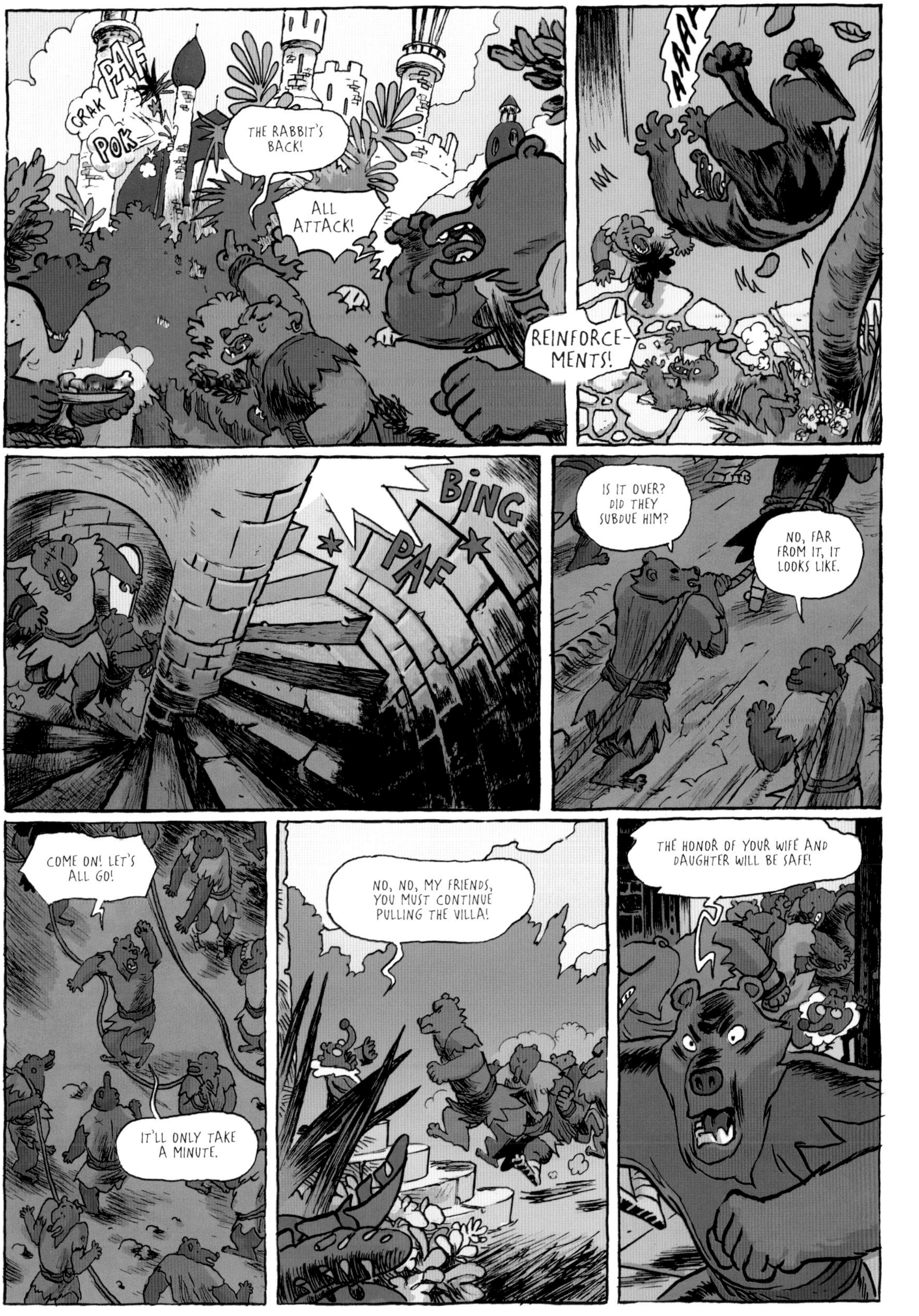
PAF
CRAK
POK
THE RABBIT'S BACK!
ALL ATTACK!
AAAA
REINFORCE-MENTS!
BING
PAF
IS IT OVER? DID THEY SUBDUE HIM?
NO, FAR FROM IT, IT LOOKS LIKE.
COME ON! LET'S ALL GO!
IT'LL ONLY TAKE A MINUTE.
NO, NO, MY FRIENDS, YOU MUST CONTINUE PULLING THE VILLA!
THE HONOR OF YOUR WIFE AND DAUGHTER WILL BE SAFE!

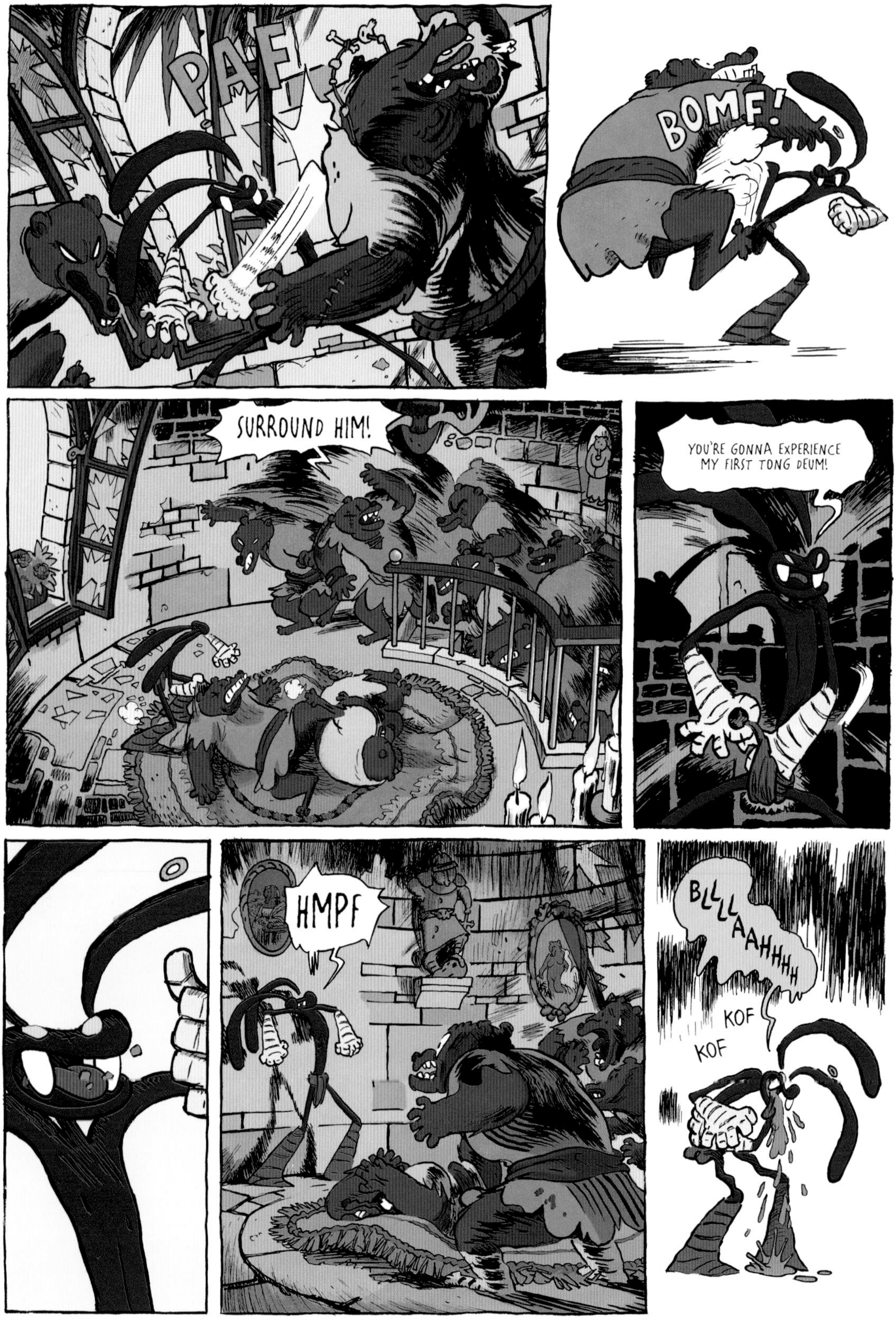
PAF!
BOMF!
SURROUND HIM!
YOU'RE GONNA EXPERIENCE MY FIRST TONG DEUM!
HMPF
BLLLLAAHHHH
KOF
KOF

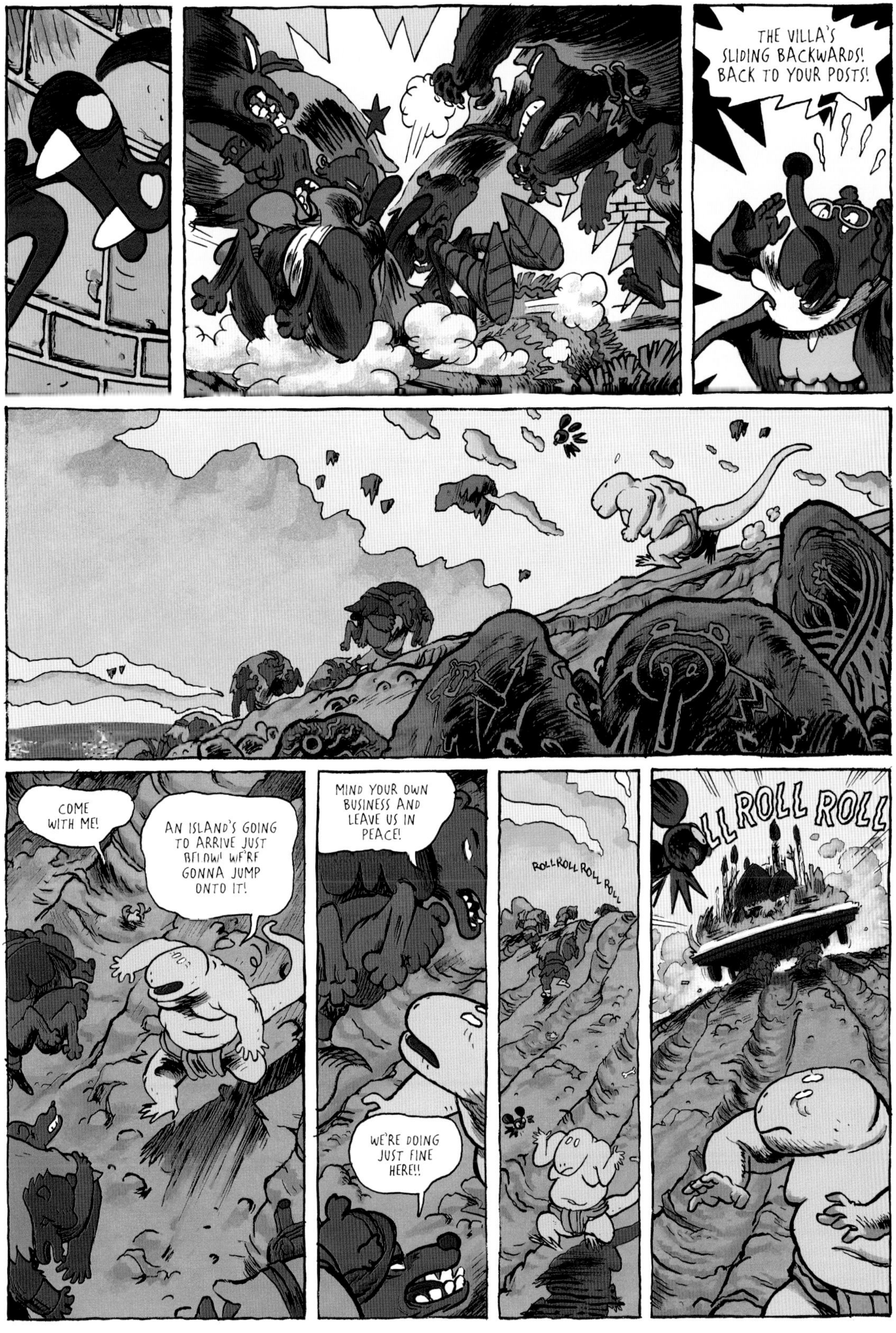
THE VILLA'S SLIDING BACKWARDS! BACK TO YOUR POSTS!
COME WITH ME!
AN ISLAND'S GOING TO ARRIVE JUST BELOW! WE'RE GONNA JUMP ONTO IT!
MIND YOUR OWN BUSINESS AND LEAVE US IN PEACE!
WE'RE DOING JUST FINE HERE!!
ROLL ROLL ROLL ROLL
LL ROLL ROLL

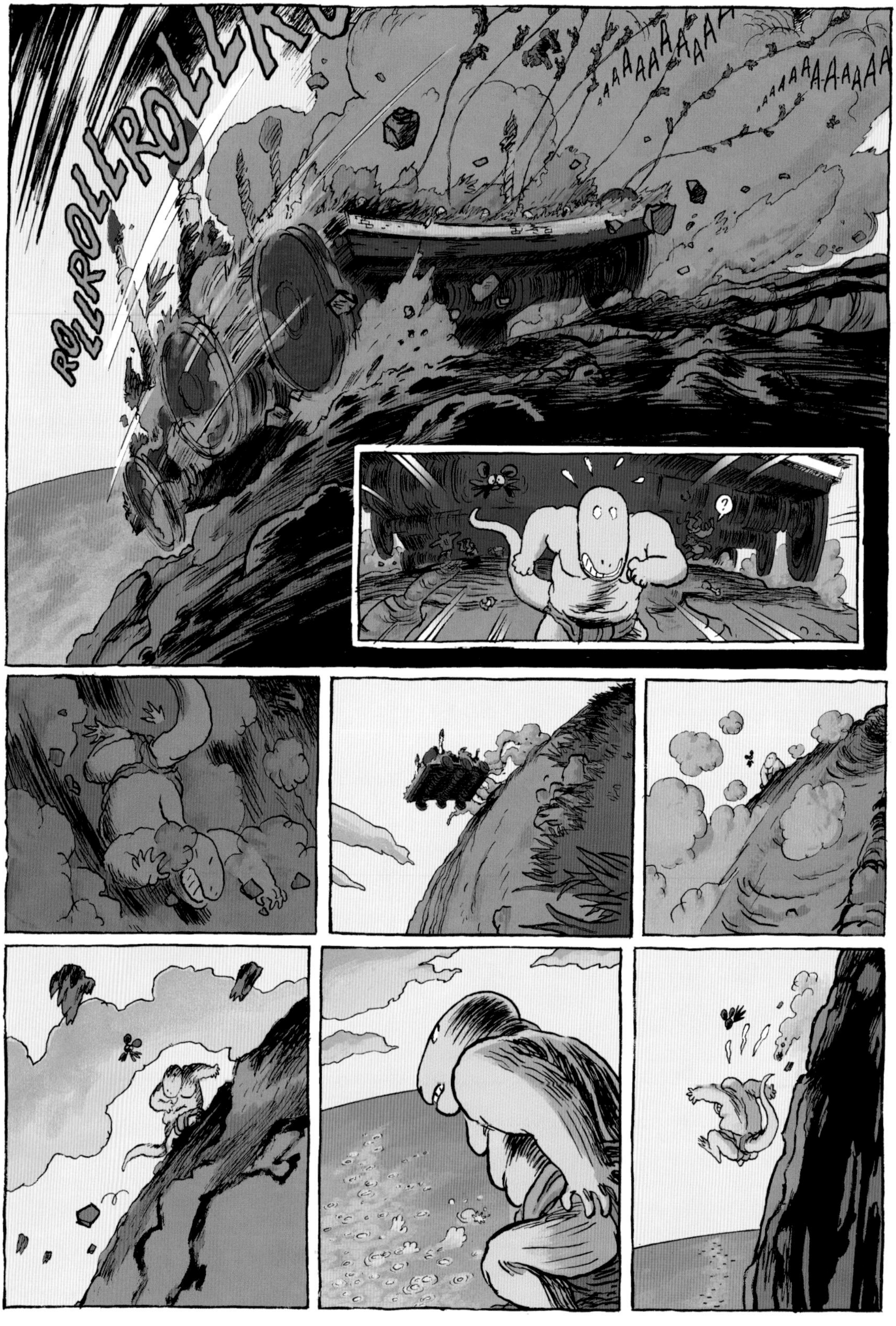
ROLLROLLROLLRO
AAAAAAAAAA
AAAAAAAAAA
?

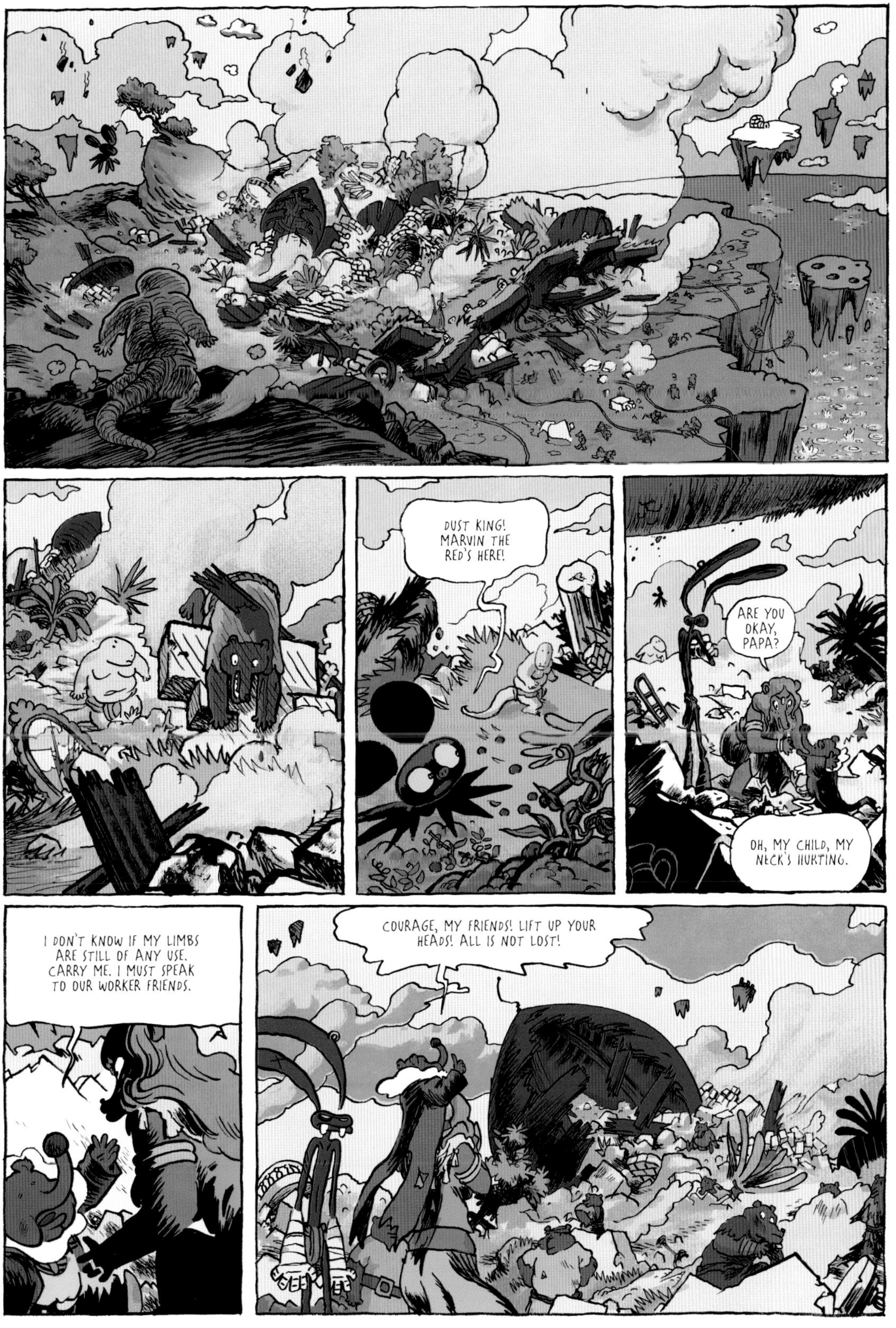
DUST KING! MARVIN THE RED'S HERE!
ARE YOU OKAY, PAPA?
OH, MY CHILD, MY NECK'S HURTING.
I DON'T KNOW IF MY LIMBS ARE STILL OF ANY USE. CARRY ME. I MUST SPEAK TO OUR WORKER FRIENDS.
COURAGE, MY FRIENDS! LIFT UP YOUR HEADS! ALL IS NOT LOST!

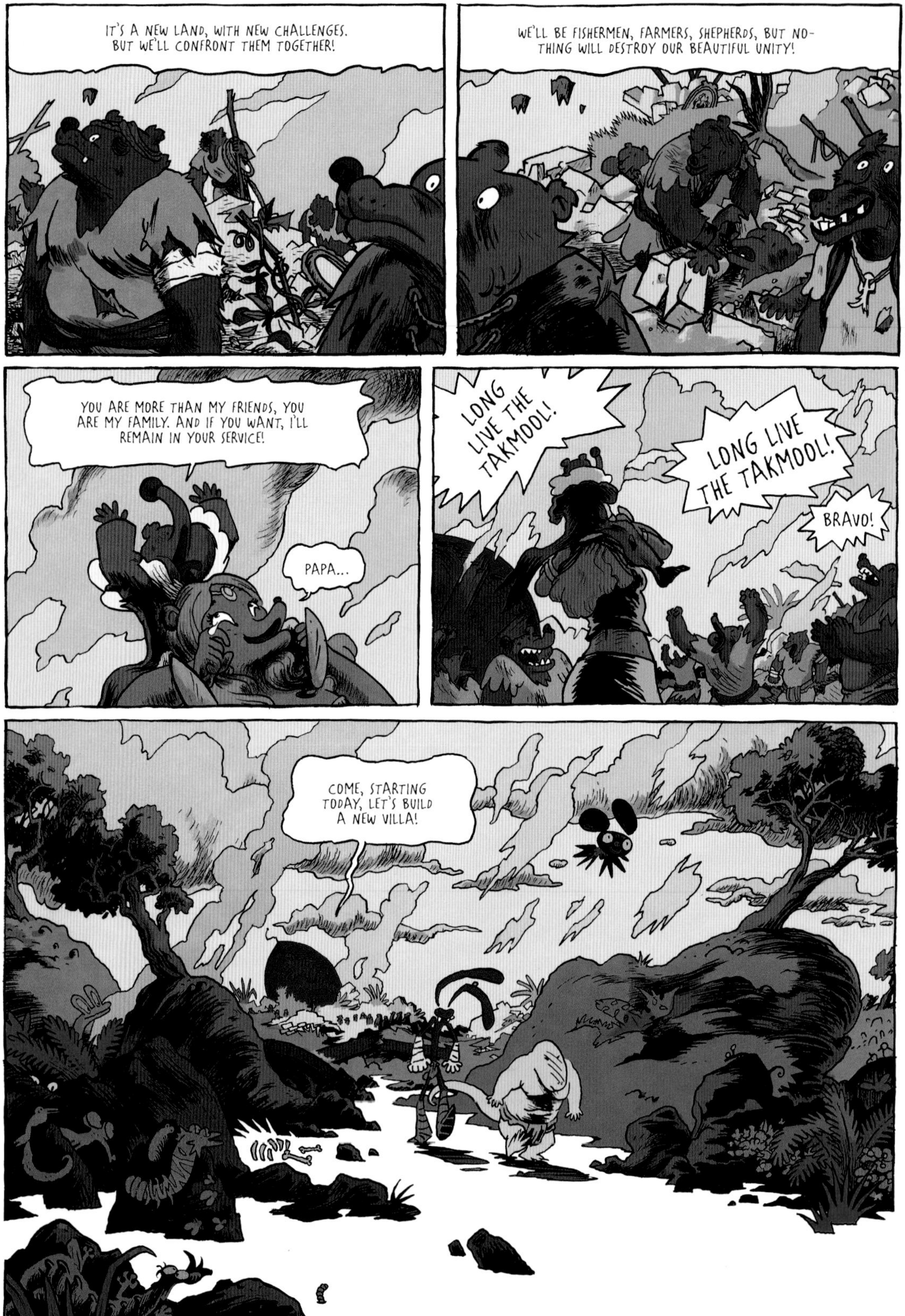
IT'S A NEW LAND, WITH NEW CHALLENGES. BUT WE'LL CONFRONT THEM TOGETHER!
WE'LL BE FISHERMEN, FARMERS, SHEPHERDS, BUT NOTHING WILL DESTROY OUR BEAUTIFUL UNITY!
YOU ARE MORE THAN MY FRIENDS, YOU ARE MY FAMILY. AND IF YOU WANT, I'LL REMAIN IN YOUR SERVICE!
PAPA...
LONG LIVE THE TAKMOOL!
LONG LIVE THE TAKMOOL!
BRAVO!
COME, STARTING TODAY, LET'S BUILD A NEW VILLA!